Finance for the Non-accountant

Finance for the Non-accountant

L. E. Rockley
BCom (Lond), MPhil (Warwick), IPFA, MBIM

Fourth edition

Business Books

London   Melbourne   Sydney   Auckland   Johannesburg

Business Books Ltd

An imprint of the Hutchinson Publishing Group

17–21 Conway Street, London W1P 6JD

Hutchinson Group (Australia) Pty Ltd
30–32 Cremorne Street, Richmond South, Victoria 3121
PO Box 151, Broadway, New South Wales 2007

Hutchinson Group (NZ) Ltd
32–34 View Road, PO Box 40–086, Glenfield, Auckland 10

Hutchinson Group (SA) (Pty) Ltd
PO Box 337, Bergvlei 2012, South Africa

First published 1970
Reprinted 1970 (twice), 1971 (three times),
1972 (three times), 1973, 1974, 1975
Second edition 1976
Third edition 1979
Reprinted 1981, 1982
Fourth edition 1984

Printed in Great Britain by The Anchor Press Ltd
and bound by Wm Brendon & Son Ltd
both of Tiptree, Essex

British Library Cataloguing in Publication Data

Rockley, L. E.
　Finance for the non-accountant. – 4th ed.
　1. Corporations – Finance　　2. Industrial
　management
　I. Title
　658.1′5　　HG4026

ISBN　0 09 153090 3 (cased)
　　　　0 09 153091 1 (paper)

To Anne and Richard

Contents

Part 1   Financial analysis

1   Introduction   19

The form of accounts – Definitions of a limited company and the 1981
Companies Act; the public limited company and the private limited company –
Layout of final accounts – Accounting conventions and practices; true and fair
view.

2   The balance sheet   26

The static picture: a statement of corporate net wealth – Capital expenditure and
revenue expenditures: their impact on the balance sheet and a profit and loss
account – Doctrines of matching and materiality – The circulation of current
assets; the available fund for settlement of current liabilities – Balance sheet
developments on company formation and growth: subscribed capital and
reserves: the total shareholders' interest and net asset worth of one ordinary
share – Retained profit as part of shareholders' investment in the company –
Working capital, current and liquid ratios as measures of corporate creditworthiness – Reserves and the growth in corporate net wealth – Introduction to funds
flow and the analysis of successive balance sheets – 1981 Act balance sheet
formats.

3   Depreciation and the determination of income   46

Functions of depreciation: a cost of use of fixed assets for more realistic profit
determination – Comparability of profits and the need for consistency in
depreciation accounting – SSAP12 and SSAP19; rules for charging depreciation
and the exemptions for investment property companies – Straight-line,
reducing-balance and sum-of-the-digits methods of formulating a cost of use of
fixed assets: the effect of the various methods upon corporate income and net
asset worth – A company depreciation code – Repairs and maintenance and the
choice of depreciation method – Replacement and historical cost bases for
calculating the depreciation charge : revaluation, current value and index

methods of establishing a cost/value of fixed assets – Depreciation and
availability of funds for asset replacement.

Functions of the profit and loss account – Comparisons of income and
expenditure with receipts and payments – The concept of matching and the
relevance of prepayments and accruals – Stock cost flows, stock valuation and
accounting profit: the effect of valuations of stock on successive profit and loss
accounts – Methods of allocating raw materials costs to operating accounts;
accounting routines for determining materials expenditure: FIFO, LIFO, etc. –
Examples of the effect on final accounts and reported profitability of corporate
activity.

   Value of stock and work-in-progress: inclusion/exclusion of overhead costs
in/from stock valuation: basic principles: standard practices for valuing stocks –
Recommendations of the Accounting Standards Steering Committee – 1981 Act
required disclosures; a comparison with SSAP9.

Further developments in corporate structure – The recording of trading profit,
its impact on company cash holdings and the funds flow statement – Taxation:
appropriations of profit, transfers to reserves and declaration of dividends – The
implications of transfers to reserve – Depreciation charges quantified: their
effect on book worth of assets, on income and the calculation of cash flow –
Gearing; its definition, assessment and appraisal – The narrative balance sheet
and its advantages – 1981 Act balance sheet formats compared – The assessment
of corporate net worth – Various expressions of the concept of capital employed:
reasons for choice of method.

Retained profits and cash flow from trading operations: impact of depreciation
charges and stock valuations upon cash flow calculations – Depreciation, profit
and return on capital employed: comparative balance sheets and profit and loss
accounts in narrative style.

   Further demonstrations of the funds flow statement – Using funds flow
statements to ascertain corporate financing and asset acquisition policies.

The planning process and the maintenance of corporate liquidity status: the cash
budget and the liquidity path – A case study of the developing firm: practical
impacts of receipts and income, payments and expenditure – Cost of resources
used in generating output; the importance of the gross profit percentage:
availability of funds, transfers from profit to reserves and the growth of total
shareholders' interest – Forecast return on capital employed, mark-up on sales
and turnover of capital – introduction to the use of business ratios – 1981 Act
profit and loss account formats and the disclosures of information.

The interdependency of return on capital employed, mark up on sales and
turnover of capital employed: various expressions of capital employed and the
measurement of return – The importance of creditworthiness: ratios of solvency:
working capital, current and liquid ratios re-examined – The importance of the

inventory to working capital ratio: stock turnover ratios – Credit manipulation: emergence of overtrading: debtor and creditor ratios – periods of credit allowed and taken.

Evaluation of business worth: viewpoints of different interested parties – The power of retained earnings to increase market worth of ordinary shares: the value of dividends as compared with earnings: dividend yield, earnings yield and the P/E ratio.

Post-tax earnings under imputation: nil, net and actual earnings: advanced corporation tax (ACT) and overseas earnings: effects of imputation upon earnings based ratios.

capacity – Criticisms of the conventional break-even chart – Profit/volume ratio as a guide to profitable product mixes: the need to consider working capital investment: the use of contribution and P/V ratios. Effect on profitability of fall in activity level: profit volume graph – Introduction to marginal costing.

12 Cost analyses and management decisions

Variable costs and the impact of management decisions: relevance for the recovery of fixed costs – Determination of overhead total costs: allocation to product lines: the problem of minimum structure costs – Apportionment routines: percentage on direct materials, on direct wages and on prime costs: machine and labour hour rates.

Absorption and marginal costing, numerical examples: departmental profitability: stock valuation and profit trends – Standard costing: minimum requirements: types of standard – Variances: their meaning, use and their dangers; reasons for variances – Numerical examples of variance analysis: budgeted profit and loss statement.

Part 3 Investment analysis

13 Capital expenditure evaluation

The specific nature of capital assets: problems of choice between alternatives: the essential requirements which criteria of appraisal should satisfy – Techniques for evaluating capital expenditure proposals – Payback; the initial screening device and risk-period rating: determination of maximum pay-back index – Rates of return on book cost: return per £ invested: average annual income per £ invested: average annual income as a percentage of book value of investment – Discounted cash flow methods of appraisal: yield, net present value and annual value: discounted pay-back: the importance of the time pattern of cash flows – Comparisons of yield, net present value and annual value: rate of earning power and growth in wealth – Constituents of annual value concept: the annual capital charge and its relationship with the notion of annuity: annualising cash flows – Investment chains – The operation of a sinking fund.

14 The cost of capital

Sources of capital finance and their cost: fluctuating costs of the various types of finance: the concept of the planned capital structure – Return to the ordinary shareholder; past achieved rates of return and future long-term expectations – Dividend yield plus dividend growth, the earnings yield as measures of investors' expectations – Impact of taxation upon the 'cost' of retained earnings – Loan capital interest costs and the reverse yield gap: the real and monetary returns for the providers of capital finance.

The weighted average cost of capital and its applications – The moving marginal weighted average cost of capital – Divergences of practice and the use of equity cost as the sole basis for determining a corporate cost of capital: the risk premium – Objects of cost of capital determination: project profiles and the relevance of a realistic cost of capital for yield and net present value – Cut-off rates: the relevance of corporate policy and long-term strategy in the application of cut-off rates: managerial limitations on the adoption of investment proposals.

15 Analysis of project returns

Proposal acceptability rating and corporate long term strategy – Criteria of choice as aids for the decision maker: use of investment profiles in locating yield, etc.: the interest rate and its impact on DCF yield: short cut methods for ascertaining yield – Returns to sample projects: NPV for each year of project life – Treatment of taxation, writing-down allowances and development grants in project appraisal: timing of receipt of grants: allowing revenue costs and capital costs in cash flow determination – Regional development area grants and their influence on location of investment projects – Treatment of asset scrap value and of working capital investment in a complete project appraisal – The Annual Capital Charge and investments with no cash inflows; appraisal of optimum vehicle life: lowest annualised cost; lease, hire purchase and purchase alternatives: appraisal of financing costs.

Preface to second edition

When *Finance for the Non-accountant* was first published in 1970 it was given a most favourable reception. The first edition's twelve impressions evidence the continued popularity of the book, and a strong support for its sympathetic approach to an education in the general subject area of Business Finance.

Much has changed since 1970: the problems of accounting for inflation are discussed more widely now than then. Therefore this edition contains a careful exposition of the two main proposals for dealing with the impact of inflation upon company accounts. Over the years, also, I have received many letters asking for specific matters to be given some prominence in a new edition. It is a great pleasure and very helpful to have this kind of guidance to readers' needs. In response I have devoted more space to such topics as Funds Flow, Stock Valuation, Marginal Costing, Standard Costing and Variance Analysis. My Glossary of Common Accounting and Financial Terms, which first saw the light of day in my book *The Meaning of Balance Sheets and Company Reports*, has been enlarged. It will continue to be developed in all my future works.

Chapters on Investment Analysis have been rewritten to reflect current thinking and to show the effects of existing grant and taxation allowances which are available for relevant capital expenditures. Fresh examples of project appraisal have been devised to cover transport costs, leasing and hire-purchase, etc.

Kenilworth 1976   L. E. ROCKLEY

Preface to third edition

The principal objective of *Finance for the Non-accountant* has always been to encourage students and businessmen, of diverse persuasions, to develop an informed understanding of finance and accounts. The continuing high demand for the book is evidence of the success of its philosophy and the treatment it has given to accounting concepts and practices.

The second edition, by its handling of financial management issues and topics, has continued to receive considerable support. However new controversies arise, other concepts and methods of quantifying and appraising business activity come to the fore. Therefore this third edition includes a new chapter devoted to a study of value added, and its related corporate partnership team. Furthermore, the debate on accounting for inflation necessitates an examination of the Hyde Report and its interim guidelines for the preparation of profit and loss accounts. Chapter 8 has been extended to cover these matters.

Kenilworth 1979   L. E. ROCKLEY

Preface to fourth edition

In this fourth edition *Finance for the Non-accountant* has been completely revised to take account of recent Companies Acts' legislation which has specified certain formats regarding the style and content of company balance sheets and profit and loss accounts.

The reader is introduced to the new styles of layout and content in gradual stages, thus enabling comparisons of the (now) legally required formats with the conventional two-sided and narrative forms of accounts which have been the practice in past years. At the same time new features, examples and explanatory tables have been devised so that non-financial executives and students alike may achieve an even greater appreciation of the financial and accounting operations of companies and firms.

The chapter on Accounting for Inflation has been rewritten to give an account of the various proposals which have followed upon the CPP standard, issued in 1974, up to the publication of SSAP16 in 1980. Furthermore a new series of self-examination questions and reading references are presented to encourage the reader to test his/her progress in the achievement of full understanding of the subject, as it is developed through each chapter.

I acknowledge the kind permission of Her Majesty's Stationery Office to reproduce data, from the Companies Acts publications, in this new edition. Similarly my thanks are due to Courtaulds Plc and Simon Engineering Plc for their continued permission to reproduce (in this instance) value added data from their published accounts booklets.

Kenilworth 1983   L. E. ROCKLEY

Part 1
Financial
analysis

1   Introduction

The form of accounts

The content and layout of the published accounts of UK limited companies, together with the considerable amount of data to be given in explanatory notes attached thereto, have been the subject of much Companies Acts legislation in recent years. In particular the requirements of the 1980 and 1981 Acts will have major impacts upon the extent and type of published information becoming available to all students of Finance – especially in the realm of company affairs.*

Finance For the Non-Accountant has always had as its prime objective the explanation and exemplification of business finance so as to enable the reader to achieve a better appreciation of the whole subject, and a clearer understanding of its many applications. In this context it is therefore necessary to recognise that the accounts of companies, and their explanatory notes, will be available to the analyst

(*a*)   as published prior to the 1980/81 Acts' specifications;
(*b*)   in 1980/81 Act published formats;
(*c*)   in whatever form a company may deem to present its accounting statements, for *internal* management uses.

Furthermore the definitions of the two main types of limited company, and their various powers, must be understood in order that the reader may be aware of the type of corporate body which he/she is appraising.

The ensuing chapters therefore will, where appropriate, present balance sheets and profit and loss accounts giving both the pre- and post-1980/81 Act forms and contents. The demonstration of accounts examples will

*For a complete study of the new requirements on data being disclosed, for the analysis of published balance sheets and profit and loss accounts, by UK companies see *The Meaning of Balance Sheets and Company Reports – a Guide for Non-Accountants*, Second Edition, by L. E. Rockley, Business Books (1983).

proceed from the simplest (conventional) two-sided form of these accounts; we shall develop the explanations and examples gradually to the point where statutory new forms of layout and content are introduced. Where the new formats are given they will be shown adjacent to the conventionally drawn (past practice) accounts. Thus, during the process of recognising and understanding the many features of business finance, the reader will be encouraged to apply his/her newly acquired knowledge in analyses of the different forms of accounting statements which legislation now demands.

Limited companies defined

Prior to the operation of the 1980 Companies Act, the two main types of limited liability company registered in the UK have had a common form of identification. This has been incorporated as a part the company's name which was shown at the head of its published balance sheets and profit and loss accounts thus:

The Standard Company Limited

In such a title, it was the term 'limited' which constituted the public announcement of the limitation of the liability of the owners (i.e. the shareholders) of that company.

Now the 1980 Act requires that the status of limited liability companies will be identified as follows:

a public company – by the title 'The Standard Public Limited Company'
or 'The Standard Plc';

a private limited company – by the title 'The Standard Company Limited'.

Their powers and constitution are explained below.

The Public Limited Company is defined as one which

(*a*)   is limited by shares and has a share capital;
(*b*)   has a memorandum (the statement of corporate trading objectives) which states that the company is to be a public company;
(*c*)   has at least two members;
(*d*)   has a name which ends in 'Public Limited Company', or the abbreviation 'Plc'*, and
(*e*)   has an *allotted* share capital which has a nominal value not less than £50,000.

Furthermore the powers implicit in a public limited company to raise capital

*The Welsh equivalents to these two English titles are permitted for companies having their registered office situated in Wales.

20

by the issue of shares and/or debentures continues, though subject to stringent regulations relating thereto.

The Private Limited Company will always be so called unless it meets the specified definition of a public limited company. The private company is one which

(*a*) has a share capital and continues to be registered as a private limited company;

(*b*) has a memorandum which states that the company is a private company;

(*c*) has at least two members;

(*d*) has a name which ends in 'Limited'.

More importantly a private *limited* company is forbidden to issue its shares or debentures to the public. The transfer of its shares between the *members* of the company is still permitted.

Layout of final accounts

The 1981 Companies Act specifies required formats for the final accounts of all limited companies registered in the UK. Companies can choose from two forms of balance sheet and four forms of profit and loss account layouts when they publish their yearly accounts. One of the permitted balance sheet formats, which is detailed in the Act, is given in Exhibit 1 in order to acquaint the reader with that new style which will be used in later chapters, where appropriate comparisons of old and new balance sheet layouts are to be shown.

Some items may be shown in either of the two positions given in Exhibit 1 – at the choice of the accountants/directors responsible for preparing or signing the balance sheet in question.

Appendix A (see pages 339–47) reproduces* the complete alternative styles of balance sheets and profit and loss accounts styles (which are specified in Schedule 1 of the 1981 Act) together with notes of explanation relating to certain items shown in those formats.

Accounting conventions and practices

In order for business accounts to have wide credibility and usefulness to students, investors and analysts etc., it is essential that their preparation and completion should be based upon universally accepted principles. Securing

*With the kind permission of Her Majesty's Stationery Office.

21

Exhibit 1

Balance sheet layout
Format 1

A *Called up share capital not paid*

B *Fixed assets*

    I Intangible assets

        1 Development costs

        2 Concessions, patents, licences, trade marks and similar rights and assets

        3 Goodwill

        4 Payments on account

    II Tangible assets

        1 Land and buildings

        2 Plant and machinery

        3 Fixtures, fittings, tools and equipment

        4 Payments on account and assets in course of construction

    III Investments

        1 Shares in group companies

        2 Loans to group companies

        3 Shares in related companies

        4 Loans to related companies

        5 Other investments other than loans

        6 Other loans

        7 Own shares

C *Current assets*

    I Stocks

        1 Raw materials and consumables

        2 Work-in-progress

        3 Finished goods and goods for resale

        4 Payments on account

    II Debtors

        1 Trade debtors

        2 Amounts owed by group companies

        3 Amounts owed by related companies

        4 Other debtors

        5 Called up share capital not paid

        6 Prepayments and accrued income

    III Investments

        1 Shares in group companies

        2 Own shares

        3 Other investments

    IV Cash at bank and in hand

D *Prepayments and accrued income*

E *Creditors: amounts falling due within one year*
    1 Debenture loans
    2 Bank loans and overdrafts
    3 Payments received on account
    4 Trade creditors
    5 Bills of exchange payable
    6 Amounts owed to group companies
    7 Amounts owed to related companies
    8 Other creditors including taxation and social security
    9 Accruals and deferred income

F *Net current assets (liabilities)*

G *Total assets less current liabilities*

H *Creditors: amounts falling due after more than one year*
    1 Debenture loans
    2 Bank loans and overdrafts
    3 Payments received on account
    4 Trade creditors
    5 Bills of exchange payable
    6 Amounts owed to group companies
    7 Amounts owed to related companies
    8 Other creditors including taxation and social security
    9 Accruals and deferred income

I *Provisions for liabilities and charges*
    1 Pensions and similar obligations
    2 Taxation, including deferred taxation
    3 Other provisions

J *Accruals and deferred income*

K *Capital and reserves*
    I Called up share capital
    II Share premium account
    III Revaluation reserve
    IV Other reserves
        1 Capital redemption reserve
        2 Reserve for own shares
        3 Reserves provided for by the articles of association
        4 Other reserves
    V Profit and loss account

this objective approach to the valuation and recording of appropriate transactions in company accounts has been one of the prime aims of the Accounting Standards Committee which issues mandatory guidelines to those who are responsible for preparing and presenting the published final accounts of their companies. The work of the Committee and the importance of the accounting standards are supported by the Council of the London Stock Exchange in that the Exchange's Listing Agreement states:

> The Council expect the accounts of listed companies incorporated within the UK and Ireland to comply with UK accounting standards approved by the principal professional accountancy bodies of the UK and Ireland.
>
> Any significant departure from or non-compliance with the applicable standards must be disclosed and explained.

Therefore the importance of accounting standards in the preparation of final accounts is given added emphasis, and in the forthcoming chapters appropriate references to these standards will be given where it will enhance the reader's understanding.

Accounting practices and policies – basic concepts – which are to be followed in producing final accounts include:

true and fair view
going concern
consistency
accruals
prudence.

True and fair view
The first of these – true and fair view – has been a feature of Companies Acts since 1948 but has never been defined. The 1981 Act reaffirms that, in respect of all limited companies registered in the UK,

(*a*) every balance sheet shall give a true and fair view of the state of affairs of the company as at the end of its financial year, and

(*b*) every profit and loss account shall give a true and fair view of the profit or loss of the company for the related financial year.

The meaning of the term 'true and fair view' has come to be accepted as referring to accounts which

(*a*) are prepared and presented in accordance with recognised accounting principles and standards, and contain data which are as objective as reasonably possible;

(*b*) are free from deliberate falsehoods or bias and do not conceal material facts about the company;

(*c*) therefore result in successive final accounts being reasonably comparable, enabling fair appraisals of corporate wealth and progress to be made.

The remaining four of the five concepts noted above have been part of the Accounting Standards Committee's Second Statement since January 1972. They have now been given legal status by their inclusion in the 1981 Companies Act, and a brief statement of their substance is given below:

Going concern
Data in final accounts are to be based upon the assumption that the company intends to stay in busines; there is no intention to liquidate the business in the near future.

Consistency
The accounting treatment of similar types of transaction, in separate reporting periods, should be followed consistently.

Accruals
The expenditures involved in earning an income should be matched with that income – they will reflect the whole costs necessary to attain the income, whether the expenditure has been paid or not: the income will reflect the results of that expenditure whether the related cash or benefit has been received or not.

Prudence
Here a conservative approach to the inclusion and valuation of data in final accounts will be followed. It implies that losses will be shown in the accounts as soon as their likelihood is apparent – even though their cash effects have not yet been realised. Profits or gains in value will be accounted for when actually realised in cash. (This does not deny the need to revalue specific corporate assets when inflationary costs, or technological changes, can be seen to suggest asset values different from those given in the accounts and statements of the company.)

2 The balance sheet

Introduction

Accountancy is a service: it is the service that gathers all the data and the facts about the operations of a business, or of a specific activity, and presents this information in financial terms to the business managers. The skill with which the information is presented and the facts that can be deduced from it may be referred to as 'financial analysis'. The use to which the data is put in influencing business decisions is called 'financial management'. To achieve a fluency in accounts interpretation – financial analysis – does not necessitate a detailed knowledge of the techniques of book-keeping and accounting which recorded all of the information and distributed it around the various ledger accounts. It is more important for the reader to acquire this interpretive skill by seeking a clear understanding of the nature and content of the two principal accounting statements, the profit and loss account and the balance sheet. Moreover it will be necessary to appreciate the relationship that exists between these two statements and the cash account.

Looking at any balance sheet the reader will see, at the top, the name of the company and the fact that it is a balance sheet which was drawn up at a particular date. The object of this statement is to give a picture of the firm at a specified point in time: therefore a balance sheet will be styled 'as at 31 December 19..' or at some other date. It is not a description of what has happened to the firm, nor does it describe a continuing process. It is simply a static picture of the firm at the close of business on the date stated in the balance sheet heading. As an immediate comparison, the profit and loss account is a recording of the events in the making of a profit or a loss during the period which ended on the specified date. This period is always given in the title at the head of the account itself. Customarily we shall have a profit and loss account for a period of, say 12 months, showing the financial consequences of the firm's activities during the 12 months. On the other hand the relevant balance sheet would be drawn up on the last day of that 12 month period: it would show the book value of the firm's wealth in net assets at that date.

Capital and revenue

Earlier on it was stated that a balance sheet presents a picture of a firm at the close of business on the date of the statement. Thus it is emphasised that a balance sheet describes a state of affairs which existed at one point in time only. But business is dynamic. Firms are trading continuously and even though a balance sheet might show that a business possessed so much cash and had so much money owing to it, i.e. debtors, on the balance sheet date, the transactions of the following day will most likely effect a complete change in the pattern of corporate assets. For example if a debtor paid cash in settlement of his debt, on that next day, the picture of the firm's possessions will have changed immediately. Cash will be increased and debtors decreased and the previous day's balance sheet would not show the true *current* position of the firm's possessions.

Such a process of change goes on whilst the firm is in business. Raw material stocks are bought on credit, they are passed to the shop floor, become work-in-progress subsequently being converted into finished goods which are sold – in many instances on credit, thus becoming debtors in the firm's balance sheet. The process continues when the debtor pays the amount due and the company treasurer uses that cash receipt to settle debts owed *by* the firm. These interactions of the various aspects of a dynamic business could be reflected in the drawing up of many balance sheets. We could prepare a daily balance sheet but it is customary, and more sensible, to show the results of the day to day operations of a firm in the profit and loss account. Here we shall record the total of the firm's expenditures and the total of its incomes for the specified period of trading. At the end of the period the worth of the firm as represented by the things it possesses, such as finished goods and debtors, will have increased if the business was trading at a profit. The profit and loss account demonstrates this clearly because the incomes total would be greater than the expenditures total – the value of the goods and services consumed in the production and selling processes will be exceeded by the value of the related sales. Now the balance sheet will also report this growth in wealth (so far as it is retained in the firm and not paid out in dividends) which stems from profitable operations and thus we can accept that a profit and loss account is the trading link between two successive balance sheets. The increase in wealth, generated by trading profit, is explained in detail in the profit and loss account: it will be, moreover, incorporated in the balance sheet at the end of the period. In this way some of the growth in wealth exhibited in the second of two balance sheets is explained.

At this stage we really must consider why the profit and loss account always contains certain kinds of expenditure but not all, and why the balance always deals with other types of expenditure. The content of these two statements depends upon the *nature* of the expenditures involved. Here we have to examine the accounting terminology which segregates corporate spending into two principal initial categories. These two categories are termed 'capital expenditure' and 'revenue expenditure'. The first of the two categories relates to expenditure on, or the acquisition of, assets of a more or less permanent nature. Such long-lived assets will include land and buildings, plant and machinery, vehicles and to some extent loose tools. Furthermore capital expenditure will embrace extensions of existing assets and major modifications to existing assets, provided the expenditure is expected to add to their permanent worth. Here is the vital point which determines whether an item should be classified as capital expenditure – at the time of the relevant expenditure the intention of the spender should be that the asset acquired or improved will have a life longer than one accounting period. Capital expenditures refer to assets which are expected to contribute to the outputs of several accounting periods. Therefore it would be wrong to place these expenditures in a profit and loss account which related to a single accounting period. Capital expenditures will be located in the balance sheet, where they will be recorded under the heading Fixed Assets.

On the other hand revenue expenditure denotes short-term commitments. There is no sense of permanence about these items. Revenue expenditure covers the day-to-day operating costs of a company and it includes a multitude of items such as rent, rates, insurance, salaries, wages, repairs, maintenance, licences, petrol and oil. The essential feature of this particular expense category is that it relates to goods and services which are *entirely consumed* in the administration and production etc. processes of the current period. Nothing is left for consumption and use in any future period. Therefore revenue expenditure finds its way into the revenue, i.e. the profit and loss account. It gives a money value to the goods and services consumed in earning the income – and hence the profit – of one trading period only. But so far as capital expenditure is concerned, one cannot similarly say that such assets will be used up entirely in a relatively short period of industrial activity. At the end of a normal trading period the fixed assets will remain and we could not say that the firm's expenditure on these items had been wholly and completely absorbed in the output of the business during that limited trading period. In a subsequent chapter we shall argue that some of the expenditure has been consumed and at that time the relevance of the depreciation charge, as a measure of the consumption of fixed assets, will be examined.

The doctrines of matching and materiality

Repeated references to the short period has in mind the normal accounting period of 12 months. Thus where the balance sheet shows fixed assets of land and buildings, this is an acknowledgement of the fact that these possessions are available for continued use in productive activities. More importantly it demonstrates that these assets have not been entirely consumed in that production/selling process. Here we can give emphasis to our understanding that a capital good lasts, whilst a revenue good will be used up, during the current period, in the business venture for which the revenue good was acquired. The essence of charging revenue expenditure to the profit and loss account of a specific trading period involves the concept of matching – matching the cost of goods and services consumed with the benefits, i.e. output, sales, achieved by those expenditures in that particular period.

Materiality is another important accounting concept. It concerns the significance of business expenditures and the worthwhileness of applying the capital and revenue expenditure distinction in too rigid a sense. Clearly a desk reading lamp or a pen rack might be used for several years in the secretary's office. Therefore their costs could be classified as capital expenditure. But whether we match such small items of expense against one year's sales or against several years' sales will make little difference to the declared year by year profitability of the business. It would be relatively immaterial to a realistic accounting for corporate profit. So we shall find that such items are charged entirely to the profit and loss account of the period in which the expenditure was incurred. This action will be acceptable provided that realistic accounting information continues to be produced at a sensible cost. If the action were to distort the comparability of year by year accounting data, then that action could not be justified. In fact the principle of materiality would not be being applied.

The doctrines of matching and materiality should explain the existence of current assets in a balance sheet. Amongst this grouping of assets we shall find raw material stocks, work-in-progress and finished goods. The reader may have thought that stock (for example) once purchased for the purpose of business operations is intended to be used up and therefore should not appear in a balance sheet at all but that its cost ought to be listed amongst the expenses of a profit and loss account. The misapprehension can be quickly dispelled when the reader considers that a business manager must look ahead and plan for his future activities. The act of planning will result in the acquisition of stock in order to meet the anticipated future needs. Therefore we shall have a storehouse in which stocks of materials and components, to be used in the manufacturing and selling processes, are stored. Once an item leaves the storehouse and is embodied in a product being made then that expenditure has been absorbed, that current asset stock has been used and its appropriate financial value which is shown in the profit and loss account will describe the cost of materials consumed in the manufacturing of the firm's output. The doctrine of matching expenditure with income (output) has been observed.

The goods which are left in the storehouse and available for use in future business operations are the firm's short-term assets. They will be recorded in a balance sheet drawn up at that time. They are listed in the balance sheet under a heading 'Current Assets' because they are assets of the *current* period only and are not possessions held for repeated, continuous use in several future trading periods. In so far as goods remain in the storehouse, or products are in course of manufacture (work-in-progress) at the date of the balance sheet, in so far as finished goods remain in the warehouse and not yet sold to customers, these possessions are assets of the current period only. In a few days, weeks or months they will no longer be assets of the firm for they will have passed into the hands of customers and will be replaced in the balance sheet by the asset 'debtors'. As debtors pay to the firm the amounts they owe then the worth of the commodities produced is represented by cash. The cash thus received, itself a current asset, will be used to settle amounts owing to the creditors of the firm. In this way the balance sheet description of a business, and its worth in terms of possessions and liabilities, can be changed in a vital fashion. Sometimes the group of assets called current assets are referred to as 'circulating assets'. The reason for this name is explained by the fact that they do not (in a dynamic concern) remain in one condition for any length of time. Circulating assets are constantly on the move, reverting into cash, cash settling creditors' bills, more stock being purchased, and so on.

The notion of circulating assets is demonstrated by Exhibit 2. Much of business activity is represented by transactions financed by credit and, in the course of trading, stock will be purchased on credit (items 1 and 2). As soon as the raw material stock is issued to the shop floor it is termed 'work-in-progress' thus describing material which is in process of being changed into a new product, a saleable finished article. The exhibit displays the changing nature of stock: it shows its new state at item 3. The production cycle continues with the emergence of the finished article (item 4) which is then sold on credit to some other person or firm. At this stage the asset called 'finished goods' is replaced by the asset called 'debtors'. Now when debtors pay the amounts they owe, they will be replaced by the asset cash (items 5 and 6). At the end of the business round, money received from the sale of goods produced is available to pay the company's creditors. It is of course used for other matters also. It enables a growth of working capital and/or the purchase of more fixed assets.

Exhibit 2
Circulating assets

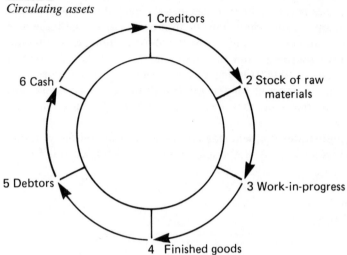

1 Creditors

2 Stock of raw materials

3 Work-in-progress

4 Finished goods

5 Debtors

6 Cash

The impact of trading

The following series of hypothetical balance sheets will show the interaction of the assets and liabilities as they would appear in a balance sheet drawn up immediately after each separate transaction.

In Exhibit 3 a business, the Standard Plc, has issued 10,000 Ordinary

Exhibit 3
The Standard Plc
Balance Sheet as at …

	£		£
Subscribed Capital		*Current Assets*	
10,000 Ordinary			
shares of £1 each	10,000	Cash	10,000
	£10,000		£10,000

shares of £1 each and has received the money from those members of the public who subscribed for the shares. The balance sheet thus shows the company's liabilities at £10,000 worth of issued shares and, amongst the current assets, cash of £10,000. The reader may wonder why shares of £10,000 are shown amongst the liabilities in the balance sheet, even though the owners of the Ordinary shares are really the residual proprietors of the business. This arises because the firm has its own legal identity and one of the objectives of any balance sheet must be to show the firm's liabilities and assets – its sources and uses of funds. Now the above exhibit shows that the Standard Plc have received from the shareholders a total of £10,000 in response to the issue of 10,000 Ordinary shares. The liability therefore rests upon the company to account for the £10,000 to those shareholders who have purchased the shares and thereby subscribed money for the company's initial operations.

Exhibit 4 demonstrates the next stage in the life of our company. Using the cash which was received from the shareholders, buildings costing £4,000

Exhibit 4
The Standard Plc
Balance Sheet as at …

	£		£
Subscribed Capital		*Fixed Assets*	
10,000 Ordinary		Buildings	4,000
shares of £1 each	10,000	Plant & machinery	3,000
		Current Assets	
		Cash	3,000
	£10,000		£10,000

and plant and machinery costing £3,000 have now been purchased. It can be seen that cash in the balance sheet has decreased to account for the payments made for the buildings and machinery purchased. The firm now possesses *fixed assets* worth £7,000; this kind of spending we have referred to previously as *capital expenditure*, being expenditure on items that are not going to be used up in a short period. These assets should remain for the firm's use over several years and they should contribute to its profit earning operations in each of those future years.

Exhibit 5 shows the firm now ready to go into production. It has bought stocks of raw materials for £3,000 but has not paid for them, obtaining the goods on credit. Thus stock is listed amongst the current assets at its cost price, whilst on the liabilities side of the balance sheet we have recorded the liability of the business to meet this particular debt. The new liability, a debt of the current period, is shown under current liabilities. Normally referred to as a trade creditor, it refers to the £3,000 owing for the stock bought on credit.

At this stage we can emphasise an important note about one of the functions of a balance sheet. It is that the left-hand side of a balance sheet

Exhibit 5
The Standard Plc
Balance Sheet as at …

	£		£
Subscribed Capital		*Fixed Assets*	
10,000 Ordinary		Buildings	4,000
shares of £1 each	10,000	Plant & machinery	3,000
Current Liabilities		*Current Assets*	
Creditors	3,000	Stock	3,000
		Cash	3,000
	£13,000		£13,000

shows where the firm obtained its money or credit – the sources of its funds – thereby showing how it has been financed in the circumstances existing at the date of the balance sheet. The right hand side shows how that money and credit was used – the applications of the funds: it shows what the funds have purchased in terms of goods not yet used up in the production process.

Let us now assume that our businessmen engage in production using some of the stock and paying cash for the labour involved in the manufacturing processes: they produce goods which are sold on credit for £5,000. These goods we shall assume were produced at the expense of the consumption of £2,000 worth of stock and the payment of £2,000 to the work force. This is a simple example which ignores all other factors such as rent, rates, light and heat, etc. The amended balance sheet would appear as shown in Exhibit 6.

Exhibit 6
The Standard Plc
Balance sheet as at …

	£		£
Subscribed Capital and Reserves		*Fixed Assets*	
10,000 Ordinary		Buildings	4,000
shares of £1 each	10,000	Plant & machinery	3,000
Profit	1,000		
Current Liabilities		*Current Assets*	
Creditors	3,000	Stock	1,000
		Debtors	5,000
		Cash	1,000
	£14,000		£14,000

The sale of goods on credit for £5,000 is represented by the item 'debtors £5,000' amongst the current assets. At the same time a consumption of £2,000 worth of materials has reduced the stock figure to £1,000 whilst the payment of £2,000 to the work force has reduced the balance of cash to £1,000. Clearly the difference between the costs of manufacturing the goods and the relevant sales income is £1,000. This sum is the profit made on the series of operations. Our profit of £1,000 must now be shown in the balance sheet, adjacent to the proprietors' subscribed capital. It is recorded there because the profit has been made by the business, a business which the shareholders theoretically own and to whom the profit belongs.

Consequently the section of the balance sheet which was previously entitled 'subscribed capital' is now called 'subscribed capital and reserves'. This title will include any unused balance remaining on the profit and loss account because profit left in the business, referred to as retained earnings, is in fact a reserve created out of its profitable workings. It is being invested in the continuing operations of the firm. A brief appraisal of the firm will show that it possesses assets with a *book* worth of £14,000 and it owes £3,000 to its suppliers. Therefore the book worth of the shareholders' investment in the company is £11,000, which corresponds with the summation of the £10,000 subscribed plus £1,000 of retained profit. The book worth of one Ordinary share, or the net asset worth as it is described, is £1.10.

The company's next transactions are revealed by the balance sheet shown in Exhibit 7. In this balance sheet we can see that some of the debtors,

Exhibit 7
The Standard Plc
Balance Sheet as at ...

	£		£
Subscribed Capital and reserves		*Fixed Assets*	
10,000 Ordinary		Buildings	4,000
shares at £1 each	10,000	Plant & machinery	3,000
Profit	1,000		
Current Liabilities		*Current Assets*	
Creditors	3,000	Stock	1,000
		Debtors	2,500
		Cash	3,500
	£14,000		£14,000

£2,500 worth, have settled their debts with the company. As a result the debtors figure is reduced by that amount and the cash figure increased. If the reader examines these last two balance sheets, he will see that this sort of transaction has not affected the worth of the business to the shareholders. The *net worth* still remains at £11,000 and the total assets owned by the company still have a book worth of £14,000. All that has been varied is the asset mix.

Total shareholders's interest

Now our next statement of the company's possessions shows that creditors have been settled to the tune of £2,500. The balance sheet (Exhibit 8) shows that cash has been disbursed to the extent of £2,500 by payments to creditors: as a result of this action the total of the creditors' accounts still awaiting payment and therefore still a liability of the firm, is shown in the balance sheet at £500.

Exhibit 8
The Standard Plc
Balance Sheet as at ...

	£		£
Subscribed Capital and Reserves		*Fixed Assets*	
10,000 Ordinary		Buildings	4,000
shares at £1 each	10,000	Plant & machinery	3,000
Profit	1,000		
TOTAL SHAREHOLDERS'		TOTAL FIXED ASSETS	7,000
INTEREST	11,000		
Current Liabilities		*Current Assets*	
Creditors	500	Stock	1,000
		Debtors	2,500
		Cash	1,000
	£11,500		£11,500

Clearly our company possesses assets, fixed and current, totalling £11,500. At the same time it owes £500 to persons and other firms who have traded with it, leaving £11,000 to be expressed as the worth of the proprietors' interest in the business. It should be noted particularly that in this balance sheet the total of £11,000 has now been given a name, 'total shareholders' interest', being an expression of the worth of the business to those who hold shares in it. Beyond saying that this monetary expression of worth is based upon the book values of the assets – not market values – nothing more will be said at this stage except to repeat that the net asset (book) worth of each £1 Ordinary share remains at £1.10. One other addition to the balance sheet information is the totalling of the values attributed to fixed assets: thus we have a section of the statement called 'total fixed assets'. The analyst can conclude that 64 per cent of the total shareholders' interest is invested in long-term lasting assets thus providing a solid backing for their investment – provided that the fixed asset values have not been unrealistically quoted.

Exhibit 9 shows that the Standard Plc is preparing for another cycle of production and has enlarged the scope of its activities. The firm has

Exhibit 9
The Standard Plc
Balance Sheet as at ...

	£			£
Subscribed Capital and Reserves		*Fixed Assets*		
10,000 Ordinary		Buildings		4,000
shares at £1 each	10,000	Plant & machinery		3,000
Profit	1,000	Vehicle		1,000
TOTAL SHAREHOLDERS'		TOTAL FIXED ASSETS		8,000
INTEREST	11,000			
Current Liabilities		*Current Assets*		
Creditors	4,000	Stock	3,500	
		Debtors	2,500	
		Cash	1,000	7,000
	£15,000			£15,000

purchased a vehicle for £1,000 and bought £2,500 worth of stock, all of these purchases being made on credit. Therefore the left hand side of the balance sheet shows an increase in the statement of amounts due by the firm, to those who trade with it, from £500 to £4,000.

The reader should note that in the section 'current liabilities', creditors may refer to fixed asset purchases as well as current assets, e.g. stock, purchases. Where these creditors are described as 'trade creditors' however, it may be taken to refer to stock and component suppliers only.

Working capital

The important point about the current liabilities is the fact that they must be regarded as liabilities for the *current period* only, and therefore will become due for payment in the next accounting period. This does not mean that the current liabilities will always be totally eliminated in the succeeding cycle of operations because the continuous nature of business brings forward other credit transactions. Whilst the particular creditors shown in Exhibit 9 will be discharged they will be replaced by other creditor amounts arising from the company's purchases in that next operating period. The relationship of current liabilities with current assets leads on to the concept of working capital. Now current assets are comprised of those assets most readily convertible into cash and they describe the fund from which the current liabilities can expect to be paid. This conversion process is the object and result of production operations (see Exhibit 2 on page 31): the rate of turnover of stock and its conversion into debtors and cash is a vital factor in appraising the adequacy of the working capital sum.

If we refer to Exhibit 9 we can see that the immediate debts are £4,000 whilst the assets of the current period are £7,000. These current assets have been totalled in order to facilitate comparison with current liabilities and therefore the reader can see that the Standard Plc had a working capital of £3,000 (£7,000 − £4,000) on the date given in the balance sheet heading. The relationship between current assets and current liabilities can be expressed as a ratio, thus:

Current assets/Current liabilities
= 7,000/4,000
= 1.75 : 1

The ratio given here indicates that the company has £1.75 worth of current assets for every £1 of current liabilities. This vital subject of corporate liquidity and credit worthiness will be examined in a later chapter but, for the moment, we will say that the 1.75 ratio reveals a satisfactory state of solvency.

For the purposes of the next statement we will assume that production was commenced and that stocks of raw materials were transferred into the production process. Exhibit 10 shows the balance sheet which would be drawn up before the production operations were completed, before the labour force was paid and before any goods could be sold. The only change in this next balance sheet demonstrates the transfer, from stock, of materials worth £1,500 to the shop floor where they are being worked upon but not yet converted into finished saleable products.

Exhibit 11 now incorporates the results of the completed manufacturing cycle. The company has sold goods worth £5,000 on credit. In producing these goods the work-in-progress was finished, further raw material stocks costing £500 were utilised and the labour force was paid £2,000. Therefore the cost of achieving the sales was £4,000 which results in a further profit of £1,000 for the firm. This £1,000 is the difference between the sales value of £5,000 of goods sold to debtors, and their costs of production, £4,000. The additional profit is added, with that previously made and retained in the company, to the shareholders' interest which is thereby increased to £12,000.

Exhibit 10
The Standard Plc
Balance Sheet as at ...

	£			£
Subscribed Capital and Reserves		*Fixed Assets*		
10,000 Ordinary		Buildings		4,000
shares of £1 each	10,000	Plant & machinery		3,000
Profit	1,000	Vehicles		1,000
TOTAL SHAREHOLDERS'		TOTAL FIXED ASSETS		8,000
INTEREST	11,000			
Current Liabilities		*Current Assets*		
Creditors	4,000	Stock	2,000	
		Work-in-		
		progress	1,500	
		Debtors	2,500	
		Cash	1,000	7,000
	£15,000			£15,000

Exhibit 11
The Standard Plc
Balance Sheet as at ...

		£			£
Subscribed Capital and Reserves			*Fixed Assets*		
10,000 Ordinary			Buildings		4,000
shares of £1 each		10,000	Plant & machinery		3,000
Profit		2,000	Vehicles		1,000
TOTAL SHAREHOLDERS'			TOTAL FIXED ASSETS		8,000
INTEREST		12,000			
Current Liabilities			*Current Assets*		
Creditors	4,000		Stock	1,500	
Bank overdraft	1,000	5,000	Debtors	7,500	9,000
		£17,000			£17,000

During this recent trading cycle when goods worth £5,000 were manufactured the payment of £2,000 to the work force used up the entire cash resources of the firm as shown previously in Exhibit 10. An overdraft of £1,000 was negotiated with the bank and this amount is now recorded as a current liability. The important factor for the reader to observe in this balance sheet is that the retained profit of £2,000 cannot be identified with any specific asset or liability in that statement. Thus the popular conception of reserves, e.g. profits retained, representing a quantity of cash available for use, is completely denied: the firm does not have any cash. Even the originally subscribed sum of £10,000 has been spent: it was used in establishing the basic asset requirements of a firm setting up in business. The essential nature of reserves in a balance sheet is that they describe the increase in wealth which the firm has generated for itself. So far as retained profit and other revenue reserves are concerned the increase in wealth comes from profitable trading activities. In Exhibit 11 the firm's wealth is embodied in the general quantum of assets less liabilities and equates with the total shareholders' interest of £12,000. As a further result of the profitable trading, the net asset worth (the book worth) of each Ordinary share in the Standard Plc becomes £1.20. The working capital is now £4,000 due to the profit on trading operations and the current ratio is 1.8. A satisfactory liquidity state is indicated despite the overdraft, for we recognise that debtors of £7,500 hold the promise of a future cash inflow for the business.

Funds flow analysis

At this point we can demonstrate how the firm's liquid cash and credit resources have been employed by preparing a Funds Flow Statement. It will give emphasis to an understanding of the means by which increases in the firm's wealth have been acquired. In order to complete a Funds Flow Statement we need to compare the data in two balance sheets, and Exhibit 12 does this by reproducing in vertical form the balances given in Exhibits 5 and 11.

The exhibit shows that liabilities have increased by £4,000 in the period between the two balance sheets. Clearly it evidences an increase in the total funds becoming available to the firm: had there been a decrease in any of the liabilities then such a decrease would have shown that corporate assets, e.g. cash, had been used to redeem those liabilities.

On the other hand certain assets have increased in book value during the period between the two balance sheets: by the same token some assets have been reduced in book value. Now an increase in the value of some assets will normally indicate an expenditure of funds on the acquisition of those asset increases. Conversely a decrease in the value of assets will normally reveal a using up, or a sale of those particular assets. (This is a simple example: no problems of asset revaluation or depreciation are being encountered.) Armed with this information and using the variations in the firm's assets/liability state as shown in Exhibit 12 we can prepare an informative statement of the sources and applications of corporate funds (see Exhibit 13).

The exhibit explains that the firm has invested £8,500 in vehicles and debtors and that this investment was financed by the five separate fund sources shown in the statement. In particular it shows that profit is only *one* of

Exhibit 12
Balance Sheet Variations

	Exhibit 5	Exhibit 11	Variations	
			−	+
	£	£	£	£
Liabilities				
Ordinary shares	10,000	10,000	—	—
Profit	—	2,000	—	2,000
Creditors	3,000	4,000	—	1,000
Bank overdraft	—	1,000	—	1,000
TOTALS	£13,000	£17,000	—	£4,000
Assets				
Buildings	4,000	4,000	—	—
Plant & machinery	3,000	3,000	—	—
Vehicles	—	1,000	—	1,000
Stock	3,000	1,500	1,500	—
Debtors	—	7,500	—	7,500
Cash	3,000	—	3,000	—
TOTALS	£13,000	£17,000	£4,500	£8,500

Exhibit 13
The Standard Plc
Funds Flow Statement for the period ended ...

	£
Sources of Funds	
Profit	2,000
Creditors increase	1,000
Bank overdraft	1,000
Cash	3,000
Stock decrease	1,500
	£8,500
Applications of Funds	
Vehicles	1,000
Debtors	7,500
	£8,500

the sources of corporate funds and that this source of funds *has been used* – with other items – to provide the necessary finance for the growth in the Standard Plc's asset strength.

Dividend payments

To continue with our company's business activities, we will assume that the directors have decided to recommend payment of a dividend to the shareholders. We will further assume this dividend to be a 10 per cent dividend based upon the nominal value of the issued shares. Thus with a subscribed share issue of £10,000 nominal value, a 10 per cent dividend will result in a payment to the shareholders of £1,000. In our next balance sheet (Exhibit 14) the dividends payable are shown amongst the current liabilities.

Exhibit 14
The Standard Plc
Balance Sheet as at …

	£			£
Subscribed Capital and Reserves			*Fixed Assets*	
10,000 Ordinary			Buildings	4,000
shares at £1 each		10,000	Plant & machinery	3,000
Profit		1,000	Vehicles	1,000
TOTAL SHAREHOLDERS'			TOTAL FIXED ASSETS	8,000
INTEREST		11,000		
Current Liabilities			*Current Assets*	
Creditors	4,000		Stock	1,500
Dividends			Debtors	7,500	9,000
payable	1,000			
Bank				
overdraft	1,000	6,000		
		£17,000		£17,000

Now, recognising that dividends are payable out of profit, the balance sheet shows that the amount which has been set aside for payment to shareholders has been deducted from the profit figure of £2,000. The retained profit therefore stands at £1,000, and the total shareholders' interest is reduced from £12,000 to £11,000. At the same time the net asset value of one Ordinary share in the company is reduced from £1.20 to £1.10 per share. The reader should find this quite reasonable to accept because the company has publicly stated its intention to return to the shareholders a sum of £1,000 from the totality of their invested interest in

41

the company. One final point: the proposed dividend has increased the Standard Plc's *current* liabilities without any corresponding increase in the current assets. Working capital has thereby been cut to £3,000 and the current ratio is only 1.5. Such a trend in the current liquidity of a firm would need to be watched to ensure that no further erosions of working capital were occasioned.

End of a trading cycle

Our next balance sheet (Exhibit 15) will show the results of several transactions. Here we assume that certain debtors have paid £6,000 to the firm's cashier, on account of the sums owing by them. We further assume that

Exhibit 15
The Standard Plc
Balance Sheet as at …

	£			£
Subscribed Capital and Reserves		*Fixed Assets*		
10,000 Ordinary		Buildings		4,000
shares of £1 each	10,000	Plant & machinery		3,000
Profit	1,000	Vehicles		1,000
TOTAL SHAREHOLDERS'		TOTAL FIXED ASSETS		8,000
INTEREST	11,000			
		Current Assets		
		Stock	1,500	
		Debtors	1,500	3,000
	£11,000			£11,000

the £6,000 has been used to pay the whole of the creditors, to pay the dividends due to the shareholders, thus leaving £1,000 to eliminate the bank overdraft. Our final balance sheet demonstrates that, after a period of considerable business activity, the company owns assets of £11,000 and owes liabilities of £11,000. In this instance the liabilities represent the liability of the firm to account to the shareholders for their total interest in this business. The total shareholders' interest has grown in book value, during the short life of the company, from £10,000 to £11,000 even after shareholders have had a return of £1,000 in the form of dividend.

Balance sheet layout – new format

The foregoing exhibits have demonstrated how a conventional balance sheet reports – amongst other things – a listing of the sources of funds and credit on the left-hand side, together with a detailed statement on the right-hand side of how those funds were invested in corporate assets. However the 1981 Act now gives some prominence to the presentation of balance sheets in vertical form (see page 92 on narrative balance sheets). As an example of one of the prescribed formats Exhibit 16 below shows the new layout as it would be applied to the data in Exhibit 14.

Exhibit 16
The Standard Plc
Balance Sheet as at...

		£	£	£
B	*Fixed assets*			
	I Intangible assets			—
	II Tangible assets			8,000
	III Investments			—
C	*Current assets*			8,000
	I Stock			
	1 Raw materials		1,500	
	II Debtors			
	1 Trade debtors		7,500	
			9,000	
E	*Creditors:* amounts falling due within one year			
	2 Bank overdraft	1,000		
	4 Trade creditors	4,000		
	8 Other creditors – dividends	1,000	6,000	
F	*Net current assets*			3,000
G	*Total assets less current liabilities*			£11,000
K	*Capital and reserves*			
	I Called up share capital			10,000
	V Profit and loss account			1,000
	TOTAL SHAREHOLDERS' INTEREST			£11,000

It should be noted that the various distinguishing letters and numbers, which relate to the several groups of assets and liabilities, do not have to be reproduced in published accounts BUT the description of each balance sheet group and item must be as given.

We can still identify

(*a*)   the source of funds and credit, i.e. creditors (formerly called current liabilities), shareholders' capital and reserves, totalling £17,000.

(*b*)   how the funds and credit were invested in corporate assets, by the £17,000 represented in fixed assets and current assets.

The reader can also see that the amount of working capital – net current assets – is now provided in the new format at item F.

Self-examination questions

1   How does a balance sheet come into existence? Where does the information which it gives originate?

2   What is meant by the 'net worth' of a company and how is it shown in a convential balance sheet? How is the concept styled and presented in the balance sheet formats specified in the 1981 Companies Act?

3   What does the net book worth of one Ordinary share mean? Has the notion any real value for portfolio investment appraisal?

4   Why is a company's profit shown amongst the corporate liabilities in its balance sheet?

5   In determining the sum of working capital why do we limit our assessment to a comparison of current assets with current liabilities, whilst ignoring the value of the fixed assets?

6   Define capital expenditure and revenue expenditure, and give four examples of each of these categories. Why is it so necessary to classify correctly a firm's expenditures in this way?

7   Define the following accounting conventions and explain their import-ance in appraisals of published accounts of companies.

(*a*)   true and fair view;
(*b*)   going concern;
(*c*)   consistency.

Recommended reading

ROCKLEY, L.E., *The Meaning of Balance Sheets and Company Reports*, Second Edition, Business Books (1983).

LANGLEY, F.P., *Introduction to Accounting for Business Studies,* Butterworth (1978).

PIZZEY, A., *Accounting and Finance,* Holt, Rinehart and Winston (1980).

3 Depreciation and the determination of income

Introduction

In Chapter 2 we were able to see how the company progressed through a trading cycle, how the changing nature of the company was reflected in the various balance sheets and how a simple statement of profit had its impact upon the amalgam of assets and liabilities appearing in the balance sheet. The perceptive reader will have had certain reservations concerning the profits shown in the previous chapter. These reservations would have referred to the lack of charge against the sales for the use of the capital equipment. Therefore we must now give consideration to the nature of the capital assets and the part they play in industrial and commercial activities.

In any business environment fixed assets are held not for resale but with the object of enabling the firm to carry on its business and earn its profits. Therefore any surplus of income over expenditure which is earned by a business, must be regarded as having been made with the aid of its fixed assets. Consequently, for a more realistic determination of profit, some estimate of the cost of use of capital assets, or of the deterioration in their worth to the company, must be made. Whatever sum we calculate to be the cost of using an asset, that amount must be set against income before a profit or loss is determined. This particular expense is called 'depreciation'. The term has many connotations and opinions differ about its objectives. Primarily, depreciation describes that part of the initial acquisition costs of an asset which is not recovered by the owner when the asset is sold by him. Moreover it is a measure of the wearing out, or loss in value of a capital asset and it arises from

Use
The passage of time
Obsolescence.

Assessing the total amount of fixed asset depreciation and apportioning

46

that total sum over the several accounting periods of the asset's economic life are matters of considerable importance. If the apportionments are not made on consistent bases, or if the total sum is unrealistically determined, then the comparability of profits in one period with another would be seriously affected. Essentially any depreciation calculations must involve

1   The original acquisition and installation costs of the plant, etc. (or its valuation where a revaluation has occurred).
2   An estimate of its sale value at the end of the expected useful life, and
3   A forecast of the asset's expected useful life in the service of the firm.

The difference between the sums specified at 1 and 2 above, the net cost of the asset to the business, will represent the total amount to be set against the profits of the various accounting periods during which the asset is retained by the firm.

We are not concerned at this stage with problems of replacing plant and equipment and other fixed assets where such replacement costs will be – more often than not – considerably higher than the original (historic) purchase price. The part played by depreciation charges in financing the replacement of capital assets will be discussed later in this chapter. But here we shall regard the cost-of-use of fixed assets being charged against income, as merely a means of allocating total net cost over life.

Opinion in final accounts

Calculating the depreciation sum to be charged against each year's income will involve an amount of personal opinion. It is here that balance sheet data reflect the views of persons who provide that data. Clearly there is ample room for judgement and opinion in assessing the expected economic life of a capital asset – for this is capable of determination only within wide boundaries, with the exception of leaseholds where the life is precisely stated. In the case of a mine or quarry, plant and machinery depreciation may be governed by the rate of extraction of raw material from the mine. For other businesses the rate of depreciation will be based upon the amount of use envisaged for the fixed assets AND the expected obsolescence arising from the impact of new technology or from market changes. Furthermore we have to consider whether maintenance can improve the performance of an asset or increase its life: whether continual use will reduce efficiency.

Each of these and other factors will have some impact upon the assessment of useful life for capital assets, and thus upon the yearly depreciation charges. Occasionally one finds that reassessments of expected asset lives and their money values are made during the periods of active use. Again, the amount of the yearly depreciation charge will be affected by such re-assessments. Past records or other information will always be of use when making estimates, but estimates they are and estimates they will remain. Then once an economic life is decided upon, the business manager has to evaluate another future occurrence – the expected receipts to be obtained from selling the asset upon its retirement. It is this sum which is deducted from the original acquisition costs (or valuation) to give the net cost of the asset to the business.

The above component parts affecting the depreciation calculations are relevant only when an asset is to be depreciated in the company's books of account. But many firms have not, in the past, depreciated their buildings and have not charged the income account with a 'cost-of-use' for corporate buildings. This despite the fact that buildings have a limited economic life and therefore should be treated in the same way as other limited life capital assets, e.g. plant and machinery. There is a difficulty in assessing buildings depreciation: it concerns the separation of the capital cost of the buildings from that of the land on which the buildings stand. (The land is not depreciated because land is indestructible and it has a limitless useful life.) But most buildings have a useful life of 50–60 years and thus the effect of minor errors in forecasting, upon the annual charges for depreciation, would not have a material impact upon the year by year comparability of reported profits. This comment is reasonable enough where a firm's buildings do not constitute a large proportion of its asset strength. The situation is more important for property companies, however, where buildings are the principal capital asset. The difficulty of determining a building's capital cost or value has been intensified by the considerable variations in property values during recent years. How much of those variations should be ascribed to the buildings and how much to the land?

Nevertheless it was recommended by the Accounting Standards Committee (in Statement of Standard Accounting Practice Number 12) that all firms should provide for depreciation of their buildings, and make appropriate charges for that depreciation in their annual profit and loss accounts. However, after further debate and in view of:

(a) the difficulties, reiterated by the British Property Federation and property companies, of ascertaining the separate values to be attributed to land and to the buildings situated thereon – both in respect of their historical acquisition costs and in respect of any periodic asset revaluations

and

(b) the above companies' concern for the effect of suddenly introducing depreciation charges for buildings upon their reported profits and on their aggregate reserves,

a new statement SSAP19 has been issued. It relates specifically to accounting for investment properties. Here the requirement to depreciate investment properties over their useful economic lives has been withdrawn. The Standard states that 'investment property need not be subject to

48

periodic charges for depreciation so long as the property is included in the balance sheet at its open market value'. It also suggests that the aforementioned market values should be updated each year, and be supported by an external valuation every five years.

It must be noted that SSAP19 does appear to contravene the 1981 Companies Act, but it can be said that the instruction NOT to depreciate investment properties may be necessary in order to comply with the Act's overriding requirement to give a 'true and fair view'. However, companies other than property investment companies would be in breach of the 1981 Act if they do not provide in their annual accounts for the depreciation of buildings.

In this connection it should be noted that when a firm's buildings are to be depreciated for the first time, any comparability of past and current year's profitability and asset worth would be weakened. We would have to determine the amount of depreciation which should have been charged in those prior years had the policy of accounting for buildings depreciation been operated at that time. The assessed total sum for the prior years should be deducted from the balance sheet asset values at the beginning of the year AND it should be deducted from the balance of profit brought forward from the previous year(s). For a more detailed comparative analysis, some apportionment of the extra depreciation charges over the past 3 or 4 years should be made. In this way fresh trends of profitability and asset worth could be established, against which forecasts of future expectations can be matched.

Now there are several methods of apportioning the cost of an asset over its useful life and the ones most generally used are the straight-line method and the reducing-balance method. The first, dealt with below, is the straight-line method.

Straight-line method of depreciation

Using the initial cost less an estimated amount to be received on retirement of the asset, this method gives the total sum to be divided by the expected number of years of useful life of the asset. In this way an equal annual charge to the profit and loss account will be established. The point to notice is that the charge against profit will be the same each year: a fixed proportion of the cost of the asset to the business is then recovered from each year's income during the asset's operating life. Here we have a rudimentary assessment of the cost of providing the asset's services in producing turnover and earning profit. This particular method is used widely in this country, the United States and Canada.

The reader must remember that the depreciation charge will affect both the profit and loss account AND the balance sheet. The charge to the profit and loss account enables a more realistic statement of profit to be achieved, in that the account thereby includes not only the day to day costs of business operations, but also an estimate of the costs of the fixed asset capacity necessary to those operations. So far as the balance sheet is concerned, the annual provision denotes some reduction in value or fall in worth of the asset as a result of its use or its wear and tear. The annual depreciation amount may be credited to the asset account, thus reducing its money value in the books of account and hence in the balance sheet. It is more likely however that it will be credited to a separate account called 'provision for depreciation'. This latter account, which will grow year by year as each year's depreciation sum is transferred to it, is then offset against the asset's acquisition cost in the balance sheet. The asset net cost, i.e. initial cost less aggregate depreciation, describes the unrecovered part of the initial acquisition cost or valuation of the asset and it is shown in the balance sheet.

We will now take the data of buildings, plant and machinery as shown in Exhibit 6 and assume operating lives of 60 years for the buildings and 10 years for the plant. Additionally a residual value of £400 for the buildings and a nil value of the plant at the end of expected life will be assumed. Thus the annual charges for depreciation would be determined as shown in Exhibit 17.

Exhibit 17

Buildings	$\dfrac{\text{Cost less residual value}}{\text{Number of years of life}}$
	$= \dfrac{£4,000 - £400}{60} = \dfrac{£3,600}{60}$
	$= £60$ per annum
Plant and machinery	$\dfrac{\text{Cost}}{\text{Number of years of life}}$
	$= \dfrac{£3,000}{10}$
	$= £300$ per annum

The effect of these costs upon one year's profit and upon the asset values shown in the balance sheet is now demonstrated by amending the balance sheet given in Exhibit 6 (page 33) and presenting it as shown in Exhibit 18. A balance sheet drawn up at the end of the next year – the second year in the life of the fixed assets – would show their book values as in Exhibit 19, whilst the next profit and loss account for that second year would be charged with that second year's £360 depreciation only. On the other hand a balance sheet must show the total of the depreciation amounts thus far charged, up to the date of the balance sheet. This is demonstrated in Exhibit 19 where the asset values of £3,880 and £2,400 describe the remaining proportions of the acquisition costs (or valuation) which have not yet been charged to any operating profit and loss account.

Exhibit 18
The Standard Plc
Balance Sheet as at ...

	£	£		£	£
Subscribed Capital and Reserves			*Fixed Assets*		
10,000 Ordinary shares at £1 each	10,000		Buildings at cost	4,000	
Profit	1,000		Less depreciation to date	60	3,940
Less depreciation	360	640	Plant at cost	3,000	
			Less depreciation to date	300	2,700
TOTAL SHAREHOLDERS' INTEREST		10,640	TOTAL FIXED ASSETS		6,640
Current liabilities			*Current Assets*		
Creditors		3,000	Stocks	1,000	
			Debtors	5,000	
			Cash	1,000	7,000
		£13,640			£13,640

The straight-line method is simple to operate and easy to calculate and understand. Furthermore it ensures an even spread of a fixed cost through the several years of an asset's life and in many instances this is a reasonable allocation of the acquisition costs. The method is most suitable for leases

Exhibit 19

	£	£
Fixed Assets		
Building at cost	4,000	
Less aggregate depreciation	120	3,880
Plant at cost	3,000	
Less aggregate depreciation	600	2,400

and for assets such as plant equipment and furniture where the economic life is capable of ready assessment. But plant and machinery in certain industries might be subject to early obsolescence due to (unforeseen) technological changes. Such an occurrence would mean that the profit and loss accounts relating to the asset's past operational life should have borne higher depreciation charges than were actually accomplished. After all, the object must be to recover the asset's cost from the income generated during its active life. Thus where an asset's life is not certain or where there could be a rapid decline in its competitive usefulness, we should ensure that the earlier years of expected economic life bear a much larger proportion of the net acquisition costs. Depreciation charges will need to be higher in the first few years. Such a requirement can be met by the reducing-balance method outlined below.

Reducing-balance method of depreciation

When using this method the previous information is still required, i.e. original costs, estimated residual value and the expected useful life of the asset. The reducing-balance method does not result in a uniform depreciation charge in successive years' profit and loss accounts. This is because each year's depreciation amount is derived by applying

1   A constant percentage rate of depreciation
    to the
2   Net book value of the asset shown at the commencement of the year.

The percentage rate is the same in each year but it is applied to *an original cost as reduced by* the total of the depreciation sums charged in previous years. In a simple example we will apply the method to the plant of £3,000, again from Exhibit 6 on page 33. We will assume the annual rate of depreciation to be 25 per cent:

		£
Year 1	Cost of plant at beginning of year	3,000
	Depreciation: 25 per cent of cost	750
	Written-down value at end of year	2,250
Year 2	Depreciation: 25 per cent of written-down value	562
	Written-down value at end of year	1,688

Year 3	Depreciation: 25 per cent	422
	Written-down value	1,266
Year 4	Depreciation: 25 per cent	317
	Written-down value	949

The forecast life of the plant has been given as 10 years: therefore by continuing the above calculations for that period, we would arrive at a book value of £169 at the end of the tenth year. The reader should note the two main features of the reducing-balance method:

1   It will not entirely delete the asset from the firm's books: the annual charge is a constant percentage of a positive book value.
2   It involves relatively higher charges in the earlier years of life of the asset.

Also, it is important to realise that the annual rate of depreciation, required under the reducing-balance method to write the asset down to its residual value by the end of its expected useful life, needs to be two or three times greater than the percentage rate used in the straight-line method.[*] The impact of this method upon the asset values shown in the balance sheet and upon profit is now shown in the revised balance sheet (Exhibit 20) based upon Exhibit 6. Depreciation in respect of the buildings has been left at £60, the straight-line charge.

Again if we prepared a balance sheet at the end of the next year – the second year in the life of the fixed asset – the fixed asset book values would appear as shown in Exhibit 21. However the profit and loss account for that second year would be charged with £622 (see Exhibit 22) depreciation, compared with the £810 charged in the first year.

Decreasing depreciation charges

If it is considered advisable to charge depreciation on a reducing cost basis in successive years, it does not follow that the reducing-balance method is the only way of accomplishing this objective. A much simpler method, which is in greater use in the USA than in the UK, is the sum-of-the-digits method. Here the numbers of each year in an expected economic life are added together: annual depreciation charges are then based upon specific proportions of the total of life/years. Again we will refer to the above plant with a forecast life of 10 years and if we add the numbers of the years 1 to 10

---

[*]The formula for precise calculation of the depreciation rate is

$$1 - \sqrt[n]{(s/c)}$$

where n is the number of years of expected life for the asset, s the scrap value or resale value on retirement and c the initial acquisition cost or valuation.

Exhibit 20
The Standard Plc
Balance Sheet as at ...

	£	£			£	£
Subscribed Capital and Reserves				*Fixed Assets*		
10,000 Ordinary shares of £1 each		10,000		Buildings at cost	4,000	
Profit	1,000			Less depreciation to date	60	3,940
Less depreciation	810	190		Plant at cost	3,000	
				Less depreciation to date	750	2,250
TOTAL SHAREHOLDERS' INTEREST		10,190		TOTAL FIXED ASSETS		6,190
Current Liabilities				*Current Assets*		
Creditors		3,000		Stock	1,000	
				Debtors	5,000	
				Cash	1,000	7,000
		£13,190				£13,190

Exhibit 21

	£	£
Fixed Assets		
Building at cost	4,000	
Less aggregate depreciation	120	3,880
Plant at cost	3,000	
Less aggregate depreciation	1,312	1,688

Exhibit 22

	£
Buildings depreciation – straight line	60
Plant depreciation – second year of reducing balance	562
TOTAL	£622

together, we arrive at the sum of 55. Each year's depreciation charge and the resultant asset value in the balance sheets will then be determined as shown in Exhibit 23, and so on until the tenth year of life would result in a charge of £56 for asset use. Two observations arise in connection with sum-of-the-years' digits: they are

1　An asset can be completely eliminated from the books of the firm.
2　The rate of decline in asset values and profit and loss account charges is not so great as in the reducing-balance method.

Exhibit 23
Sum-of-the-years' digits: annual depreciation charges and asset values

Year	Formula	Charge in Profit and Loss Account £	Net asset value in Balance Sheet £
1	$\dfrac{10}{55} \times £3,000$	545	2,455
2	$\dfrac{9}{55} \times £3,000$	491	1,964
3	$\dfrac{8}{55} \times £3,000$	436	1,528

Now without a precise scientific examination of the impact of corporate activity upon asset efficiency and contribution to earnings it would be difficult to *assert* which of the above two methods is the more realistic. Indeed the appropriate level of a depreciation charge for a capital asset will vary from company to company. These circumstances might lead business managers to establish their own depreciation codes, based upon their own past experiences of asset lives and operating efficiencies. Such a company code is exemplified in Exhibit 24.

1981 Act balance sheet formats

The balance sheets given in this chapter's exhibits have continued to be drawn in the conventional two sided form of presentation, in order to facilitate the reader's appreciation of the progress of our company in its use of funds to obtain assets for business operations. Exhibit 25 below now shows the data given in Exhibit 20 – but in one of the 1981 Act's required layouts.

An important point arises. The practice of showing the related year end totals of (for example) groups of assets, and of the final balance remaining on the profit and loss account, enables a balance sheet in sharper, clearer

Exhibit 24

Company depreciation code

Details		Forecast economic life in years		
		2	5	7
		%	%	%
Proportion of	1	60	40	35
initial outlay	2	40	25	20
cost to be	3		20	12.5
charged in	4		10	12.5
years	5		5	10
	6			5
	7			5

Exhibit 25
The Standard Plc
Balance Sheet as at…

		£	£
B	*Fixed assets*		
	I Intangible assets		—
	II Tangible assets		6,190
	III Investments		—
			6,190
C	*Current assets*		
	I Stock		
	1 Raw materials	1,000	
	II Debtors		
	1 Trade debtors	5,000	
	IV Cash in hand and at bank	1,000	
		7,000	
E	*Creditors:* amounts falling due within one year		
	4 Trade creditors	3,000	
F	*Net current assets*		4,000
G	*Total assets less current liabilities*		£10,190
K	*Capital and reserves*		
	I Called up share capital		10,000
	V Profit and loss account		190
	TOTAL SHAREHOLDERS' INTEREST		£10,190

outline to be published. It gives the principal facts about the firm without the potential confusions of too much detail. Such a method does not mean that the disclosure of information, which is legally required, is being avoided. Such data can be, and is most frequently given in explanatory notes attached to the published accounts.

Exhibit 26 below is an example of such a note: here it provides a detailed composition of the fixed asset total of £6,190 which is recorded in Exhibit 25. Exhibit 26 also includes descriptions of some fixed asset transactions which might take place in a company's accounting year and would need to be disclosed to meet the requirements of law.

Exhibit 26
Movements in fixed assets during year

Details	Freehold Buildings	Plant	Total
	£	£	£
As at 1st January	4,000	3,000	7,000
Plus additions	—	—	—
revaluations	—	—	—
Less disposals	—	—	—
depreciation in year	60	750	810
As at 31st December	£3,940	£2,250	£6,190

Clearly some numerical reference relating the item in the published balance sheet to its explanatory note, which enlarges upon the figures in the balance sheet, is necessary. Such guidance is always given.

Now we have not yet produced separate profit and loss accounts relating to the balance sheets shown in our various exhibits. However, for the purposes of our examinations, we will assume that the profit before depreciation was £1,000 (as in fact is reported in Exhibit 20). In this case a further explanatory note would be published, as shown in Exhibit 27, to

Exhibit 27
Profit and Loss Account

The profit was arrived at after charging:	
	£
audit fees	—
interest payable	—
directors' fees	—
depreciation for the year	810

show the disclosure items which have affected the determination of the profit and loss amounts shown in the balance sheet.

Again the exhibit includes the description of some of the items found in profit and loss accounts and which are subject to the disclosure requirements of the Companies Acts 1948–81.

Repairs and maintenance

Text books and other theoretical appraisals of accounting practices point out that plant and machinery, in the earlier years of economic life, suffer less from the need for repairs and maintenance. Thus in those earlier years of life the profit and loss account bears a lower charge for keeping the assets in good operating condition than is experienced in the later years. Consequently it is argued that the calculation of depreciation by the reducing balance method (and other similar methods) should result in a more even total charge against income for the use and operation of those assets. The argument is based upon a presumed rising annual cost of maintenance. The case has its defects, particularly when we consider settling-in costs, initial trial and testing costs, pre-production runs for some new item of plant and machinery. These costs can be quite substantial. They result in the first year of a new plant's life being the most expensive period of its operating life, contributing little to the overall productive efficiency of the firm.

Now one cannot foresee with any certainty the future trend of repairs and maintenance expenditure for all types of plant, though good plant records will be of some help. Repairs and maintenance costs may increase at a gradually growing rate, or they may not present any particular pattern at all especially when a major overhaul becomes necessary. Such comments all point to the fact that it is not possible to forecast all future repairs and maintenance costs with any certainty. In many instances however we can indicate that, in the first year or years of life of expensive complicated machinery, installation and running costs may be inordinately high in comparison with succeeding years. In view of these comments it does not s sound principle to opt for a reducing cost method of depreciation simply because it *may* have the function of spreading more evenly over the life of an asset the costs of having it and using it in business operations.

Review of basic data

Whichever method is adopted for the calculation of depreciation, the bases upon which those calculations are made, i.e. expected useful life, expected residual value, should be reviewed periodically. Many years ago one of our most famous companies reviewed its depreciation charges which were calculated on the straight-line basis. Attention was paid to initial cost, expected life, expected residual value and, in this instance, to replacement cost also. During their review, the company's accountants discovered that depreciation charges which had been levied in past years had resulted in an overcharge (in total) of depreciation to those past years, simply because it was evident that the plant and machinery were going to last longer than was originally estimated! Here then was the problem: should the accountants re-open the past years' accounts and charge to those accounts revised computations of depreciation? Or should they re-calculate the depreciation charges for the future years only bearing in mind the now extended expected future life of the assets involved? What actually happened was the latter: the balances remaining in the books represented the unrecovered net costs of the assets – to be spread over a longer period in the future than was originally thought.

In succeeding years the charge for depreciation, still calculated by the straight-line method, in respect of those assets was therefore automatically reduced.

Replacement of historical cost

So far we have been concerned with depreciation as a means of recovering the original cost of the asset less its expected sale value on retirement. In his *Principles of Economics*, Pigou says 'the manufacturer knows that his machinery wears out, and if his capital is to remain unimpaired he must set aside something annually to replace it. If he is to secure a permanent profit he must reckon these amounts as part of his expenses'. If, as may be implied here, depreciation must be regarded also as a means of providing for the replacement of assets when they wear out, then some consideration must be given to the possible costs of replacing the assets, especially in times of inflation. Having studied the impact of depreciation upon building and plant values shown in the balance sheets of Exhibits 18 and 20, the reader has seen the effect upon profit also: it was reduced by the depreciation charge.

Appreciating this impact on profit is important because the *net* profit, remaining after all operating costs and taxation charges have been met, is the source of dividends and appropriations for the growth and development of the business. Thus it is clear that decisions affecting the calculation of annual depreciation charges may have a decisive impact on the rate of dividends being paid. The depreciation charge can have the effect of a *conserver* of corporate cash resources in that the consequent reduction in post-tax profits should act to prevent unreasonably high dividend distributions. At least the Board's dividend decision will be made within the context of more realistic profit reporting. The size of the depreciation charge is an important feature in the 'realistic profit' notion when we realise that the charge can be based upon

1   The historical acquisition of costs of the asset.
2   Its current replacement cost.
3   Some future replacement cost.

Again we must return to the question of 'what is the object of the depreciation charge?' If the object is to evaluate a cost of use of the assets then we have to decide which of the above three costs should be regarded as the basis of the depreciation calculations. Added emphasis has been given to the answer to this question by a continuing high rate of inflation and strong arguments are put forward for the replacement cost concept. At least the cost-of-use charge in the profit and loss account will match the better with other current operating costs, and with the income they generate.

The conventional profit and loss account has always used factual historical cost data, but the picture is changing. Accounts or subsidiary statements which demonstrate the financial/cost effects of an unstable monetary unit form the subject of specific recommendations for company reporting. Such information is essential for a better appraisal of corporate worth and profitability – the limitations upon the worth of reported *money* profits are thus exposed. The need for a more realistic value when accounting for the consumption of business assets in generating income has given rise to several methods for dealing with the effects of changing price levels. These are explained, briefly, below.

Replacement cost method

This method envisages that depreciation charges will be based upon the estimated replacement cost of the fixed asset involved. But some doubt surrounds the estimation of a replacement cost. Except in the very short period it cannot be calculated with great accuracy: therefore personal opinion must influence the valuation and consequently the size of the annual depreciation charge. Furthermore one cannot be sure that a piece of plant and equipment will be replaced by a similar item. Whilst the improbability of replacing one item of plant by another piece of *similar* equipment is not a major criticism of the method (a firm may wish to change its product lines or methods of production), the difficulties of assessing future replacement costs are too great to ignore.

Revaluing or writing-up method

Reference has been made earlier to revaluing fixed assets to bring their balance sheet worth into line with current levels of worth. Such a process has the effect of treating the business as though it had just started, with current values being attributed to its capital assets and thus shown in its accounts and balance sheet. Where this method is used, depreciation is charged on the higher values and a greater charge is levied against current income before profit is determined. Objective revaluations of capital assets should be accomplished by applying a specific industry plant-cost index to historic cost values. The influences of the opinions of interested parties would be minimised thereby.

The current-value method

Here the object of the cost-of-use assessment is to charge for the consumption of capital assets at current values, not as an allocation of an historical cost. Depreciation would be regarded as a measure of the consumption of asset values at the current prices, as if the assets had been bought at those prices. Again it is emphasised that opinion – rather than fact – will determine the current values selected, unless some independent index of value changes is used.

Index of purchasing power

The above methods of reporting changes in the values of fixed assets, and thus 'revaluing' the annual depreciation charges, do not envisage examinations of all other current asset values or of liabilites. A more refined method of judging the change in value of an asset can be effected by the use of a general index – an index of the purchasing power of money. The method recognises that the problems of replacement accounting and determination of profit revolve around the fact that an income obtained from the sale of commodities is expressed in terms of today's values. The same comment applies to most of the expenditures incurred in generating the income. But the capital assets used in producing the turnover are expressed in the currency of the period when those assets were bought. They are recorded in yesterday's prices. Now in a period of inflation, these two groups of monetary value measures are by no means comparable: a result of this inequality is that depreciation is based upon money values of some years ago, whilst rent and wages, etc., reflect the current year's values.

The object of the purchasing power index method – for determining depreciation – would be to eliminate the differences arising from inflation between the monetary values given to the other cost/income items and the monetary values given to the cost of use of assets. In practice the method would be applied to the historical cost of the assets so as to increase their book values by the amount of the change in the index. Depreciation would then be calculated by reference of the adjusted book values. But there is another considerable advantage which accrues to the operation of the purchasing power index method. Its application is not restricted to fixed assets only. Variations in the index are applied to the other aspects of business operations also and here current assets, liabilities and the remaining cost/income items will undergo adjustments which reflect the impact of changes in the value of money. Its effect is more comprehensive; its full practical operation will therefore be demonstrated in a later chapter.

Funds for asset replacement

The reader should remember that, in discussing replacement cost accounting, much of the emphasis has been laid on rising prices. The experiences of recent years have naturally stimulated the thinking which has concentrated attention on replacing capital assets at increasing acquisition costs. But if such a system is used for replacement cost accounting, then it must be used consistently. However unlikely it may seem, the consequences of falling price levels must be considered also. In these instances the replacement of plant and equipment would cost less than in the past and adjusted depreciation charges would not be sufficient to eliminate the original cost of an asset from the firm's books. We return to the problem of defining profit. If we say that profit is the excess of income over the cost of getting that income we must remember that 'cost' includes capital costs as well as revenue costs. If profit is achieved after accounting for the replacement cost, or current cost, of capital assets, then that definition must apply in periods of falling prices also.

Now depreciation charges do not produce a cash income for the firm. This is done by selling goods at a profit – a result of the costs of operations being less than the income from the sales produced by those operations. Depreciation merely reduces the *accounting* profit by charging some part of an asset's book value against income before profit is calculated. Whilst this reduction in accounting profit does not result from a cash outflow of money, it does act to retain cash within the firm in that dividend payments will be constrained to more realistic levels.

Even so we have to recognise that a company's cash inflow will be available for all corporate uses. It is used to invest in working capital and to meet the expenses of expansion and diversification. Therefore, unless amounts of cash equivalent to the depreciation charges are invested elsewhere, it does not follow that ready money will be available for asset replacement when it becomes necessary to retire a piece of plant. Such is not the automatic function of charging for depreciation: corporate financial planning must prepare for those requirements. Here it is appropriate to reflect on the effects of replacement cost accounting upon depreciation charges. Whilst the cost of an asset is rising, each separate year's profit and loss account will bear a charge based upon the increased cost of asset replacement. It does so however in that year's account only. No action is taken to recover increased depreciation costs from previous years' accounts and therefore any summation of the year by year depreciation charges could not hope to match the rising replacement costs or represent a fund of money available to pay for the new, more costly replacement asset. Again the reader is referred to the function of corporate financial planning and to the problem of defining income.

Self-examination questions

1   The accountant is concerned with achieving a realistic – rather than an exact – description of a company's wealth. How does the principle of charging for fixed asset depreciation assist, or deny, the achievement of this aim?

2   Why should we charge for depreciation in a profit and loss account when the current values of the related assets are rising?

3   Describe and appraise two commonly accepted methods of determining charges for fixed asset depreciation.

4   What does replacement cost mean and how would you assess it? What is the object of valuing fixed assets at their replacement costs?

5   Does the act of charging for depreciation ensure the availability of funds for asset replacement when that need arises?

6   A balance sheet is merely a valuation statement. Discuss.

Recommended reading

ICA, 'Accounting for Depreciation' (SSAP12) and 'Accounting for Investment Property' (SSAP19): Publications Department, Institute of Chartered Accountants in England and Wales, PO Box 433, Moorgate Place, London EC2P 2BJ.

ROCKLEY, L.E. *Finance for the Purchasing Executive*, Business Books (1978), pp. 8–12 and pp. 61–2.

BAXTER, W.T., and DAVIDSON, S., *Studies in Accounting*, ICAEW (1977).

NOKE, C., 'The Reality of Property Depreciation', *Accountancy* (November 1979), pp. 129–30.

4　Stock valuation and the determination of income

Introduction

The objective of the profit and loss account is to show how the profit was made, or loss incurred during a specified period. Here it is important to note that the heading of the account will always give the period to which it relates. The heading or title to the account (see Exhibit 28) states that it is the Profit and Loss Account *for the year ended* 31 December 19.. or some other relevant period and date. Consequently the reader knows that each of the

Exhibit 28
Profit and Loss Account for the year ended ...

Expenditure	*Income*
1　Goods and services consumed leading to cash outflows	1　Sales, turnover – leading to cash inflows
2　Depreciation charges – not leading to cash outflows	
3　Profit (accounting net income) – where income exceeds expenditure	2　Loss – where expenditure exceeds income

items of expenditure and income relate to the costs and gains of that period only. Now when the accountant talks of expenditure and income he has a mental picture of the value of goods and services consumed in producing a quantity of sales. The fact that some of this resource consumption, or sales output, may not have been paid for is not a criterion for judging the money values to be entered in profit and loss accounts. Naturally the businessman must pay for the resources he uses, and will expect to be paid for the sales he achieves but such *money* transactions will be found in the cash account – another name for which is the receipts and payments account.

The 1981 Companies Act

The final accounts used in later exhibits have been limited in their content in order to present, in clear fashion, the consequences of different methods of stock valuation. The accounts have moreover been drawn in formats which the reader will meet in practical business situations. However the 1981 Act sets out four profit and loss account formats in which published accounts may be presented (see Appendix A). Companies may choose one of these forms of layout, and would be expected to use the same style in publishing accounts for subsequent financial years, unless the directors consider that there are special reasons for changing the format. If the format is changed the directors must disclose the reasons.

The reader should note the considerable variations in the disclosure requirements of the different formats. Styles 2 and 4 report the cost of raw materials consumed during the period of the account; this is an item of great value in calculating the company's stock turnover rates in each year (see page 135). We can thereby evaluate the efficiency of the company's stockholding and usage policies. On the other hand, formats 1 and 3 do not ask for this information to be given but they do require that gross profit, distribution costs and administration costs should be revealed (with depreciation reported in a note attached to the profit and loss account). So the permitted formats vary greatly and company directors will choose the type which suits their own needs for confidentiality. Clearly distribution cost data would be a vital factor for a company engaged in the distributive trade, and such a firm might not wish to follow formats 1 and 3.

Income and expenditure

The essential difference between expenditure and payments, between income and receipts, must be appreciated before any further understanding of finance can be pursued. Broadly, expenditure relates to the total cost of the *resources used up* during the period stated at the head of the account. Payments, on the other hand, refer to *money paid* during the same operating period for those goods and services, which the business has used or will use *at any time*. Payments, although made during an operating period, do not necessarily relate to resource consumption in that particular period only. Some amounts may be paid in advance of next year's planned output: some amounts may be paid in arrear, being outstanding debts from last year's trading. Again, income represents the value of sales achieved by the firm during the period given at the head of the account. The total of sales achieved should agree with the total value of goods despatched to customers from the factory or shop during that same period – after adjusting for returns and goods out on approval. Receipts describe money transactions, actual cash received for goods and services delivered by the firm whether those goods and services were provided during the period of account or not.

Thus we return to the concept of 'matching', explained in Chapter 2, and emphasise that the type and size of the expenditures listed in the profit and loss account will denote those expenditures which were a necessary concomitant to the incomes shown in that account. No item of expenditure will be included in the left-hand side of the profit and loss account unless it forms part of the total resource consumption required to achieve the output of goods and services, shown as income on the right-hand side of the account. 'Matching' necessitates an understanding of the acts of accrual and prepayment which bring to profit and loss accounts a closer definition of income. 'Accrual' refers to those items of expenditure or income which have not yet reached the account books of the firm, but which need to be recorded in order to attain a more realistic profitability reporting. The following items are good examples of accruals:

1   An electricity bill, not yet received for entering in the books of account or the profit and loss account, but relating to electricity consumed during the period of account.
2   Rent income relating to the period of the account but not yet billed to the tenant.

Item 1 would increase the electricity charge in the profit and loss account and be shown as a creditor in the balance sheet's current liabilities section – both for the estimated amount of the account. Item 2 would increase income in the profit and loss account and be shown as a debtor amongst current assets – again both for the expected amount of rent due.

'Prepayment' involves an appraisal of the relationship of certain cash payments with the expenditure content of a profit and loss account. For example, the rates due to a local authority are frequently paid at the commencement of a specific rating year or half year. To the extent that the payment relates to a period beyond that of the current profit and loss account, it is said to be 'rates prepaid'. The amount of such a prepayment must be recorded amongst the current assets in a balance sheet drawn up on the last day of the account period. The remainder of the payment becomes part of the local authority services applicable to the period of the account.

In the foregoing paragraphs we have examined the content of profit and loss accounts by comparing the accounting concepts of income and expenditure with the more widely understood notions of receipts and payments. These two definitions of two groups of business transactions, the consuming and the paying functions, are but further analyses of the main categories of commercial spendings – capital expenditure and revenue expenditure. The reader will be acquainted with the impact of capital expenditures upon the balance sheet picture of the firm, and with the impact of revenue expenditures upon the profit picture of the firm. This knowledge must now be used to emphasise the potentially serious effects of erroneous categorisation of expenditures. Thus, if capital expenditures of significant amount were treated as revenue and charged to the profit and loss account, then the reported profitability of the company would be markedly at fault: comparisons with other years and with other firms would result in misleading conclusions. There would be an apparent, but erroneous, lessening of corporate profitability. At the same time the firm's asset status, the total shareholders' interest, the book value of the ordinary shares would be similarly misrepresented at lower (than expected) book values. On the other hand, should revenue expenditure be recorded amongst fixed assets in the balance sheet, the reverse position would be the result. Again, profitability and asset worth would be misrepresented at relatively higher levels. But throughout this argument we have to remember the doctrine of materiality, for it is only when items of material money size are involved that firm application of the capital and revenue expenditure categorisation must be adhered to.

Expenditure flows

We have faced the problem of assessing the cost of fixed asset use in seeking to attain a more realistic statement of corporate profit. But this is not the only area where subjective allocations of expenditure flows can make a significant impact upon the determination of accounting profit. The cost of raw materials or goods consumed in a production process or retail trade and the consequent valuation of year end stocks, can also be computed by different routines. Each of these various stock cost routines will result in different expenditure totals being charged against the income shown in a profit and loss account. Thus the book profit reported in that account will be affected.

The simple profit statements shown in Exhibits 29 and 30, which cover two years of a firm's life, are presented in a form different from that outlined in Exhibit 28. These accounts are written in narrative (vertical) form rather than the conventional two sided style. The narrative style seems easier to follow, it takes up less space, therefore accounts for several periods can be placed side by side. Cost and profit comparisons can be more effectively observed, as these exhibits will demonstrate. The exhibits emphasise the importance of stock cost allocation and stock valuation in any appraisal of corporate net income, the book profit referred to in the previous paragraph.

An essential feature to note in these exhibits is the fact that the closing stock value of year 1 equates with the opening stock value of year 2. This fact must remain unless some readjustment of stock values takes place in year 2, and unless losses of stock arise through fire or theft immediately

Exhibit 29

Stock cost flows, stock valuation and book profit

Year 1	£	£	Year 2	£	£
Sales		2,000	Sales		2,400
Cost of goods sold:			Cost of goods sold:		
Opening stock	100		Opening stock	150	
Purchases	1,050		Purchases	1,350	
	1,150			1,500	
Less closing stock	150	1,000	Less closing stock	300	1,200
GROSS PROFIT		£1,000	GROSS PROFIT		£1,200

Exhibit 30

Stock cost flows, stock valuation and book profit

Year 1	£	£	Year 2	£	£
Sales		2,000	Sales		2,400
Cost of goods sold:			Cost of goods sold:		
Opening stock	100		Opening stock	250	
Purchases	1,050		Purchases	1,350	
	1,150			1,600	
Less closing stock	250	900	Less closing stock	300	1,300
GROSS PROFIT		£1,100	GROSS PROFIT		£1,100

after the close of business at the end of the year 1. Now when the profitability in year 2 (Exhibit 29) is compared with that for year 1, a satisfactory position is given, in that

Sales have increased by 20 per cent.
Profits have increased by 20 per cent.
Gross profit as a percentage of sales in each year stands at 50 per cent.

We will now assume that a different view of allocating costs of materials consumed, and therefore of valuing the year 1 closing stocks, was taken. Exhibit 30 shows the result.

In order to highlight the effect of different methods of stock valuation and of calculating cost of materials consumed, all other data have been left unchanged. A radically different picture of the firm's profitability progress is revealed when, again, year 2 is compared with year 1. Thus –

Sales have increased by 20 percent.
Profit remains unchanged.

Gross profit as a percentage of sales has declined from 55 per cent in
year 1 to 45.8 per cent in year 2.

Exhibits 29 and 30 show the effect on profit of a variation in the routine
of calculating the cost of materials consumed in business activities. Such a
variation affected the valuation of the end year stocks of unused materials in
year 1. Now the year end stocks will be assets of the current period and as
such must be shown in the appropriate balance sheet. Clearly then, the
routine of calculating a cost of materials consumed – the flow of materials
costs – through its impact upon year end stock valuations, will affect the
asset worth of the firm also. Similarly, variations in reported profits will
have an impact upon the book value of the total shareholders' interest. This
is because profit is shown in the balance sheet grouping of issued shares and
reserves. Thus materials cost flows, stock valuations, depreciation charges
and fixed asset book valuations each have a power to affect data in both
profit and loss accounts AND balance sheets. Any conclusions drawn from
those two statements must be conditioned by materials cost flow assumptions and by choices of methods for calculating depreciation.

But different methods of materials cost allocations and stock valuation
will have a significant effect on profit, etc., only when replacement stocks of
materials or components are bought at differing prices (an oversimplifica-
tion which will not detract from the ensuing explanations). Here it is
essential to our understanding of materials expenditure determination that
we recognise the essential similarity of many of the materials and
component items used in production and other commercial activities. In a
period of inflation especially, it is the *price* of the goods which changes: the
raw materials, stocks or components purchased by a business will be
fundamentally the same. Where there is no distinction in the physical
properties and uses of items purchased at different times, there can be no
need to ensure that when such a good is consumed or used in the business
activity the item is linked with its *own* purchase price for the purpose of
expenditure calculation.

FIFO and LIFO

Two of the accounting routines for arriving at materials expenditure to be
charged in a profit and loss account will now be examined. These two
examples are known as

1   The first in, first out method (FIFO).
2   The last in, the first out method (LIFO).

The descriptions relate to unit cost movements; they are statements about a
systematic flow of *costs* which aggregate to expenditure totals in a profit and
loss account. FIFO demands that when physically interchangeable items are

issued from stock to be consumed in a production or retailing activity, the profit and loss account will be charged with the purchase prices of the first of those goods to be received in the firm's storehouse. On the other hand, LIFO will ensure that the profit and loss account is charged with last cost received into the firm's storehouse. FIFO and LIFO do not depict a situation where the date of receipt of a stores item determines the order in which goods are issued to a production or other trading activity. They are not routines which report and control the physical movement of goods: they are concerned with accounting for the costs to be entered in profit and loss accounts in ways which ensure a consistent approach to expenditure determination.

The next exhibits present simple numerical examples of the FIFO and LIFO cost flow routines. The examples (see Exhibits 31–33) portray a firm using two components A and B in the products it makes and sells. Furthermore, we assume a sequence of component purchases, bringing goods into the storehouse, before any items are issued to production.

If we assume that the manufacturing process commences after the above purchases, and consumes 900 units of A and 1800 units of B, our materials expenditure totals will be calculated as shown below. At the same time the valuation of the items remaining in the storehouse appears as a summation of the item/costs left in stock.

The final accounts

The materials expenditure and stock valuations which derive from the above FIFO and LIFO calculations are now incorporated into alternative profit and loss accounts and balance sheets of the firm. They are the only items in these statements which show any change in money value so that the consequences of the two cost flow routines are shown clearly. The reader should note that

1 Under FIFO the profit is higher than under LIFO: thus it may be said that FIFO overstates the profit.
2 Under FIFO the value of the net assets is higher than under LIFO.
3 Under FIFO the net asset worth of a £1 Ordinary share is £1.18 whilst under LIFO it is £1.15.
4 Under FIFO the net profit to sales ratio is 12 per cent whereas under LIFO it is 9.9 per cent.
5 Under FIFO the amount of working capital and the current ratio will be larger than under LIFO.

And so the comparisons could continue but an important qualification remains. These situations arise because the examples given in the Exhibits 31 to 34 reflect the consequences of *rising* prices, a result of persistent

Exhibit 31
Component purchases

Details	Component A			Component B		
	Number purchased	*Unit price, £*	*Total purchase price, £*	*Number purchased*	*Unit price, £*	*Total purchase price, £*
1st purchase	250	45	11,250	400	27	10,800
2nd purchase	150	46	6,900	350	29	10,150
3rd purchase	300	48	14,400	400	31	12,400
4th purchase	200	49	9,800	400	32	12,800
5th purchase	350	50	17,500	450	34	15,300
TOTALS	1,250	—	£59,850	2,000	—	£61,450

Exhibit 32
FIFO routine
Materials expenditure and stock valuation

Details	Units consumed				Total purchase prices		Expenditure and stock valuation totals £
	A	Unit price, £	B	Unit price, £	A £	B £	
1st purchase	250	45	400	27	11,250	10,800	
2nd purchase	150	46	350	29	6,900	10,150	
3rd purchase	300	48	400	31	14,400	12,400	
4th purchase	200	49	400	32	9,800	12,800	
5th purchase	—		250	34	—	8,500	
TOTAL UNITS CONSUMED	900	—	1,800	—			
Materials expenditure – to Profit and Loss Account					42,350	54,650	97,000
Number of units remaining in stock	350	50	200	34	17,500	6,800	24,300
Stock valuations							
TOTAL PURCHASE DATA	1,250	—	2,000	—	£59,850	£61,450	£121,300

Exhibit 33
LIFO routine
Materials expenditure and stock valuation

Details	Units consumed				Total purchase prices		Expenditure and stock valuation totals, £
	A	Unit price, £	B	Unit price, £	A £	B £	
5th purchase	350	50	450	34	17,500	15,300	
4th purchase	200	49	400	32	9,800	12,800	
3rd purchase	300	48	400	31	14,400	12,400	
2nd purchase	50	46	350	29	2,300	10,150	
1st purchase	—	—	200	27		5,400	
TOTAL UNITS CONSUMED	900	—	1,800	—			
Materials expenditure – to Profit and Loss Account					44,000	56,050	100,050
Number of units remaining in stock	100	46	200	27			
	250	45					
Stock valuations					15,850	5,400	21,250
TOTAL PURCHASE DATA	1,250	—	2,000	—	£59,850	£61,450	£121,300

74

Exhibit 34

Stock valuation and corporate performance

Income for the year

FIFO	£	£	LIFO	£	£
Sales		150,000	Sales		150,000
Cost of sales:			Cost of sales:		
Purchases	121,300		Purchases	121,300	
Less closing			Less closing		
stock	24,300	97,000	stock	21,250	100,050
GROSS PROFIT		53,000	GROSS PROFIT		49,950
Other			Other		
expenditure	20,000		expenditure	20,000	
Depreciation	15,000	35,000	Depreciation	15,000	35,000
NET PROFIT		£18,000	NET PROFIT		£14,950

Balance Sheets at year end

	£	£		£	£
Fixed assets	100,000		Fixed assets	100,000	
Less deprec'n	15,000	85,000	Less deprec'n	15,000	85,000
Current assets:			Current assets:		
Stocks	24,300		Stocks	21,250	
Debtors	17,000		Debtors	17,000	
Cash	3,700		Cash	3,700	
	45,000			41,950	
Less creditors	12,000		Less creditors	12,000	
WORKING CAPITAL		33,000	WORKING CAPITAL		29,950
		£118,000			£114,950
TOTAL SHAREHOLDERS'			TOTAL SHAREHOLDERS'		
INTEREST:			INTEREST:		
Shares		100,000	Shares		100,000
Net profit		18,000	Net profit		14,950
		£118,000			£114,950

inflation for example. Should the position be reversed and a pattern of falling prices be demonstrated, each of the above conclusions 1 to 5 would be reversed also.

Valuation of stock and work-in-progress

The cost flow routines previously outlined may be applied both to the issue of materials in a manufacturing business and to goods issued for sale in a retail concern. But where raw materials or components are used in a manufacturing operation, then the particular cost flow routine which is used will have its impact on valuations of work-in-progress also. Moreover, within the context of stock valuations, should we not also consider the firm's overhead expenses? These expenses relate to a firm established in a specific type of business, ready to operate at a certain level of activity; without the firm itself there would be no stock, either of raw materials or work-in-progress, etc!

Now there have always been different views as to whether some of the overhead expenditures should be included in valuations of stock and work-in-progress, in attempting to quantify the whole costs of bringing such stocks *to their existing state and location*. In this matter overhead expenditures will include plant depreciation, rent, rates, administration, etc. But for the purposes of stock valuation, selling and distribution overheads would be ignored for they do not relate to the cost of holding stock, they deal with passing stocks away from the firm. Clearly when some of the overhead expenses are allocated to stocks, their computed book value – not market value – will rise. The book profits will be affected also, as we have seen in Exhibits 29 and 30.

Arguments which are said to support the inclusion of some overhead expenditures in stock valuations rest mainly upon the matching principle (see page 29). Thus, in so far as overhead expenses are included in stock valuations, they are carried forward from one year to the next succeeding year. When goods are sold in the second year, the overhead expenses carried forward will be effectively charged against that sales income which they generate. Though some of the corporate overhead expenses will be related to the existence of stocks *only in a very indirect sense*, their inclusion in the valuation of stocks ensures that they are NOT effectively charged against income until the relevant sales are accomplished. This is the application of the matching principle which is the basis of the argument.

The contrary view to that which recommends the inclusion of some overhead expenses in stock valuations, deals with the 'marginal' costs of goods and work-in-progress in stocks. The marginal view contends that most overhead expenses arise from the existence of the firm itself: they do not relate directly to the level of activity of the firm's business. In other words, overhead expenses are incurred irrespective of the levels of stock and work-in-progress and therefore should be excluded from any stock valuations. Furthermore, the money values of the overheads aggregate largely through the passage of time and here plant depreciation, rent, rates, etc., are good examples of this point. When this stand is taken, when

76

unrelated overhead expenses cannot be held to be *caused* by stock holding and therefore are excluded from stock valuations, then the true costs of having specific levels of stock or work-in-progress are revealed. Business decisions will be guided by data which reflect more realistically the financial consequences of the decisions. It is here that marginal analysis assumes its most important role.

Specific aspects of the inclusion/exclusion of overhead expenses controversy will now be examined. Clearly, the case for the exclusion of overhead expenditure is strong if:

1 The level of business activity remains reasonably constant.
2 The nature of the firm's business is highly competitive and subject to price cutting by other firms.
3 Overhead charges accrue mainly on a time basis.

With regard to (1) any allocation of these expenses to stock will have little comparable effect on the book profits of successive years. But when the variation in activity levels is marked, the case for excluding (unrelated) overhead expenses is equally marked. Such expenditure would have to be met by the firm irrespective of its stock holding operations.

On the other hand, a case can be made for the inclusion of overhead expenditure in stock and work-in-progress valuations if

1 The production cycle is a long one.
2 Firms engage in contract work extending over a period longer than one year.

To do otherwise could result in abnormal, unrealistic, profit/loss declarations in successive years. The concept of matching must be applied with the object of achieving a more equitable reporting of corporate net income in successive years. In any situation, allocations of overhead expenditure to stock valuations must be based upon the firm's normal activity levels. In this context strikes and machinery breakdowns should not result in lower levels of stocks and outputs bearing a greater proportion of overhead expenses than would *normally* be the case.

Stock valuation – accounting standards and the law

In dealing with the question of whether or not to include overhead expenses in the valuation of stocks, an overriding requirement remains that such valuations do not exceed current replacement prices for the stocks involved. In the past it has been recommended that published accounts should state the bases used in valuing the stocks shown in those accounts. Notes appended to the accounts have reported that stocks had been valued by reference to their

(*a*) cost, or
(*b*) cost plus a proportion of variable overheads, or
(*c*) cost plus a proportion of manufacturing and administrative
overheads.
Other explanations included statements such as
(*d*) at the lower of cost or net realisable value, or
(*e*) at the lowest of cost, net realisable value, or replacement price.

The special problems of retail stores, with many separate items for sale, were met by adopting the method which valued stocks by taking the items' current selling prices (or proposed 'sales' prices) and then deducting the firm's normal gross profit margin.

The Accounting Standards Committee's current recommendations are embodied in a statement of standard accounting practice (SSAP9) issued in 1975, and the terms of this standard accord with Standard Number 2 of the International Accounting Standards Council. Broadly the Accounting Standards Committee opts for the matching concept in relation to the allocation of some overhead expenditures to stocks and work-in-progress, and to the periodic recognition of profit/loss on long term contracts. Clearly when these recommendations were first implemented, they resulted, in some instances, in increases in the values attaching to stocks and work-in-progress. With the matching of expenditure and income, the valuation of stocks, work-in-progress and finished goods should now include such expenditures[*] as arise in the normal course of trading and are necessary to bring the goods into their present location and condition.

The Standards Committee's statement of standard accounting practice sets out to establish common bases for valuation of stocks, in the hope that relevant data in the accounts of different companies will be reasonably comparable. But the original concept of standard accounting practices had the aim of reducing the element of subjectivity in the information content and values found in company accounts. To some extent it is questionable whether a more realistic set of values will emerge, because increasing elements of subjective judgement will be necessary to determine

(*a*) the appropriate proportion of overheads to be allocated to the
various categories of stocks, and
(*b*) the appropriate method(s) by which those overheads should be
further allocated to the various types and ages of stocks and products.

The 1981 Act has established new disclosure and valuation requirements for the various types of stocks held by companies. Exhibit 35 gives brief explanations of the terms of the Act and of SSAP9, together with a commentary on the implied variations in the data requirements of these two

*Costs of purchase may include items such as import duties, transport, handling and related legal costs (if any).

78

Exhibit 35
Comparison of stock disclosure and valuation rules

Items	1981 Companies Act	SSAP9	Comments
1 Disclosure	Stocks *must* be analysed, in balance sheets, between (a) raw materials (b) work-in-progress (c) finished goods (*Schedule 1, Section 8* – see Appendix A, page 339)	Stocks and work-in-progress *should* be analysed in balance sheets (or in explanatory notes attached thereto) in a 'manner which is appropriate to the business', showing the total values in each of the main groups. (*Paragraph 29*)	The 1981 Act is more specific in its balance sheet data requirements. SSAP9 allows corporate management to classify stocks in the balance sheet in a 'manner which is appropriate …' and thus avoids problems of transfer pricing disclosures.
2 Cost of purchases	The methods of costing which may be used are (a) FIFO (b) LIFO (c) weighted average price (d) any other similar method (e.g. standard costing) The directors of the company to decide on the method which appears to be most appropriate for the business. (*Schedule 1, Section 27*)	Corporate management to choose that method which gives the 'fairest approximation to actual cost'. e.g. (a) unit cost (b) average cost (c) FIFO LIFO is *not acceptable* as it does not give that 'fairest approximation to actual cost'. (*Appendix 1, paragraphs 11 and 12*)	The 1981 Act would enable the directors to elect to use LIFO where they judged it most appropriate to the circumstances of their business. SSAP9 does not accept the use of LIFO, but the overriding 1981 Act requirement to present a 'true and fair view' may give the directors power to use LIFO.

(continued on p. 80)

Exhibit 35 *(Continued)*

Items	1981 Companies Act	SSAP9	Comments
3 Production cost (e.g. work-in-progress and finished goods)	To be determined by the cost of purchases (see 2 above) plus a reasonable proportion of the indirect costs attributable to the *production* of the asset, so long as these indirect costs relate only to the period of production. Such indirect cost additions must not include distribution costs. (*Schedule 1, Section 26*)	To be determined by the cost of purchases (see 2 above) plus costs of conversion such as (a) *production* overheads attributable to a normal level of activity; (b) other overheads necessary to bring the product to its existing location and condition. (*Paragraphs 19 and 20*)	Little difference between the two, except for the purchase price problem of LIFO.
4 Limitations on stock valuations	In regard to (a) cost of purchase (b) production cost where balance sheet values, thus determined, differ materially from replacement cost at the date of the related balance sheet, the amount of the difference must be disclosed in an explanatory note attached to the accounts.	Balance sheet values of stocks, work-in-progress and finished goods should be derived from the lower of cost or net realisable value, and the accounting policies used in arriving at these valuations should be disclosed. (*Paragraph 11*)	(a) Net realisable value means the proposed or forecast selling price less (i) all other costs necessary to complete the item, and (ii) all other costs necessary in marketing, selling and distributing the products involved. (b) Replacement cost means the cost of acquiring or manufacturing an identical asset.

80

authorities. The exhibit does not detail the principles of valuing long- and short-term contract stocks, in the view that such matters are for more advanced study. However the Act's references to contract stocks do not imply much variation from SSAP9, because it states that

> only realised profits at the balance sheet date may be included in a profit and loss account
>
> *(Schedule 1 paragraph 12)*

and

> profits of a company fall to be treated as realised profits in accordance with generally accepted accounting principles which govern the preparation and presentation of those accounts
>
> *(Schedule 1, paragraph 90)*

Therefore the SSAP9 recommendation that profits on long term contracts should be included in profit and loss accounts, though at first seemingly at variance with the terms of the Act, must be acceptable in the light of the 'generally accepted accounting principles' which the Accounting Standards Committee promulgates for the UK.

Self-examination questions

1 Why does the profit and loss account include incomes and expenditures rather than receipts and payments?

2 What is the object of making charges in a profit and loss account for the depreciation of fixed assets? Do you consider that all companies should make provision for the depreciation of their buildings?

3 Describe the narrative form of the profit and loss account. What advantages stem from its use?

4 Describe the FIFO and LIFO routines for determining
   (a) expenditure on raw materials and components, and
   (b) the values of stocks remaining in the storehouse.

5 How does SSAP9 define 'cost of purchase' and why does the standard reject LIFO as a method of costing for raw material consumption?

6 To what extent should overhead costs be included in valuations of stocks, work-in-progress and finished goods?

7 Compare the requirements of the 1981 Act with those of SSAP9 in regard to the classification of stocks in a balance sheet.

Recommended reading

PARKER, R.H., and HARCOURT, G.C. (Editors), *Readings in the Concept and Measurement of Income*, Cambridge University Press (1969).

LANGLEY, F.P., *Introduction to Accounting for Business Studies*, Butterworth (1978).

HART, H., *Overhead Costs: Analysis and Control*, Heinemann (1973).

PIZZEY, A., *Accounting and Finance*, Holt, Rinehart and Winston (1980), see chapters 7, 14 and 15.

ICA, 'Accounting Standards 1982'.

5   Cash flow and funds flow: I

Introduction

Using Exhibit 15 on page 42 as our starting point we will now trace the further development of the Standard Plc and examine the effects upon the firm's final accounts of a continuing series of business transactions. The balance sheets resulting from these transactions will be used to demonstrate various styles of Funds Flow statements. Furthermore the value of these statements, for revealing how the firm has changed and how that change has been financed, will be emphasised.

Financing expansion

The first group of transactions which resulted in the Balance Sheet of Exhibit 36 are given below:

1   New machinery costing £500 was purchased on credit.
2   Additional stock at £1,500 was purchased on credit.
3   £500 was received by the company's cashier, from a debtor.

Here, as in other examples, the reader must note that the purchase of fixed assets on credit will affect working capital in the same way as the purchase of current assets, e.g. stock. Exhibit 36 shows a reasonable liquidity state when we consider the amount of working capital and the related current ratio. However, the liquid ratio does not present such a confident picture with only 75p worth of liquid assets being available to meet each £1 of current liabilities. The essential principle to note is that long life assets such as plant and machinery should not normally be financed from short-term credit facilities. If this kind of operation is repeated too frequently, the working capital will be eroded: it can be replaced only by an injection of fresh long-term funds, by the cash flow generated by profitable trading operations or by the sale of corporate fixed assets.

Exhibit 36
The Standard Plc
Balance Sheet as at ...

	£			£
Subscribed Capital and Reserves		*Fixed Assets*		
10,000 Ordinary		Buildings		4,000
shares of £1 each	10,000	Plant & machinery		3,500
Profit	1,000	Vehicles		1,000
TOTAL SHAREHOLDERS'		TOTAL FIXED ASSETS		8,500
INTEREST	11,000			
Current Liabilities		*Current Assets*		
Creditors	2,000	Stock	3,000	
		Debtors	1,000	
		Cash	500	4,500
	£13,000			£13,000

A further group of transactions involving fixed asset growth is given below:

1 Land and buildings were purchased on credit for £2,000.
2 New plant and machinery costing £500 was purchased for cash.
3 An old vehicle was sold for £500 cash (for the purpose of the example the asset's *book* value is presumed to be £500)
4 Additional stock at £4,000 was purchased on credit.
5 The cashier paid £2,000 to creditors and received £1,000 from debtors.
6 Using stock valued at £3,000 and paying £3,000 for manufacturing expenses, the company sold goods on credit for £10,000.

The resultant balance sheet is shown in Exhibit 37, where it can be seen that the current ratio has declined from 2.25 to 1.47, partly as a result of buying £2,500 of fixed assets by means of short term credit finance. Even though the liquid ratio appears satisfactory, the adequacy of the total fund of current assets to act as cover for the current liabilities should begin to give some concern.

Now the data given in transaction 6 will enable us to prepare a simple profit and loss account to show the operating results of this period. In its most rudimentary form such an account would be drawn as shown in Exhibit 38.

This profit of £4,000 is shown in Exhibit 37 to have been added to that profit recorded in the previous balance sheet, and the total shareholders' interest becomes £15,000. Therefore the net asset *book* worth of each £1 Ordinary share is now £1.50 – as a result of profitable use of the corporate assets.

Clearly in the simplest form of profit statement as given in Exhibit 38, the profit figure of £4,000 could represent the assessment of cash currently

Exhibit 37
The Standard Plc
Balance Sheet as at ...

	£			£
Subscribed Capital and Reserves		*Fixed Assets*		
10,000 Ordinary		Land and buildings		6,000
shares of £1 each	10,000	Plant & machinery		4,000
Profit	5,000	Vehicles		500
TOTAL SHAREHOLDERS'		TOTAL FIXED ASSETS		10,500
INTEREST	15,000			
Current Liabilities		*Current Assets*		
Creditors	6,000	Stock	4,000	
Bank overdraft	3,500	9,500	Debtors	10,000	14,000
		£24,500		£24,500

Exhibit 38
The Standard Plc
Profit and Loss Account for the year ended ...

	£		£
Stock consumed	3,000	Sales	10,000
Manufacturing			
expenses	3,000		
Profit	4,000		
	£10,000		£10,000

flowing to the firm as a result of its manufacturing and trading operations. This 'cash flow' assessment depends upon all of the items in the account being cash receipt or cash payment transactions: there is no non-cash expense such as depreciation. Turning to the balance sheet which includes this profit, the total value of the assets is shown to be £24,500: the firm has grown from an asset strength of £13,000 – an improvement of £11,500. This growth in asset strength contains the answer to why the cash balance of £500 in Exhibit 36 has been turned to an overdraft of £3,500 in Exhibit 37, despite the £4,000 net gain from profitable trading. A simple Funds Flow statement comparing the company state in Exhibit 36 with that demonstrated in Exhibit 37 (see Exhibit 39) explains how the cash has been used: a balance sheet variation statement similar to that shown on page 40 has not been

Exhibit 39
The Standard Plc
Funds Flow Statement for the period ended ...
(i.e. Exhibit 37)

	£
Sources of funds	
Profit	4,000
Increase in creditors	4,000
	£8,000
Applications of Funds	
Increased expenditure on fixed assets	2,000
Increased expenditure on stocks	1,000
Increase in debtors	9,000
	£12,000
Net cash movement	−£4,000

(Therefore £500 cash in hand becomes £3,500 overdrawn)

prepared here, for the reader can do that himself to verify the entries in the Funds Flow exhibit.

Appropriations of profit

The net profit referred to above is an important figure. It is from this sum that amounts due for taxation on profits are deducted: furthermore it represents the fund (post-tax) from which transfers to reserves may be made, and dividends paid. The pre-tax profit is also one area of a vital business ratio – return on sales. In this instance the £4,000 profit would be expressed as 40 per cent of sales. In commercial parlance our profit and loss account shows a return before tax of 40 per cent on sales.

It now remains to demonstrate the process of sharing out the profit between taxation, reserves and dividends, as well as bringing to account the impact of charges for depreciation. In this next example the amount given as the company's corporation tax assessment is not a precisely calculated sum, but a figure used for the purpose of demonstration only. This amount, and other transactions to be incorporated into our next balance sheet are as follows:

1 Debtors paid £5,000 to the company.
2 Inland Revenue agreed a Corporation Tax assessment of tax payable –
   £2,000.

86

3 Stock in Exhibit 37 to be divided into the following groups:
   (*a*) Raw materials, £2,500.
   (*b*) Work-in-progress £1,000.
   (*c*) Finished goods £500.
4 For entry in the balance sheet, work-in-progress is to be valued at £1,250: the increase of £250 represents cash spent on manufacturing operations.
5 For entry in the balance sheet, finished goods are to be valued at £1,000: the increase of £500 represents the cost of manufacturing operations: of this sum £250 has been paid in cash and £250 is still owing.
6 Transfer £2,000 from profit and place in a general reserve.
7 Pay creditors £1,500.

The balance sheet of the company after taking note of the above adjustments is shown at Exhibit 40.

Exhibit 40
The Standard Plc
Balance sheet as at ...

	£	£		£	£
Subscribed Capital and Reserves			*Fixed Assets*		
10,000 Ordinary shares		10,000	Land & buildings		6,000
of £1 each			Plant & machinery		4,000
General reserve	2,000		Vehicles		500
Profit	1,000	3,000			
			TOTAL FIXED ASSETS		10,500
TOTAL SHAREHOLDERS' INTEREST		13,000			
Current Liabilities			*Current Assets*		
Creditors	4,500		Raw materials	2,500	
Expenses due	250		Work-in-progress	1,250	
Taxation due	2,000		Finished goods	1,000	
Bank overdraft	500	7,250	Debtors	5,000	9,750
		£20,250			£20,250

The directors' decision to transfer £2,000 to a general reserve indicates that they consider this sum to represent a part of the *permanent* growth in the firm's asset strength. If the £2,000 had been left in the profit and loss account, it would appear to be available for future dividend payments. Should dividend payments, involving this total sum, be envisaged then the firm would have to

Sell some of their assets, *or*
Negotiate a larger bank overdraft

to provide the cash for the dividend to be paid! Again, it is stressed that retained profits, e.g. reserves, do NOT necessarily measure available resources of cash: they demonstrate a growth in corporate net wealth which must be retained within the firm to ensure its continued existence.

Now it would seem that, with a post-tax profit balance of £1,000, some dividend could be paid to the shareholders. With a subscribed share capital of £10,000 of Ordinary shares, a 10 per cent dividend would absorb the whole of this post-tax balance. But, as was argued in Chapters 3 and 4, profits result from the consumption of goods and services in the efficient production of goods for sale. The price at which the firm's output is sold must in the long run cover not only the materials and labour charges, but also the costs of use of capital assets such as plant and machinery. Therefore, in order to come to a more realistic cost of converting raw materials into products ready for sale, further adjustments must be made to the balance sheet in Exhibit 40, to take account of the capital assets used in the production process.

In making the conventional 'rule of thumb' calculations for depreciation we will apply the straight-line method outlined on pages 49–52. Furthermore, the adjustments to asset values and retained profit, demonstrated in Exhibit 41, have derived from assuming

1   A sixty year life for the buildings.

Exhibit 41
The Standard Plc
Balance Sheet as at …

	£	£	£		£	£
Subscribed Capital and				*Fixed Assets*		
Reserves				Land & buildings		
10,000 Ordinary shares				at cost	6,000	
of £1 each			10,000	Less depreciation	100	5,900
General reserve		2,000		Plant & machinery		
Profit and Loss Account	1,000			at cost	4,000	
Less depreciation				Less depreciation	400	3,600
charges	625	375	2,375	Vehicles at cost	500	
				Less depreciation	125	375
TOTAL SHAREHOLDERS'						
INTEREST			12,375	TOTAL FIXED ASSETS		9.875
Current Liabilities				*Current Assets*		
Creditors		4,500		Raw materials	2,500	
Expenses due		250		Work-in-progress	1,250	
Taxation due		2,000		Finished goods	1,000	
Bank overdraft		500	7,250	Debtors	5,000	9,750
			£19,625			£19,625

2   A ten year life for plant and machinery.
3   A four year life for vehicles.

With a final assumption that these assets will have nil salvage values at the end of their expected lives, then the annual charges for depreciation are shown to be:

1   Land and buildings – one sixtieth of cost, i.e. £100.
2   Plant and machinery – one tenth of cost, i.e.£400.
3   Vehicles – one quarter of cost, i.e. £125.

As a result of the above subjective decisions being applied to the assets and profit shown in Exhibit 40, the revised picture of the firm now emerges as given in Exhibit 41.

The full effect of 'charging for use' of the fixed assets is now seen to reduce

1   The book value of each fixed asset.
2   The book value of the total fixed assets.
3   The balance on the profit and loss account.
4   The value of the total shareholders' interest.
and thus:
5   The value of the whole firm as it is represented in the totals of the balance sheet.

It should be noted further that the profit after tax, after transfers to general reserve, and after depreciation charges, is now reduced to £375. In these circumstances a dividend of £3.75 per cent is all that the directors ought to recommend, if the general reserve is to be ignored. Expressed in another way, the charges for depreciation have reduced the sum of money which the firm might distribute in the form of dividend from £1,000 to £375. So we can say that charging for depreciation has not only produced a more realistic profit statement, but it has resulted in the company being persuaded to conserve some of its cash resources by *not* paying out *un*realistic dividends.

Continuing our analysis of the growth of the Standard Plc., we will assume that the directors have decided to recommend a 3 per cent dividend. Furthermore, being concerned about the firm's lack of liquid resources and the need to finance further expansions, they also issued £5,000 of 10 per cent debentures which were secured by a mortgage on the fixed assets of the company. Exhibit 42 shows the state of the company after these transactions have been entered in the accounts.

The profit and loss account balance has been reduced by the 3 per cent dividend, the amount of which now becomes a current liability, assuming that the dividend is voted by the shareholders at their annual general meeting. The total of the proposed dividend has been transferred from the profit and loss account balance to current liabilities because it will be

Exhibit 42
The Standard Plc
Balance Sheet as at ...

	£	£	£		£	£
Subscribed Capital and Reserves				*Fixed Assets*		
				Land & buildings at cost	6,000	
10,000 Ordinary shares				Less depreciation	100	5,900
of £1 each			10,000			
General reserve		2,000		Plant & machinery at		
Profit & Loss Account	375			at cost	4,000	
Less dividend	300	75	2,075	Less depreciation	400	3,600
				Vehicles at cost	500	
TOTAL SHAREHOLDERS'				Less depreciation	125	375
INTEREST			12,075			
Loan Capital				TOTAL FIXED ASSETS		9,875
10% Debentures (secur-				*Current Assets*		
ed on the fixed assets)			5,000	Raw materials		
Current Liabilities				Work-in-progress	2,500	
Creditors		4,500		Finished goods	1,250	
Expenses due		250		Debtors	1,000	
Taxation due		2,000		Cash	5,000	
Dividends payable		300	7,050		4,500	14,250
			£24,125			£24,125

payable by the company within the current operating period: it cannot therefore by definition be a part of retained profits.

Additionally a new form of liability grouping called Loan Capital has been introduced. This kind of company financing does not form part either of the corporate share capital or of the total shareholders' interest. It is quite simply a long term loan which will have to be paid back some day.

Finally the firm's liquid position has improved considerably from having an overdraft of £500 to where a healthy bank balance of £4,500 is displayed. The creditworthiness of the Standard Plc is also on a sounder footing with the

current ratio improvement from 1.34 to 2.02,
liquid ratio improvement from 0.69 to 1.35,

and the growth in working capital from £2,500 to £7,200.

Gearing

The new form of liability grouping, referred to above as loan capital, brings forward an important area of long-term financing of corporate activities.

Now debentures and other forms of longer term borrowing, such as bank loans and loan stock, are also referred to as 'prior capital'. This descriptive title arises from the fact that the liability for their annual interest is payable before the ordinary shareholder receives any dividend at all. Furthermore, debenture and other long-term loan interest amounts must be paid each year whether the company is profitable or not. Such annual rates of interest will be quoted in the debenture etc. deeds. They are also disclosed when the company publishes its annual accounts where they may be recorded in the balance sheet, as in Exhibit 42, or in the explanatory notes accompanying the final accounts.

Another form of prior capital, the preference share, is of lesser importance than debentures or loan stocks. The preference shareholder's annual rate of *dividend* (NOT interest) will be quoted also, either in the balance sheet or in the related explanatory notes, but it will be paid only when there are sufficient post-tax profits available to meet the total dividend sum. Both of these forms of prior capital are notable for the fixed rate of their annual return – that is the debenture-holder's fixed rate of interest and the preference shareholder's fixed rate of dividend. The ordinary shareholder's rate of dividend has no fixed limit laid upon it other than the availability of post-tax profits from which the directors will decide whether or not to pay an ordinary share dividend and, if so, what dividend per share they will recommend.

The relationship between issued ordinary shares and the various types of prior capital is called 'gearing' – the financial gearing which is embodied in the corporate long term financing policy. Calculation of the gearing level is found by application of the following formula:

$$\frac{\text{Preference shares plus long term debt}}{\text{Ordinary shares}} \times 100$$

and for the Standard Plc the gearing rate is

$$\frac{5{,}000 \times 100}{10{,}000} = 50 \text{ per cent}$$

which indicates a low geared company: its borrowed capital is but one half of the subscribed risk capital – the ordinary shares. A figure of 100 per cent would describe a medium geared company where ordinary shares and prior capital were equal to one another in total. 150 per cent would indicate a high geared company where prior capital was the predominant factor.*

*A more detailed account of the consequences of varying levels of gearing upon a company's (a) financial status (b) the priority ratings of the several types of its long term finances and (c) the market value of its ordinary shares, is given in *The Meaning of Balance Sheets and Company Reports,* Second Edition, by L.E. Rockley, Business Books (1983), see Chapters 6, 7 and 9.

The essential feature for the reader to recognise is the liability of a company to pay interest on its long term debts (which debts will frequently be secured on the firm's assets). Clearly when a company follows a policy of continually increasing its gearing rating, its liability for annual interest payments will be absorbing more and more of its income until insufficient remains for the company's own uses. Modernisation and improvements to production facilities may be delayed or cancelled, creditors may be paid less promptly, all due to the reduced cash flow; creditworthiness will suffer and the threat of insolvency looms ahead.

The narrative balance sheet

So far the balance sheets of the Standard Plc have been set out in the conventional two-sided form. We can, however, present this same information in an entirely different way. This other method of presentation, called the *narrative* form of balance sheet, is given in Exhibit 43. It is the form of layout which will be adopted throughout the remainder of this book.

In the narrative layout details of the fixed assets are shown first because they are an expression of the firm's permanent operational capacity, its power to produce and deliver its goods. Next in order of priority, the sequential positioning of current assets and current liabilities enables the amount of working capital to be revealed. This presentation of corporate financial data reflects the businessman's approach to planning when he thinks of the cost of setting up and running a commercial enterprise. A business manager would estimate the total investment in a venture to consist of

the cost of the fixed assets – the capacity, *plus*
the amount of working capital

needed to run the concern. Exhibit 43 gives that total sum and specifies it as 'Net capital employed, £17,075'.

The value of the debentures has been deducted from the total net capital employed to give a book value of the net worth of the company. Net worth of a firm indicates the net *book* value of the company to the shareholders, after all corporate debts to outside parties have been accounted for. It is the book value – not the market value – of the proprietors' shareholdings and we have repeatedly referred to this as the total shareholders' interest. In the above narrative balance sheet the proprietors' interest comprising subscribed shares, reserves and profit retention, is defined as the means of financing the existence and growth of the firm up to the date of the given balance sheet. Thus we have a financial statement which shows

1   The total net capital employed and how it is made up.
2   How the working capital is comprised and its value in money terms.

Exhibit 43
The Standard Plc
Balance Sheet as at ...

	£	£	£
Fixed Assets			
Land and buildings at cost		6,000	
Less depreciation		100	5,900
Plant & machinery at cost		4,000	
Less depreciation		400	3,600
Vehicles at cost		500	
Less depreciation		125	375
TOTAL FIXED ASSETS			9,875
Current Assets			
Raw materials		2,500	
Work-in-progress		1,250	
Finished goods		1,000	
Debtors		5,000	
Cash		4,500	
TOTAL CURRENT ASSETS		14,250	
Less: Current Liabilities			
Creditors	4,500		
Expenses due	250		
Taxation due	2,000		
Dividends payable	300		
TOTAL CURRENT LIABILITIES		7,050	
NET CURRENT ASSETS (WORKING CAPITAL)			7,200
NET CAPITAL EMPLOYED			17,075
Less: Loan Capital			5,000
NET WORTH OF THE COMPANY			£12,075

The above net worth has been financed as follows:

Subscribed Capital			
10,000 Ordinary shares of £1 each			10,000
Reserves			
General reserve		2,000	
Profit and loss account		75	2,075
TOTAL SHAREHOLDERS' INTEREST			£12,075

3 The net worth of the company.
4 How the business has been financed.

The 1981 Companies Act

Exhibit 43 shows the nominal value of the debentures being deducted from the net capital employed in order to arrive at the corporate net worth. Many readers may continue to see balance sheets presented in this way, when their circulation is for internal management use only. It does not follow that this is the only style which has been, and may continue to be, used for company purposes. For example, where it was desired to emphasise the composition of the sources of long term finance, then the first section of our company's balance sheet would terminate at 'Net Capital Employed £17,075' and the statement of corporate financing would be as given in Exhibit 44.

Exhibit 44
Long-term capital employed

	£	£
Subscribed Capital		
10,000 Ordinary shares of £1 each		10,000
Reserves		
General reserve	2,000	
Profit and loss account	75	2,075
TOTAL SHAREHOLDERS' INTEREST		12,075
Loan Capital		
10 per cent Debentures		5,000
TOTAL LONG-TERM FINANCE		£17,075

As the reader is aware, the 1981 Act now specifies two forms of layout for the published balance sheets of UK registered companies and company directors may choose which format they will use in these annual statements. Exhibit 45 below shows how the balance sheet of the Standard Plc, shown in Exhibit 43, would appear when format 1 of the prescribed layouts is chosen by the company.

The reader must now compare the two styles of layout and information. Clearly there is little difference between the 1981 Act format and that which is found in Exhibit 43, as it might be amended by Exhibit 44. The data given in the 1981 Act format and its terminology have changed somewhat but we can still appraise the financial and asset state of the company by studying Exhibit 45, with the same facility as would be experienced from an

Exhibit 45
The Standard Plc
Balance Sheet as at…

Assets	£	£	£
B *Fixed assets*			
I Intangible assets			—
II Tangible assets			
1 Land and buildings			5,900
2 Plant and machinery			3,600
3 Vehicles			375
			9,875
III Investments			—
C *Current assets*			
I Stocks			
1 Raw materials		2,500	
2 Work-in-progress		1,250	
3 Finished goods		1,000	
		4,750	
II Debtors			
1 Trade Debtors		5,000	
IV Cash at bank and in hand		4,500	
		14,250	
E *Creditors:* amounts falling due within one year			
4 Trade creditors	4,500		
8 Taxation	2,000		
9 Accruals (Expenses & Divs.)	550	7,050	
F *Net current assets*			7,200
G *Total assets less current liabilities*			£17,075
H *Creditors:* amounts falling due after more than one year			
1 10 per cent Debentures			5,000
K *Capital and reserves*			
I Called up share capital			10,000
IV Other reserves		2,000	
V Profit and loss account		75	2,075
			£17,075

examination of Exhibit 43. The detailed composition of the fixed asset totals shown in the 1981 Act format will be disclosed in explanatory notes accompanying the statement. This method is just the same as has been widely practised in all forms of published accounts for many years.

Capital employed

The data recorded in our balance sheets result from transactions in the books of account. They are book figures only and they arise from dealings in the past: they do not presume to be the current market values of the items listed.* Thus in Exhibits 43 and 45 the definition of capital employed, £17,075, looks at the company's asset availability in the long term and, furthermore, it brings to account the fixed assets after their initial acquisition costs have been reduced by depreciation charges. Current liabilities also have been deducted from the total book worth of the assets because these liabilities are short-term items which fluctuate in size from month to month throughout the year. They are matched to a great extent by short-term assets such as stocks of materials, amongst current assets.

On the other hand, debentures have not been eliminated from the capital employed total because they refer to the borrowing of money for periods of, say, 20 years. Frequently debenture loans will be used to finance long-term expansion and the provision of additions to, or replacements of, fixed assets. Additionally, they may be used to finance permanent increases in working capital. The point is that the net capital employed is the financial book value of the extent to which corporate assets are held throughout the year, available for the earnings of profit.

Capital employed is also frequently referred to as total assets possessed by the firm and shown in its balance sheet – but without any deduction being made for any short term liabilities. This measures the total book value of *all* assets at the disposal of the company for its trading operations. There are other combinations of asset values which lead to different assessments of a company's capital employed. Commonly used practices include

1   Calculating fixed assets at gross cost, i.e., no depreciation.

---

*Some reservations need to be made here about the valuation of current assets. The monetary values of these assets will, indeed must, be approximating more closely to their actual values. Current assets change much more frequently than fixed assets and therefore their balance sheet values are more 'up to date'. Furthermore, any losses through, for example, obsolescence, changes in demand or bad debts, must be written off to the profit and loss account before the appropriate asset values are entered in the balance sheet. Even so, current asset valuations are relevant only for the firm in business as a going concern. Thus the value of work-in-progress can only be a value to that company intending and able to convert the work-in-progress to finished goods for eventual sale to its customers.

2 Calculating fixed assets at current cost or replacement cost – either with or without deductions for depreciation.
3 Regarding capital employed as those assets available *throughout the year*, and therefore taking the average of capital employed totals at the beginning and at the end of the year.

These other expressions of the term 'capital employed' are given to show the potential variety of the basic expression of corporate earning power. The return on capital employed is our principal ratio of comparison and appraisal of industrial performance, and therefore care must always be taken to ensure the comparison of like with like.

Whilst there are good reasons for differing computations of this concept, it is intended that we should restrict our study of return on capital employed by utilising the book value of fixed assets plus working capital as our definition of the long-term investment of funds in the firm's operations. This is because such a definition

1 Is the most common interpretation for comparison of corporate profitability.
2 Represents a view of earning power which is available to the firm in the long term, without there being too much influence of personal opinion on the valuation of assets.

However, it must be acknowledged that, for internal comparisons of the profitability of separate divisions of a large organisation, other considerations will prevail. For example, it is not uncommon in these instances for capital employed to be calculated by reference to the total gross cost of the assets available for use, excluding cash and bank balances. Cash and bank balances are eliminated from the evaluation because they represent items which are not always within the power of the divisional manager or factory manager to control. Cash and bank balance management is frequently carried out by head office staff. They should not therefore be regarded as part of the capital employed upon which the divisional and factory managers must earn a specific return.

Self-examination questions

1 Why is the appropriation account so called? What business transactions would you expect to appear in an appropriation account?

2 If the sum of reserves shown in a company's balance sheet does not represent its cash and bank balances, then what does it represent?

3 What do you understand by the term 'gearing' in relation to a company's financial structure?

4 Discuss the various definitions of the term 'capital employed'. Give reasons for your choosing any of these definitions in your appraisal of a company's (or division's) profitability.

5 What is a 'narrative' balance sheet? How does a narrative balance sheet lead to a better presentation of the data, than does a two-sided balance sheet?

6 Compare the 1981 Act balance sheet formats with the pre-1981 Act styles found in the published accounts of any UK registered company. Rewrite the balance sheet of your choice in one of the now prescribed 1981 Act formats.

Recommended reading

ROCKLEY, L.E., *The Meaning of Balance Sheets and Company Reports*, Second Edition, Business Books (1983).

ROCKLEY, L.E., *Finance for the Purchasing Executive,* Business Books (1978), see chapters 1, 4 and 5.

PITFIELD, R.R., *Business Finance*, Gee & Co. (1976), see chapters 6 and 8.

LEE, G.A., *Modern Financial Accounting*, Nelson (1976).

WATTS, B.K.R., *Business and Financial Management*, Macdonald and Evans (1978).

6   Cash flow and funds flow: II

Retained profits

In order to examine the growth in the shareholders' investment in the Standard Plc, the simple profit and loss account demonstrated in Exhibit 38 must now be revised and extended. The redrawn account will incorporate all of those trading transactions which have contributed to the increase in shareholders' wealth from that shown in Exhibit 37 to that given in Exhibit 43. Therefore the revised account shows the results of trading during the intervening period and includes details of the undermentioned operations and decisions.

1   The earnings of £4,000 profit by selling goods, costing £6,000 for £10,000 – see Exhibit 37.
2   The appropriation or setting aside of £2,000 by transfer of this sum to a general reserve – see Exhibit 40.
3   The company's liability for corporation tax of £2,000 – Exhibit 40.
4   A total charge of £625 for depreciation of fixed assets used in the production process – Exhibit 41.
5   The declaration of a dividend of £300 – Exhibit 42.

The resultant profit and loss account is given in Exhibit 46 and shows that the post-tax profit for the period was £1,375. Now if every transaction in the account had been a *cash* transaction, we could equate the post-tax profit with the total sum of cash flowing to the firm during the period given in the heading of the account. However, we know that one of the expenditure items – depreciation – is not a cash expense: it merely represents the annual apportionment of some past cash payment which occurred when the relevant fixed assets were first acquired. Thus we could say that the company's cash flow can be more realistically described as post-tax profits plus depreciation charges, i.e. £1,375 + £625 = £2,000. Such a conclusion is a reasonable expression of the amount of cash flowing to the firm as a result of trading operations in the period stated. Care must be taken

Exhibit 46
The Standard Plc
Profit and Loss Account for the period ended …

		£	£		£
(Exhibit 36)	Opening stock	3,000		Sales (Exhibit 37)	10,000
(Exhibit 37)	Purchases	4,000			
		7,000			
(Exhibit 37)	Less closing stock	4,000			
	Materials consumed		3,000		
(Exhibit 37)	Wages		3,000		
(Exhibit 41)	Depreciation		625		
	Profit before taxation		3,375		
			£10,000		£10,000
(Exhibit 40)	Corporation tax		2,000	Profit before taxation	3,375
	Profit after taxation		1,375		
			£3,375		£3,375
(Exhibit 40)	Transfer to General Reserve		2,000	Profit for the period,	
(Exhibit 42)	Dividends payable		300	after taxation	1,375
(Exhibit 43)	Balance of profit remaining to			Balance of profit from	
	carry forward to next period		75	the previous period	
				(Exhibit 36)	1,000
			£2,375		£2,375

when appraising a cash flow figure for we must remember, as in the above example, that

1   The cost of materials consumed does not specify an outflow of cash on raw materials: such an outflow would relate to goods paid for, whereas the £3,000 in Exhibit 46 being adjusted for opening and closing stocks, merely states the cost of materials *used*.

2   When business is conducted on credit, the whole of the sales income may not yet have been received in cash: in other words, debtors may have increased.

3   The corporation tax charge of £2,000 does not necessarily represent the tax *paid* during the account period: it is an estimate of the amount payable some months later but based upon the income earned during the account period given in the exhibit.

Moreover we should never expect the sum of cash flows to represent an increase in the firm's bank balance. Money flowing into a firm is used for all corporate operations, e.g. purchase and extension of fixed assets as well as increases in working capital.

Depreciation, profit and return on capital

Exhibits 41 and 46 have shown the effect, upon asset valuations and upon profits, of accounting for the cost of using fixed assets. The examples thus far have been based upon a calculation of depreciation by the straight-line method, and a total of £625 has been deducted from the acquisition cost of fixed assets in the balance sheet and has been charged in the profit and loss account. In order to demonstrate the effects of different depreciation policies, we will now substitute depreciation charges based upon the reducing-balance method for those used in previous exhibits. The reader should recall (pages 52–3) that the *annual rate* of asset diminution must be larger when using the reducing-balance method than when the straight-line method of depreciation calculation is used.

In these circumstances the three types of asset will be reduced by the following percentages per annum, remembering that this annual rate of asset diminution is not based upon cost but upon *the reduced book value* shown at the commencement of each year:

Land and buildings, 3 per cent
Plant and machinery, 25 per cent
Vehicles, 60 per cent

In the earlier exhibits when the straight-line method of depreciation was used the proportions of the initial acquisition costs, which determined each year's depreciation charge, were

Land and buildings, 1/60th (1.7 per cent)
Plant and machinery, 1/10th (10 per cent)
Vehicles, 1/4 (25 per cent)

Exhibit 47 shows the comparative annual reductions in asset values and profits, for the first four years of the firm's operations, resulting from the application of the two methods of calculating depreciation which we have just discussed. The table demonstrates the variations in individual and total amounts which could be put forward as appropriate depreciation charges i.e. the assessment of the cost of fixed asset use or the means of asset valuation. The first column, which deals with the straight-line method of calculation, is shown once only because there would be no change in subsequent years in

1   The total depreciation sum.

Exhibit 47
The Standard Plc
Depreciation charges: straight-line and reducing-balance methods

Details	Straight-line method £	Reducing-balance method			
		Year 1 £	Year 2 £	Year 3 £	Year 4 £
Land and buildings	100	180	175	169	164
Plant and machinery	400	1,000	750	562	422
Vehicles	125	300	120	48	19
ANNUAL TOTALS	£625	£1,480	£1,045	£779	£605

2   The amount of buildings' depreciation for sixty years.
3   The amount of plant depreciation for ten years.
4   The amount of vehicles' depreciation for four years.*

The figures in Exhibit 47 speak for themselves. With similar asset structures the annual depreciation charges *could* vary from £625 to £1,480 depending upon the business manager's opinion of expected asset lives, and upon his preference for one or other method of calculating the cost of fixed asset usage.

However it must be emphasised that it is not necessary – or usual – to operate only one method of calculating depreciation charges for each of the various groups of corporate assets. For example, reducing balance might be used in respect of vehicles whilst the straight-line method was being used for plant, equipment, buildings and leases. Consequently the possible variations in a company's total charge for depreciation would not be so marked as is shown in Exhibit 47. This exhibit has been so drawn as to highlight the potential effects of two of the principal methods of calculating the annual charge for depreciation of fixed assets.

Finally it must be said that the methods of depreciation used, life expectancy of the related assets, and sales values on asset retirement should not be determined by the accountant alone. He will work in consultation with production engineers and other corporate personnel who may be concerned with the effective use of the assets in question.

*The comments assume that there would be no additions to or disposals of the present group of fixed assets, and accepts that the forecasted economic lives of the assets will remain unchanged. It is also assumed that no revaluations of the asset values would be undertaken.

Returning to the contents of Exhibit 47 we shall see that the variations in total depreciation charges have a more meaningful result when they are shown in profit and loss accounts. Exhibit 48 shows the consequences for reporting accounting profit when these two depreciation methods are employed. It should be remembered, however, that variations in accounting profit, such as those recorded in Exhibit 48, will be present to some extent whatever the *mix* of depreciation methods used.

Exhibit 48
Comparative Profit and Loss Accounts: effects of various depreciation methods

Details	From Exhibit 46		Reducing-balance method					
			Year 1		Year 2		Year 3	
	£	£	£	£	£	£	£	£
Sales		10,000		10,000		10,000		10,000
Less:								
Materials	3,000		3,000		3,000		3,000	
Wages	3,000		3,000		3,000		3,000	
Depreciation	625	6,625	1,480	7,480	1,045	7,045	779	6,779
Profit before tax		3,375		2,520		2,955		3,221
Less corporation tax		2,000		2,000		2,000		2,000
Profit after tax		1,375		520		955		1,221
Profit from previous year		1,000		1,000		1,000		1,000
Available for appropriation		£2,375		£1,520		£1,955		£2,221
To General Reserve		2,000		1,220		1,655		1,921
Dividends payable		300		300		300		300
Balance to next year		75		—		—		—
		£2,375		£1,520		£1,955		£2,221

Retained earnings

Assuming a dividend policy costing £300 in each year, then the amount of book profit available for retention and transfer to reserves is shown to be:

Straight-line method

Year 1 and subsequent years = £2,000 + £75 = £2,075*

*For effective comparisons with reducing-balance method the only change in the income and expenditure of the profit and loss account is taken to be the total amount of the depreciation charges.

Reducing-balance method

Year 1	£1,220
Year 2	£1,655
Year 3	£1,921

But, as we have seen, the several depreciation expenditure items do not represent cash payments. When this is recognised, and when depreciation is regarded as a special kind of 'plough-back', then the totals of these retentions become:

Straight-line method

Year 1 and subsequent years = £2,075 + £625 = £2,700

Reducing-balance method

Year 1	= £1,220 + £1,480 = £2,700
Year 2	= £1,655 + £1,045 = £2,700
Year 3	= £1,921 + £779 = £2,700

After elimination of the £1,000 balance of profit brought forward from the previous year, we are left with a total retentions figure, attributable to the current year's operations, of £1,700. This sum describes the company's post-dividend cash flows from trading operations. Again, however, the reader is warned that the concept of cash flow should be used with some care and reservations (see page 100).

Moreover, it is the return on capital employed by which a company's profitability is so frequently judged even though there are many deficiencies in its use as a measure for comparing performance between different firms. The reader should know at this stage that subjective opinion can affect fixed asset and stock valuations in ways which will influence

the value of the return (profit), *and*
the value of capital employed

shown in the final accounts. Also the impact of inflation upon the *current* replacement values of assets will tend to distort any return on capital invested percentages unless book values are adjusted, in some way, to bring the up-to-date costs to account. (The subject of accounting for inflation is dealt with in Chapter 9.) Now Exhibit 49 has been drawn to emphasise the impact on the company's net worth and profitability rating of merely using different methods of calculating depreciation. Clearly the potential for change is great and it therefore becomes essential to ensure, for any worthwhile comparisons of profitability, that consistency of method in e.g. asset and stock valuations is followed.

If we now take the respective profits before tax from Exhibit 48 and express these as percentages of the net capital employed data as given opposite, we have

Exhibit 49
The Standard Plc
Comparative Balance Sheets showing the effects of various depreciation methods

	From Exhibit 43			Reducing-balance method	
	£	£	£	£	£
Fixed Assets					
Land & buildings					
at cost		6,000		6,000	
Less depreciation		100	5,900	180	5,820
Plant & machinery					
at cost		4,000		4,000	
Less depreciation		400	3,600	1,000	3,000
Vehicles at cost		500		500	
Less depreciation		125	375	300	200
TOTAL FIXED ASSETS			9,875		9,020
Current Assets					
Raw materials		2,500			
Work-in-progress		1,250			
Finished goods		1,000			
Debtors		5,000			
Cash		4,500			
TOTAL CURRENT ASSETS		14,250		14,250	
Less: Current Liabilities					
Creditors	4,500				
Expenses due	250				
Taxation due	2,000				
Dividends payable	300				
TOTAL CURRENT LIABILITIES		7,050		7,050	
WORKING CAPITAL			7,200		7,200
NET CAPITAL EMPLOYED			17,075		16,220
Less Loan Capital			5,000		5,000
NET WORTH OF THE COMPANY			£12,075		£11,220

The above net worth of the company has been financed as follows:

Subscribed Capital					
10,000 Ordinary shares of £1 each			10,000		10,000
Reserves					
General reserve		2,000		1,220	
P&L account		75	2,075	—	1,220
			£12,075		£11,220

105

Straight-line method:

$$\frac{3,375}{17,075} \times 100 = 19.76\% \text{ return}$$

Reducing-balance method: Year 1

$$\frac{2,520}{16,220} \times 100 = 15.54\% \text{ return}$$

Both of these rates are in respect of the same company!

Flow of funds

The balance sheets and profit and loss accounts such as have been studied so far each set out to inform the reader about specific aspects of the firm's progress. A balance sheet gives details of the firms's net wealth, though this is generally based upon certain asset values – historic acquisition costs – which may not be appropriate for *current cost* evaluations. The profit and loss account's main object must be to show how an amount of accounting profit was earned, or how trading has increased the corporate wealth. But certain of the incomes and expenditures in the account may not be shown in current cost equivalents. (The problems of accounting for the current cost equivalents, i.e. the impacts of inflation, are dealt with in Chapter 9.) Furthermore, neither of the two forms of final account give a single complete picture of all the changes which have taken place in the firm's liability/asset state during the trading period since the date of the immediately prior balance sheet. A Flow of Funds Statement is required for this purpose: sometimes called a Source and Application of Funds Statement, it gives a progress report on the changes in composition of the firm's net wealth during the specified period.

Now we have to recognise that it is vital to identify the *changes* which have taken place in a firm's wealth, and what these changes have done for the corporate well being. Therefore we will examine the firm's progress from Exhibit 36 to Exhibit 43 and, by studying a Flow of Funds Statement, show the extent of the variations in the company's assets and liabilities. The first stage in this process is, as shown on page 107, the preparation of a statement of balance sheet variations.

The variation statement of Exhibit 50 gives the *net* changes in the Standard Plc's asset/liability state: it does not show the impact of the depreciation charges upon fixed assets or upon retained profits (the increase in reserves). Therefore, to give the complete worths of the cash flow and

Exhibit 50
Balance Sheet variations

	Exhibit 36	Exhibit 43	Variations	
			+	−
	£	£	£	£
Liabilities				
Ordinary shares	10,000	10,000	—	—
Reserves	1,000	2,075	1,075	—
Loan capital	—	5,000	5,000	—
Creditors	2,000	4,500	2,500	—
Expenses due	—	250	250	—
Taxation due	—	2,000	2,000	—
Dividends payable	—	300	300	—
TOTALS	£13,000	£24,125	£11,125	—
Assets				
Land & buildings	4,000	5,900	1,900	—
Plant & machinery	3,500	3,600	100	—
Vehicles	1,000	375	—	625
Raw materials	3,000	2,500	—	500
Work-in-progress	—	1,250	1,250	—
Finished goods	—	1,000	1,000	—
Debtors	1,000	5,000	4,000	—
Cash	500	4,500	4,000	—
	£13,000	£24,125	£12,250	£1,125

fixed asset elements in the firm's progress, our Funds Flow Statement will show the

Increase in reserves as

£1,075 + £625 $\qquad$ = £1,700 (see page 104)

Increase in total expenditure on fixed assets as

£1,900 + £100 − £625 + £625 = £2,000

Furthermore, the changes in the investment in all stocks is recorded as a single item though it may well be worth giving the greater detail of variations in work-in-progress and finished goods as separate items.

The funds flow statement in Exhibit 51 is an important document. It shows how the firm is being financed and who is paying for the firm's growth.

Exhibit 51
The Standard Plc
Funds Flow Statement for the period ended ...

	£
Sources of Funds	
Cash flow from trading	1,700
Issue of debentures (loan capital)	5,000
Increase in creditors	2,500
Increase in expenses due	250
Increase in taxation due	2,000
Dividends payable	300
	£11,750
Applications of Funds	
Net expenditure on fixed assets	2,000
Increase in stocks	1,750
Increase in debtors	4,000
Increase in cash	4,000
	£11,750

Thus out of the total sources of funds of £11,750, the various groups of suppliers of funds contributed the following proportions of the total

	£	%
The company – from its cash flow	1,700	14.5
Long-term lenders – loan capital	5,000	42.5
Short-term creditors	5,050	43.0
	11,750	100.0

During the period to which the statement refers, only one-seventh of the total funds needed was provided by the residual proprietors of the company – the shareholders. This situation would have to be kept under observation, for sound financial planning does not envisage a permanent growth of loan capital beyond 100 per cent of the total shareholders' interest. Nor does it envisage a permanent growth in current liabilities beyond 20 to 30 per cent of the total shareholders' interest.

On the other hand, it is equally important to consider the implications of the various applications of the total supply of funds:

	£	%
Fixed asset expansion	2,000	17
Increased investment in stocks	1,750	15
Increased investment in debtors	4,000	34
Growth in cash balances	4,000	34
	11,750	100

Clearly the Standard Plc has found it necessary to greatly increase their investment in stocks and debtors, both of which are important components of working capital. Thus, by examining a series of funds flow statements we may be able to reach firm conclusions on the policies being implemented by the Board of Directors with respect to both financing and plant modernisation or expansion.

Self-examination questions

1 Though a company's accounts may show a satisfactory level of profits, its liquid cash resources may be declining rapidly. How might this happen and how would you explain this seeming paradox to a Board of Directors?

2 What do you understand by 'retained earnings'? If retained earnings imply the application of funds to corporate asset growth, how would you seek to verify this?

3 Do the published balance sheets of a company offer a sound basis for appraising corporate net wealth and creditworthiness?

4 What principal interest should each of the following groups of people have in a company's published accounts:
   (a) short term creditors;
   (b) long term lenders:
   (c) Ordinary shareholders;
   (d) corporate managements?

5 Why does the profit and loss account tend to supersede the balance sheet as a means of appraising the general strength and well-being of a public limited company?

6 What considerations should be taken into account by the directors of a company when formulating a dividend policy?

Recommended reading

BULL, R.J., *Accounting in Business*, Butterworth (1976)

LEE, G.A., *Modern Financial Accounting*, Nelson (1976).

HINGLEY, W., and OSBORN, F., *Financial Management*, W.H. Allen (1978).

LEE, T.A., *Company Financial Reporting: Issues and Analysis*, Nelson (1976), see chapters 4 and 5.

7 Planning and forecasting

Introduction

The management accountant is an interpreter to the business planners: he is able to represent the forecasts of production, administration and sales activities into statements of profit and company worth. The forecast profit and loss account and balance sheet are compiled from the data in a plan of proposed business development. These statements enable managers to see what the return on capital will be if the plan is put into action. Similarly, they can see whether this return will be adequate or whether other proposals should be examined to improve the forecast. Frequently areas of high cost can be studied before the event, in the search for economies and greater efficiencies which could bring the budgeted return more into line with business requirements. Profit figures and return on capital targets are thus established and, week by week, the firm's actual progress can be checked against the approved plan.

The progress of the Standard Plc is now to be followed in such an exercise. Certain plans for the company's future have been made and are presented in the case study below. Before proceeding with the preparation of a forecast profit and loss account and balance sheet, however, some recapitulation of the relationships between these statements and the cash account must be undertaken. The reader should be aware of the essential nature of the profit and loss account – it is a statement of income and expenditure. The figures of income describe the monetary values of the firm's products which have finally *left the works on their way to customers, as sales*, during the whole of the period stated at the head of the account. It is not necessary that the goods should have been paid for, before the relevant value can appear amongst the sales in the profit and loss account. *Money* receipts are entered in the cash book. Any difference between (*a*) the credit sales value, and (*b*) the cash received, at the balance sheet date, in respect of those sales, will be shown in the balance sheet amongst sundry debtors.* In the same way the profit and loss account shows expenditure, *not* payments. Expenditure is the monetary cost of the physical goods and services used, during the period of account, to make the sales shown in that account. Where such goods and services are received on credit, then those items not paid for by the balancing date will be shown amongst the various creditors under the title 'current liabilities' in the balance sheet.

The following demonstrations of the preparation of budgeted, i.e. forecast, final accounts will commence with a cash budget. This is an important document because it shows the expected cash flow during the forthcoming period. The corporate liquidity path can be traced, and a watch kept on the ability of the company to meet its debts. It is not sufficient to be profitable only: too frequently the growth of sales has been achieved at the expense of prompt payment of creditors' accounts. This kind of situation indicates a company which is overtrading: operating at a level of business beyond that which can be sustained by its own long-term financial resources. Where these circumstances are foreseen, then arrangements can be made to obviate financial embarrassment and the consequent loss of the company's creditworthy reputation. The use of short-term creditors to finance the company long-term growth is a dangerous practice which can lead to bankruptcy. Preserving the firm's liquidity or debt-paying ability may be secured by obtaining a bank loan or an overdraft, issue of shares or debentures or by the sale of investments. In each of these cases greater chances for the success of any financing operations will ensue, when the firm is able to support its requests for money with forecast cash and profit figures. Where investments are to be sold, this can be done gradually without disturbing the market. Sales can be effected at prices to suit the company – not as a result of panic measures to meet unforeseen events. This is the benefit of planning.

Exhibit 52 sets out a flow diagram of the interrelationships involved in preparing the company's activity plans. The reader will see how *all* roads lead ultimately to the cash book which contains not only day to day (running cost) payments but also payments for capital items.

CASE STUDY

The Standard Plc

CASH BUDGET, PROJECTED PROFIT AND LOSS ACCOUNT AND
BALANCE SHEET FOR NEXT THREE MONTHS

1 The Plan The Standard Plc decided to develop some of their promising lines and to enter new fields of production. A market study by a firm of

---

*This postulates that settlements are received in arrear (goods sold on credit) and that no *over*payments are received.

Exhibit 52

Development of Profit and Loss Budget

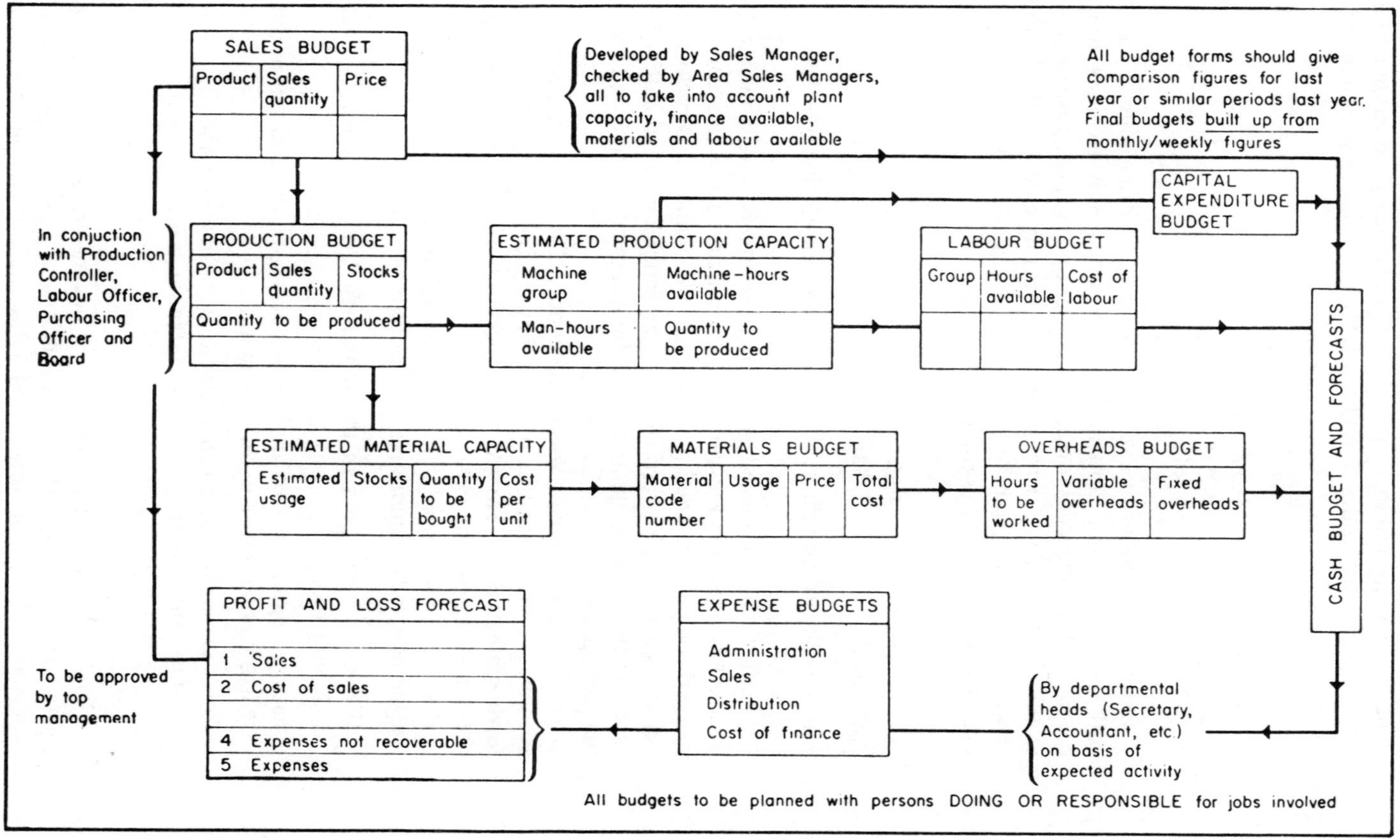

consultants indicated that, with carefully planned production and distribution arrangements, sales should reach the following targets in the next three months:

	£
1st month	6,000
2nd month	7,200
3rd month	7,800

Exhibit 49 (straight-line version) shows the existing state of the company and it soon became apparent, when production facilities were being compared with the sales forecast that additional expenditure on fixed assets would be necessary. Therefore with a re-arrangement of the layout of the shops, additional machinery was to be installed. This expenditure on machinery was phased as follows:

	£
1st month	3,000
2nd month	2,000

whilst in the 3rd month, £1,000 was to be spent on new vehicles.

2 *Budget* The proposed extension of company activity meant that fresh detailed budgets for the various departments of the company had to be worked out. With the assistance of the Finance Director, heads of departments came forward with the undermentioned estimates of expenditure for the ensuing quarter. The final agreed income and expenditure budgets are tabulated in Exhibit 53.

The Finance Director was then requested to produce a profit and loss account for the next three months showing the anticipated profit for that forthcoming period. He was also expected to show the anticipated balance sheet at the end of the period.

Past practices showed that the actual cash disbursements in respect of the above budgeted expenditures would occur as follows:

Wages ¾ being paid in the month of the statement; ¼ paid in the following month.

Factory, administration and selling overheads Paid in full in the month following that shown in the statement.

Research and development ⎱ ½ paid in the month of the statement;
Welfare and medical ⎰ ½ paid in the following month.

3 *Stocks* It was decided that enough raw materials should be purchased in each month to support the sales of that month. As the raw material cost is expected to be ¾ of anticipated sales value these purchases would be

Exhibit 53
The Standard Plc
Operating Budgets for three months ended ...

Details	Month 1	Month 2	Month 3	Totals to profit and loss account
(1)	(2)	(3)	(4)	(5)
	£	£	£	£
Wages	600	720	760	2,080
Factory overheads	500	500	600	1,600
Administration overheads	250	250	300	800
Selling overheads	500	500	630	1,630
Research and development	200	200	400	800
Welfare and medical	50	50	70	170
TOTALS	£2,100	£2,220	£2,760	£7,080

£4,500 in the 1st month. In order to build up stocks, purchases of raw materials in each month should be supplemented by additional purchases of £1,000 per month. Stocks at the end of the three-month period would be planned to achieve

	£
Raw materials	5,500
Work in progress	2,750
Finished goods	2,500

The company takes two months' credit before paying its suppliers so that purchases in month 1 are paid for in month 3. Furthermore the creditors shown in Exhibit 49 represent two months' accounts, due from the previous trading period.

4 General Other details pertinent to the planning period are given below:
(*a*) Debtors are given two months' credit.
(*b*) Taxation of £2,000 shown in Exhibit 49 as being due, is paid in month 3.
(*c*) Dividends of £300 also shown in Exhibit 49 are paid in month 1.
(*d*) Expenses of £250 shown in Exhibit 49 as being outstanding represent amounts due as follows:
   (*i*) Wages £100.
   (*ii*) Factory overheads £50.

(*iii*) Administration overheads £50.

(*iv*) Selling overheads £50.

These sums are to be paid in Month 1.

(*e*) Capital expenditure acquisitions are paid in the month of the planned installation.

(*f*) Assume depreciation to be charged for the quarter as follows:

(*i*) Land and buildings £25.

(*ii*) Plant and machinery £100.

(*iii*) Vehicles £25.

Cash budget*

The above information shows what the managers of the company think that they will be able to achieve in the next three months. Budget periods are not limited to three months – indeed many firms prepare such a statement to cover a period of 12 months. Longer-term plans are generally supported by re-examinations and revisions of the proposed activities every quarter. In those instances of quarterly (or monthly) revision, it is quite common for the planners to look forward over the *next period of 12 months from the date of revision*. Thus business forecasts may be 'rolling over' – consisting of sucessive month by month projections, each projection covering a forthcoming period of 12 months.

The cash budget for the next three months, based upon the data in the case study, is given in Exhibit 54.

The layout of the budget gives details and totals of expected receipts in each month (lines 1 to 3). Here are shown balances brought forward plus the estimated cash flow from debtors. The receipts total for each month therefore gives the assessment of monies expected to be available to meet the expenses of the firm in that month. Forecasted payments are listed for each separate group of costs and the totals of those payments are also given for each month of the plan (line 15). The difference between receipts and payments (line 16) represents the expected balance of cash at the month's end.

A note of warning must be sounded at this point. The flow of cash expressed by the cash budget does not necessarily imply that payments are made each month *after* the receipts of that month have arrived at the firm's bank account. Thus if there is an uneven or delayed stream of cash receipts

*To aid the explanation of the cash budget it should be assumed that the balance sheet in Exhibit 49 was compiled to show the position as at 31 December. In this case the debtors and creditors in that balance sheet would refer to November and December of the period leading up to 31 December. Months 1, 2 and 3 of the budget plan would then relate to January, February and March of the next year.

Exhibit 54
The Standard Plc
Cash budget for three months ended …

Line no.	Details	Month 1 £	Month 2 £	Month 3 £	Totals £	To balance sheet £
	Receipts		o/d			
1	Balances b/fwd	4,500	625	3,315	4,500	Debtors
2	From debtors	2,500	2,500	6,000	11,000	7,200 + 7,800
3	Totals	£7,000	£3,125	£2,685	£15,000	
	Payments					Creditors
4	Materials	2,250	2,250	5,500	10,000	6,400 + 6,850
5	Wages	550	690	750	1,990	190 ⎫
6	Factory overheads	50	500	500	1,050	600 ⎪
7	Admin. overheads	50	250	250	550	300 ⎬ £1,955*
8	Selling overheads	50	500	500	1,050	630 ⎪
9	Research	100	200	300	600	200 ⎪
10	Welfare	25	50	60	135	35 ⎭
11	Taxation	—	—	2,000	2,000	Capital expend.
12	Capital	3,000	2,000	1,000	6,000	6,000
13	Dividends	300	—	—	300	
14	Interest	—	—	—	—	
15	Totals	6,375	6,440	10,860	23,675	
			o/d	o/d	o/d	
16	Balances c/fwd	625	3,315	8,175	8,175	
17	Total receipts (above)	£7,000	£3,125	£2,685	£15,500	

*The figure of £1,955 represents the total due but unpaid, at the end of the budget period, in respect of the running expenses listed on lines 5–10. This amount is a liability of the firm at that date. It is therefore shown in the Balance Sheet, under the heading 'Current Liabilities' on page 127.

to match with an earlier pattern of outgoings, then the figure of cash in hand (month 1, line 16) could be misleading. It may conceal the fact that, for most of the month, there was an overdraft *not* a balance in hand. Now, to trace the completion of the budget shown in Exhibit 54, the reader must turn to Exhibit 49. Amongst the current assets, at that balance sheet date, cash is shown to be £4,500. Our forecast period is taken to be a continuation of the firm's business from the situation given in Exhibit 49. Therefore, the commencing cash balance for the forecast period must be £4,500 and this amount begins the cash budget at line 1 for month 1.

In this simple example, an assumption will be made in order to make our calculations the easier. The assumption relates to debtors and creditors which are shown as £5,000 and £4,500 respectively (see Exhibit 49). As the case study, at paragraphs 3 and 4a, indicates that the periods of credit taken and given are two months, then the totals of debtors and creditors are taken to refer in equal proportions to the final two months leading up to the balance sheet date.* This means that the total debtors of £5,000 include:

£2,500 due from November sales and
£2,500 due from December sales.

Similarly the total creditors of £4,500 relate to

£2,250 owing for November's purchases and
£2,250 owing for December's purchases.

In view of the two months' credit periods which apply to debtors and creditors it is expected that cash will be received from debtors as follows:

November's £2,500 in month 1, and
December's £2,500 in month 2.

Payments are similarly planned to be made to creditors so that the outward cash flow for these items will show that

November's £2,250 will be paid in month 1, and
December's £2,250 will be paid in month 2.

The above transactions are shown in the cash budget on lines 2 and 4, respectively.

Now paragraph 1 of the case study quoted the forecast sales during the planning period as

	£
Month 1	6,000
Month 2	7,200
Month 3	7,800

In view of the continuing credit periods of two months, these three amounts should be received in that given order, in months 3, 4 and 5. Thus the reader will find that the receipts from debtors (line 2) in month 3 are entered as £6,000. The two months still outstanding at the end of the

*Obviously in a practical situation we should *know* the periods to which debtors and creditors relate. They would rarely arise from a series of month's sales – in *equal proportions for each month*.

118

planning period will be shown in the balance sheet as 'sundry debtors' £15,000. This is recorded as a note in the final column of Exhibit 54.

The same process is repeated in respect of the cost of material purchases, but here some calculation has to be completed first. Paragraph 3 of the case study states:

'It was decided that enough raw materials should be purchased in each month to support the sales of that month. As the raw material cost is expected to be ¾ of anticipated sales value, these purchases would be £4,500 in the 1st month. In order to build up stocks, purchases of raw materials in each month should be supplemented by additional purchases of £1,000 per month.'

Exhibit 55
Raw materials: computation of expenditure and payments during the planning period

Details	Sales	Purchases of raw materials (3/4 of column 2)	Additional materials purchases	Total purchases of materials (columns 3 + 4)	Entries
(1)	(2) £	(3) £	(4) £	(5) £	(6)
Month 1	6,000	4,500	1,000	5,500	Month 3 of cash budget
Month 2	7,200	5,400	1,000	6,400 ⎫ Balance
Month 3	7,800	5,850	1,000	6,850 ⎭ Sheet
TOTALS	£21,000	£15,750	£3,000	£18,750	P&L Account

These instructions relating to the purchases of, and payments for, materials are tabulated in Exhibit 55. Here one can trace the monthly incidence of expenditure and of payments and see how they affect the cash budget demonstrated at Exhibit 54. Entries to be made in the final accounts – profit and loss account and balance sheet – will be demonstrated in subsequent pages. By this system of methodical calculation, and it is only elementary arithmetic, all of the remaining entries in the budget layout can be verified. The relevant data for verification of these other payments are found in paragraphs 2, 3 and 4 of the case study.

Paragraph 4d is of prime importance here for it explains how the item 'Expenses £250', amongst the current liabilities of Exhibit 49 is compiled. Furthermore, paragraph 2 of the plan gives details of how payments are made for the other main groups of expenses. By using these instructions, the

119

Exhibit 56
Wages: computation of monthly payments

Month	Amount due per Exhibit 53	Amount paid (3/4 × column 2)	Amount due from previous month	Total payments (columns 3 + 4)	Entries
(1)	(2)	(3)	(4)	(5)	(6)
	£	£	£	£	
1	600	450	100*	550	Cash
2	720	540	150	690	budget
3	760	570	180	750	line 5
TOTALS	£2,080	£1,560	£430	£1,990	

*This sum relates to the previous year; it forms a part of the £250 'expenses' due which are listed amongst the current liabilities of Exhibit 49.

pattern of disbursements for wages can be seen (Exhibit 56). The amount unpaid of the third month's wages, which is £190 (¼ of £760) will be found in the final column of the cash book layout.

The profit and loss account

Exhibit 57 is the completed projection of the manufacturing, trading and profit and loss accounts for the coming three months. The sequence of items in this account follows the natural progress of materials, through the production process until the results of sales are revealed in the ultimate profit or loss. The first item therefore sets out the expected consumption of raw materials in attaining the output of the budget period. Commencing stocks are brought forward from the previous account (Exhibit 49 – where they were the stocks at the *end* of that period). This amount, together with the raw materials to be purchased (Exhibit 55, column 5), gives the total value of materials available for use by the production department during the three months of the plan. As we are trying to find the accounting cost† of the goods manufactured during a specified period, then we must deduct any raw materials which remain unused at the end of that period. In this instance the value of the closing stocks of raw materials is given in the case study, at paragraph 3, as £5,500. Deducting this amount will reveal the cost of materials used to be £15,750.

†The various concepts of cost will be discussed in a later chapter.

Exhibit 57
The Standard Plc
Projected Manufacturing, Trading and Profit and Loss Account for the three months ended …

Materials consumed	£	£		£
Opening stock	2,500		Cost of goods	
Purchases	18,750		manufactured	
	21,250		transferred	
			to trading	
Less Closing stock	5,500	15,750	account	18,030
Wages		2,080		
		17,830		
PRIME COST				
Factory overheads	1,600			
Depreciation	100	1,700		
		19,530		
Add Work-in-progress				
at commencement	1,250			
Less Work-in-progress at end	2,750	1,500(CR)		
COST OF PRODUCTION		£18,030		£18,030
Opening stock of				
finished goods		1,000	Sales	21,000
Cost of goods				
manufactured		18,030		
		19,030		
Less Closing stock				
of finished goods		2,500		
COST OF SALES		16,530		
Gross profit		4,470		
		£21,000		£21,000
Administration overheads		800	Gross profit	4,470
Selling overheads		1,630		
Research and development		800		
Welfare and medical		170		
Debenture interest*		125		
Depreciation:				
Land and buildings	25			
Vehicles	25	50		
		3,575		
Profit before taxation		895		
		£4,470		£4,470

*Interest on debentures has not been introduced before this exhibit as the author wished to present the gradual development of the company, without raising too many issues at one time. Clearly all profit and loss accounts presented since the issue of debentures (Exhibit 42) should have borne an appropriate interest charge. As the P&L account above covers 3 months, the costs should include (3/12) × (10/100) × £5,000 – this being the relevant proportion of the total annual interest charge for £5,000 worth of debentures, issued at 10 per cent per annum.

The reader is reminded that here we are ascertaining income and expenditure: *cash* is not part of the profit and loss statement.* In this case, Exhibit 53, column 5 gives the planned expenditures which are expected to be incurred in obtaining the forecast income. Each item of the table can be traced to its appropriate place in the final income account shown in Exhibit 57. Only the totals appear in the account because its object is to show the aggregate income – expenditure relationships – over the period given. The division of the total expenditure into monthly amounts is an essential part of the planning process. Such greater detail of the *monthly* incidence of, for example, purchases, is necessary for the following:

1 Cash planning – cash budget.
2 Scheduling, purchasing and storing materials so that sufficient materials shall always be available to meet the requirements of the sales programme.

Similar comments explaining the month by month analyses of the likely expenditure on overheads, research and medical facilities can be specified.

To return to the manufacturing account: one item remains to be charged to the costs of manufacture, i.e., depreciation. The proposed depreciation provisions are given at paragraph 4f of the case study and it will be noted that a charge for plant and machinery depreciation has been shown in the manufacturing account. That entry is necessary because the goods produced could not have been completed without the aid of the company's machines. On the basis of assessing the total costs of manufacture, some recognition must be given to fixed asset use: this recognition is achieved in some measure by the fixed assets' depreciation charges. But depreciation of buildings and vehicles has been shown in the profit and loss account and one may wonder why some proportion of, for example, the buildings cost is not apportioned to the costs of manufacture. This is a very proper observation and in practice some allocation, of the appropriate buildings' depreciation charge, to manufacturing process, to the administration and selling departments, would be determined. The allocation could be based upon actual areas of buildings space used by the various departments. The function of the vehicles, whether for interfactory movement of goods, transfers around the shop floor, or for delivery of finished goods would determine the allocation of the depreciation charge for these assets also.

Before proceeding to examine the forecast balance sheet, a word on the transfer of balances in the profit and loss account is necessary. The

*In so far as an entry in the final accounts reflects the ultimate *movement* of cash, this statement is not strictly true of course. The amounts of cash which flow to and from the firm are shown in the cash account: the statement says therefore that entries in the profit and loss account, whilst reflecting the *movement* of cash, do not *mirror* exactly cash payments. The account is concerned with income and expenditure and nothing else.

summation of charges in the manufacturing account is described as 'cost of goods manufactured, transferred to the trading account – £18,030': this represents the total manufacturing cost of goods produced during the period stated at the head of the account. These are the goods passed to the sales and distribution departments for delivery to customers. Manufacturing costs are a part of the cost of sales of finished goods: the whole cost is shown in the trading account to be £16,530, but this figure takes into account the opening and closing stocks of finished goods. Now at this point the reader must observe one of the most important items of information which the profit and loss accounts give – gross profit. If this amount is expressed as a percentage of sales, we ascertain the mark-up which has been achieved on total sales. This mark-up or gross profit, however it is termed, is a vital absolute sum also. It is the total amount which is available from trading to meet the overhead expenses shown in the profit and loss account proper. Therefore the gross profit sum, determined in the trading account, is passed to the profit and loss account in order to be set against the expenditures of administration and selling, etc. Finally when the taxation liability is taken into account we may see how much is left for dividends or for transfer to reserves. Thus the size of the gross profit, the achievement of mark-up on sales, must ultimately influence both the shareholders' dividends and the growth of the company through retentions.

The 1981 Companies Act

The profit and loss account in Exhibit 57 has been presented in the kind of detail which would be for the use of internal management only, i.e. not published in the annual accounts booklets. Therefore some of the items listed in that exhibit would not be available for public study and analysis. However the 1981 Act, by virtue of its specified formats for the publication of the final accounts (see Appendix A, page 339), has extended the disclosure requirements which must be observed by public limited companies. We shall now adapt the detailed information from Exhibit 57 in preparing a profit and loss account in accordance with format 2 of the 1981 Act. Exhibits 58 and 59 are shown in juxtaposition so that the full specified format (Exhibit 58) can be readily compared with a published version of the internal profit and loss account (Exhibit 59).

Clearly Exhibit 59 results from a company whose activities do not embrace all of those features and transactions which would have required disclosure. Nevertheless certain matters are emphasised for the reader's appreciation, for example:

1   Items 1, 2, 3 and 4 of the 1981 Act format describe those increases in

Exhibit 58
Profit and Loss Account layout
Format 2

---

1 Turnover
2 Change in stocks of finished goods and in work progress
3 Own work capitalised
4 Other operating income
5 (*a*) Raw materials and consumables
  (*b*) Other external charges
6 Staff costs:
  (*a*) wages and salaries
  (*b*) social security costs
  (*c*) other pension costs
7 (*a*) Depreciation and other amounts written off tangible and intangible assets
  (*b*) Exceptional amounts written off current assets
8 Other operating charges
9 Income from shares in group companies
10 Income from shares in related companies
11 Income from other fixed asset investments
12 Other interest receivable and similar income
13 Amounts written off investments
14 Interest payable and similar charges
15 Tax on profit or loss on ordinary activities
16 Profit or loss on ordinary activities after taxation
17 Extraordinary income
18 Extraordinary charges
19 Extraordinary profit or loss
20 Tax on extraordinary profit or loss
21 Other taxes not shown under the above items
22 Profit or loss for the financial year

Exhibit 59
The Standard Plc
Profit and Loss Account for the three months ended ...

	£
1 Turnover	21,000
2 Change in stocks of finished goods and work-in-progress	3,000
5 (*a*) Raw materials and consumables	15,750
6 Staff costs:	
(*a*) Wages and salaries	2,080
7 (*a*) Depreciation and other amounts written off tangible and	
intangible fixed assets	150
8 Other operating charges	5,000
14 Interest payable and similar charges	125

---

corporate wealth* which have resulted from the company's own operations, but not all of these increases have been *realised* at the end of the year to which the account relates.

2   Item 6 of the format would normally contain data relating to other departments of the firm but Exhibit 59 is limited to the disclosure of relevant material from Exhibit 57.

3   Items 9 to 12 relate to those other sources of corporate wealth which do not arise from the company's own trading activities: they are not therefore grouped with items 1 to 4 above.

4   A study of items 1 to 14 will enable the corporate profit before tax to be calculated – as shown below.

The increase in corporate wealth during the period of the account is shown by Exhibit 59 to comprise:

	£
Turnover	21,000
Increase in stocks of finished goods and work-in-progress	3,000
	£24,000

whilst the expenditures incurred in achieving this growth are given as:

	£
Raw materials	15,750
Staff costs	2,080
Depreciation	150
Other operating charges	5,000†
Interest payable	125
	£23,105

So by deducting the expenditure from the income (growths in wealth) we arrive at a profit before tax of £895, as was reported in Exhibit 57.

The balance sheet

The compilation of totals for the balance sheet should now be relatively easy. As this statement presents a static picture of the firm at the end of a

*The changes in stocks of finished goods and work in progress do, in this instance, reflect increases in value; they might, however, have shown decreases.

†The other operating charges total is derived from factory, administration and selling overheads plus expenditures on research and development, together with welfare and medical costs.

series of trading transactions, it will include the results of that trading. Thus the new balance sheet will incorporate the period's profit or loss, together with any variation in the quantity of fixed assets. The other factors affected by trading, e.g. debtors, creditors and stock, will be listed at the values attributed to them on the balancing date.

Whilst the case study did not plan any effect on the firm's possessions of land and buildings, it did state that £5,000 was to be spent on machinery and £1,000 on new vehicles. Exhibit 60 shows the expected balance sheet at the end of the three months planning period.

The reader will note that the cost of land and buildings remains at £6,000, but machinery now stands at £9,000 (£4,000 + £5,000 additional expenditure). Similarly the cost of vehicles owned by the firm is shown as £1,500, after adding the expenditure of £1,000 on new vehicles. The depreciation charges which have been deducted from fixed assets are given in the case study (paragraph 4f): these amounts have already been charged to the profit and loss account. If the whole of the proposed plan is implemented therefore, the total value of fixed assets possessed by the Standard Plc will reach the sum of £15,725. Each of the remaining items in the balance sheet can now be traced either from the case study or from the various statements which have been completed in this chapter, e.g.:

Stocks Case study paragraph 3 (note also that these amounts have been deducted from the costs in the profit and loss account, as they represent the *unused part* of available materials, etc.)

Debtors, creditors and expenses Exhibit 54, final column.

Cash overdrawn Exhibit 54, line 16, month 3.

Lastly, the forecast profit of £895 shown in the profit and loss account is the only change in the shareholders' capital invested.

Whereas the balance of the profit and loss account was given in Exhibit 49 as £75, the addition of the expected £895 will bring the undistributed profit figures to £970 and the total shareholders' interest to £12,970.

We can now proceed to an evaluation of the forecast profitability of the company, as it is represented in the profit and loss account and balance sheet given in Exhibits 57 and 60. For this purpose we have to insert the appropriate figures in the following equation:

$$\frac{\text{Profit} \times 100}{\text{Capital employed}} = \frac{\text{Profit} \times 100}{\text{Sales}} \times \frac{\text{Sales}}{\text{Capital employed}}$$

Now profits and sales for the planning period are given in Exhibit 57 as £895 and £21,000 respectively. Exhibit 60 shows the book value of capital

Exhibit 60
The Standard Plc
Projected Balance Sheet as at …

	£	£	£
Fixed Assets			
Land and buildings at cost		6,000	
Less depreciation		125	5,875
Plant and machinery at cost		9,000	
Less depreciation		500	8,500
Vehicles at cost		1,500	
Less depreciation		150	1,350
TOTAL FIXED ASSETS			15,725
Current Assets			
Stock		5,500	
Work-in-progress		2,750	
Finished goods		2,500	
Debtors		15,000	
TOTAL CURRENT ASSETS		25,750	
Less: Current Liabilities			
Creditors	13,250		
Expenses	1,955		
Debenture interest	125		
Cash overdrawn	8,175		
TOTAL CURRENT LIABILITIES		23,505	
NET WORKING CAPITAL			2,245
NET CAPITAL EMPLOYED			17,970
Less 10% Debentures			5,000
NET WORTH OF THE COMPANY			£12,970

The above net worth of the company was financed as follows:

	£	£	£
Subscribed Capital			
10,000 Ordinary shares of £1 each			10,000
Reserves			
General reserve		2,000	
Profit and Loss Account:			
Brought forward	75		
Forecast	895	970	2,970
TOTAL SHAREHOLDERS' INTEREST			£12,970

employed to be £17,970. Therefore the company's expected profitability from executing the plan proposed in the case study would be:

$$\frac{895 \times 100}{17,920} = \frac{895 \times 100}{21,000} \times \frac{21,000}{17,920}$$

$$4.99\% \qquad 4.26\% \quad \times \ 1.17 \text{ times}$$

But these figures relate to a period of three months only. If this level of activity and profitability continued for the whole accounting year, the firm's return on capital would be

$$4.99\% \times 4 = 19.96\%$$

and the sales per £ of capital employed would be

$$1.17 \times 4 = 4.68$$

whilst the return on sales would remain at 4.26 per cent.

Self-examination questions

1 What do you understand by the term 'cash flow'? In what sense is it important in company planning and how does it differ from funds flow?

2 Why do most corporate budget plans commence with a proposed sales budget? In what circumstances would you expect some other factor to have a greater influence upon the business plan?

3 Define 'accruals' and 'prepayments'. Would you expect either or both of these items to have an impact upon the preparation of a cash budget?

4 How can it be said that an increase in current liabilities is a source of corporate funds? Examine the Funds Flow Statement in the published accounts booklet of a UK company, and verify the entries in that statement for variations in current liabilities.

5 As annual depreciation charges are taken into account in cash flow calculations, why do they not form part of a cash budget?

6 Define turnover, turnover of capital and return on capital. Study the published accounts of (a) a retailing company and (b) an electronics company and ascertain the values of these three appraisal criteria for each company.

Recommended reading

ROCKLEY, L.E., *Finance for the Purchasing Executive*, Business Books (1978), see chapters 1 and 5.

PIZZEY, A., *Accounting and Finance*, Holt, Rinehart and Winston (1980), see chapter 24.

LANGLEY, F.P., *Introduction to Accounting for Business Studies*, Butterworth (1978), see chapter 16.

ROCKLEY, L.E., *The Meaning of Balance Sheets and Company Reports*, Business Books (1983), see chapters 5 and 7.

8 Analysis of accounts and company worth

Introduction

At the close of the previous chapter, three measures of business performance were given. These measures, or ratios, facilitate a ready appraisal of the results of specific aspects of the firm's activities. The appraisal is made easier to comprehend because the results of business activity are reduced to simple percentages, or simple unit comparisons, of otherwise complicated aggregations of financial data. The ratios which were used on page 126 are explained below.

Return on capital employed

This is a commonly used expression for evaluating an investment in any venture. A decision to put one's money in a Building Society rather than National Savings is made as a result of, for example, comparing the rates of interest offered for deposits with either form of saving. A businessman does much the same thing if, when reviewing the profit made by his firm, he is concerned with the rate of return (*cf.* interest) which he is making on his investment. Return on capital employed is an overall average measure of a firm's efficiency-of-use of its total assets.

Mark-up on sales

Here we have a term which expresses the net profit as a percentage of the value of sales obtained during the period of account. The term 'mark-up' indicates, for an individual sale, the level of gross profit planned by a businessman; the total *net* mark-ups actually achieved are revealed by the net profit in the profit and loss account. In order to evaluate variations in the percentage rating of this ratio, all other expenditure items and groups of such expenses can be shown similarly as a percentage of sales. These subsidiary ratios will enable clarification of

1   the cost importance of each item or group of items which go to make up the total cost;
2   the impact of changes in cost structure from one period to another, i.e. whether any single expense or group of expenses threatens the firm's profitability.

Return on sales – the net profit mark-up – is a measure of the cost efficiency of the firm throughout the whole process of manufacturing and distributing its products.

Turnover of capital employed
Also referred to as sales per £ of capital employed, this ratio shows the extent to which the firm's physical assets are used to produce goods for sale. Clearly if full-time working is achieved, more goods will be produced than if short-time working is in force. Similarly, a business which has an efficient production flow on the shop floor will have a greater output, in a similar period, than a firm with disorganised workshops. Both of these instances (full-time working, efficient production flow) lead to a greater out turn of goods from identical operating assets. This is what turnover of capital employed describes: it is a measure of the efficiency of use of the available assets in producing output.

A relationship

The above three ratios are the first stages in the appraisal of a firm's business activities: they lead to a more complete evaluation of the beneficial use of resources. These indices are not independent measures however. It is pointed out that if the net mark-up on sales is raised whilst the turnover of capital remains the same, the return on capital employed will increase. These interrelationships are displayed by the equation

$$\text{Return on capital employed} = \text{Net profit on sales} \times \text{Turnover of capital employed}$$

which is more fully expressed by

$$\frac{\text{Profit} \times 100}{\text{Capital employed}} = \frac{\text{Profit} \times 100}{\text{Sales}} \times \frac{\text{Sales}}{\text{Capital employed}}$$

In order to ascertain the reasons for a particular rate of profit on sales, and for a particular rate of sales per £ of capital employed, we must examine the profit and loss account and balance sheet in greater detail.

The chart overleaf shows how the various impacts upon the corporate return on capital employed are linked to one another. The chart sets out a

Performance evaluation and ratio analysis

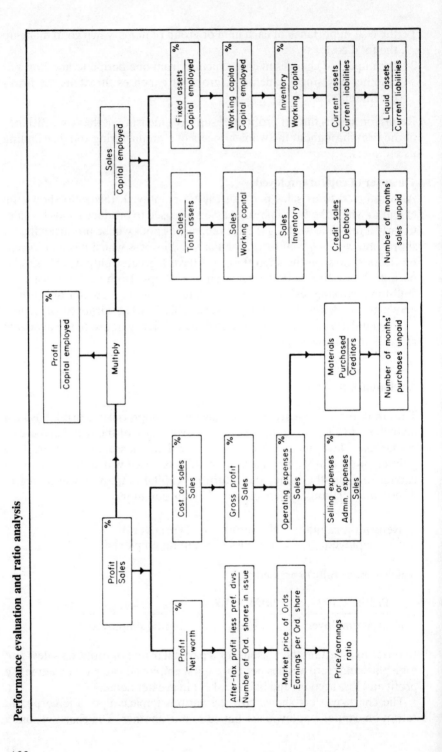

few of the operating ratios and capital asset ratios which can be used to identify areas of high cost/low profitability, etc., so that effective investigations may be pursued. Thus economies and greater efficiencies can be discovered and appropriate actions taken.

Now return on capital employed is used widely in comparisons of the profitabilities of different firms and industries. Therefore the reader should remember that the amounts of the accounting profit and of the capital employed sum can each be seriously affected by different methods of valuing assets. The impact of various ways of calculating depreciation provisions has already been shown.* Again, profit has several connotations: it may refer to

Profit before tax
Profit after tax
Profit before tax and interest
Profit before tax and depreciation

The list of alternatives is not complete. Consistency of approach is the important criterion however, and it is suggested here that profit should be taken to mean

Profit before tax and debenture interest but after depreciation.

The object of our study of return on capital employed has been the identification of efficient and profitable business activities. Profit *before tax* has been chosen for this purpose because a company's taxation charge does not rest upon the firm's efficiency or ineffeciency only. The taxation charge can be affected quite considerably by, e.g. capital allowances for new plant and machinery and in such a case the post-tax profit figure would reflect this benefit. Operational efficiencies or inefficiencies would be obscured.

Nevertheless, it must be emphasised that the post-tax figure is a vital factor affecting corporate liquidity. This is because it is only the post-tax earnings which are available for company uses and which can therefore relieve liquidity pressures. The point is an important one to bear in mind when cost inflation coupled with controls on selling prices bear down upon the company cash resources.

Solvency

The writer has stated earlier in this book that profitability and efficiency are

*Different expressions of the term 'capital employed' are used also. Such other computations will have regard to the objectives of the person making the analysis. For example, a prospective investor in ordinary shares will be concerned with the post-tax rate of return on the equity shareholders' interest. See Chapter 5 of *The Meaning of Balance Sheets and Company Reports*, by L. E. Rockley, Business Books (1983)

not the only considerations for ensuring successful business continuance. In a complete appraisal of company performance, the question of whether the firm can pay its way must be answered. Here the size of the net working capital is a vital factor in a satisfactory answer to the problem of liquidity. Now previous exhibits have demonstrated that

Working capital = Current assets − Current liabilities

At the end of the planning period in the case study (pages 112–16), working capital was expected to be £2,245 as shown in Exhibit 60. Therefore, if during the ensuing trading period current assets each realised the values attributed to them, then short-term creditors would be able to be settled from the current income. Where prompt settlement of creditors' accounts is not effected, due to lack of sufficient cash and income earning current assets, the firm will lose its good name, its creditworthy status will diminish and petitioning creditors can force liquidation. A ready appraisal of working capital, so that comparisons can be made with other periods is essential therefore. The form of a working capital ratio is calculated, and expressed in the equation below:

$$\frac{\text{Current assets}}{\text{Current liabilities}} = \frac{25,750}{23,505} = 1.09 \text{ to } 1$$

The desired level of the working capital ratio will vary from industry to industry, and at different periods of the year. A company engaged in a seasonal trade will require a larger working capital in the close season period, because at this time it will be manufacturing largely for stock. However it is generally recognised that a ratio greater than unity, i.e. current assets money value being greater than the money value of current liabilities, is desirable. A relationship of 2 to 1 is advisable for a sound financial basis for current business operations.

Even so the net working capital sum, or the equivalent ratio, is not a wholly adequate indicator of a company's liquidity. Stocks of raw materials, work-in-progress and finished goods, which are included in current assets, are vital elements in the calculation of working capital. Such goods are valued in anticipation of their being converted into sales and thus into cash flowing to the firm's bank account. Should the change from stock to sales and cash be fairly speedily completed, any risk of loss through depreciation of stock values is thereby reduced. In order to emphasise the importance of truly liquid current assets, the *liquidity ratio* is used. It is considered to be a better indicator of a firm's ability to meet the demands of its creditors and is calculated by

134

$$\frac{\text{Current assets} - \text{Stocks}}{\text{Current liabilities}} = \frac{15,000}{23,505} = 0.64 \text{ to } 1$$

Again the desired level of the liquidity ratio should be at least unity. In the example above, the liquid ratio does show the potential dependence of the Standard Plc upon its stocks for its solvency status.

The importance of observing the impact of inventories upon a working capital assessment can be brought out by showing stocks as a percentage of working capital. The company's total stocks in Exhibit 60 are valued at £10,750. Working capital is given as £2,245 and therefore if the value of the various stocks were to fall by only 20 per cent, current assets would be reduced to £23,600! In this event working capital would be cut to £95. A fall in the value of raw material stocks, of work-in-progress and of finished goods can arise relatively easily and with very little warning. Changes in consumer taste, the appearance of new products, currency valuation changes and loss of markets can each have their influence upon the worth of a firm's stocks on hand. The existence of a situation which could lead to an 'overnight' loss of working capital, in the way suggested above, can be revealed by expressing the total stocks' value as a percentage of working capital. Here stocks of £10,750 are 479 per cent of the working capital of £2,245! Though this ratio should give a warning of the true liquidity of our company, there is yet one more consideration to examine.

One must not be too rigid in the approach to this problem. It may well be advisable for stocks to be bought in a certain time in the year, because that is the best (or only) time of the year to buy them. This can apply to the supply of natural resources such as animal hides, sheep's wool etc. Again a seasonal trade may justifiably carry heavy stocks in readiness for the normal surges of trade at some other time in the year.

Stock turnover ratios

The continuing analysis of company liquidity* demands a study of inventory movement, and this means finding out how long the average item of stock remains on the company's books. The speed of transference of stock into sales is referred to as the *turnover of stock*. The greater the rate of turnover, the smaller the risk of loss of value whilst the goods are in the charge of the manufacturer. Now the turnover rate of raw material stocks is demonstrated by

*The figures used in the next series of ratios are taken from Exhibits 57 and 60, respectively.

$$\frac{\text{Cost of materials used}}{\text{Average stock of raw materials}}$$

$$= \frac{15,750^*}{4,000} = 3.9 \text{ times in the period of account}$$

As the period of account is three months, the actual time during which the material would be in stock is shown by

$$\frac{3}{3.9} = 0.77 \text{ months} = 23 \text{ days (approx.)}$$

Whether this period is a reasonable one is a matter of fact and can be determined by such criteria as

1 The time taken to obtain new supplies.
2 The optimum order size to apply when obtaining new stocks.
3 The level of activity of the works.

Work-in-progress and finished goods

The rate of turnover for these sections of the total inventory should be calculated also. The rate for work-in-progress will be arrived at by

$$\frac{\text{Cost of goods manufactured}}{\text{Average stock of work-in-progress}} = \frac{18,030}{2,000}$$

$$= 9.01 \text{ times in the period of account}$$

Again, as the period of account is three months the actual time during which work-in-progress would be passing through the works is shown by

$$\frac{3}{9.01} = 0.33 \text{ months} = 9.9 \text{ days (approx.)}$$

An efficient production control system, aided by a good shop floor layout, will operate to keep this ratio down to acceptable levels. Furthermore the quantity of work-in-progress must also be influenced by the sales programme and the need for finished goods. Thus the turnover rate for finished goods, the next ratio to be studied, will give an indication of

1 The pressure of demand for the company's goods.

*Where published accounts are used to find out the stock turnover rate, only two inventory valuations are normally available. These are the valuations at the beginning and at the end of the year and it is from these two totals that an *average* stock would be calculated. This is what has been done in the determination of materials turnover rate in this example. A more accurate turnover rate will result from calculating an average stock by using the *monthly* valuations in, say, a twelve-month period.

2   The efficiency with which they are inspected, packaged and despatched to customers.

The speed of transfer of finished goods to satisfy orders, the finished goods turnover rate, is expressed as

$$\frac{\text{Cost of sales}}{\text{Average cost of finished goods}} = \frac{16{,}530}{1{,}750}$$

= 9.44 times in the period of account

Once again the reader will appreciate that a more meaningful index is created if this ratio is converted into months or days. As the plan in the case study covered a period of three months, then the time during which the average stock of finished goods would be in the company warehouse is calculated as

$$\frac{3}{9.44} = 0.32 \text{ months} = 9.6 \text{ days (approx.)}$$

Credit manipulation

From a study of the management teams of different organisatons, one can see that some companies are marketing orientated whilst others place great stress upon the financial or production aspects of the firm's activities. On the other hand it appears that the really successful businesses base their operations upon an appreciation of the need for a complete integration of the planning and functioning of all departments. Only in this way can the progress and expansion of the business be controlled and carried out profitably and safely. In other words, it is of little use to aim for ambitious targets in one section of the firm whilst leaving the other departments to adapt themselves to the requirements of targets which have been fixed without *full interdepartmental* discussion. A rapidly expanding sales programme calls for more and more production and/or supplies of materials and finished goods. These requirements cannot be met without additional finance to

1   Pay for the increased production and additional supplies of materials which must be held in stock.
2   Furnish the greater absolute quantity of credit which follows upon an increasing number of customers at the higher level of sales.

It should be emphasised that it is the *continuous rapid* expansion of sales which gives rise to these problems of lack of adequate company finance. The first indications of corporate overtrading are revealed in the debtor-creditor relationships shown in the balance sheets. When the firm's bank balance is under pressure, the first reaction of the management may well be to seek earlier settlements of debtors' bills. At the same time creditors of the firm could find themselves waiting longer and longer for payment of sums due to them, from the company. Such a situation has the tendency to grow worse until certain creditors will wait no longer.* If this crisis arises, and the company cannot obtain sufficient extra funds, then the impatient creditors might commence legal proceedings to recover their money. Liquidation may not be far away.

Now in all businesses there are some standard relationships which have emerged during the normal trading operations. One of these is the *average collection period* for debts. The ratio is calculated from

$$\frac{\text{Debtors}}{\text{Average daily credit sales}} = \begin{array}{l} \text{Number of days that} \\ \text{accounts remain unpaid} \end{array}$$

and a study of the trend in this ratio is very material to the analysis of corporate liquidity. Conclusions drawn from this study must have regard to the terms of sale in force, because a firm operating net settlement conditions of 30 days will have a different ratio from one where a 60-day credit period is in operation. However, after allowing for particular specialities, the accounts analyst can see whether the average collection period is lengthening or shortening. To consider this concept in relation to the volume of creditors, it is necessary to compare the cash sum of outstanding creditors with the current level of material purchases:

$$\frac{\text{Current level of material purchases per annum}}{\text{Creditors}}$$

$$= \begin{array}{l} \text{Average number of months that creditor} \\ \text{accounts remain unpaid} \end{array}$$

A comparison of the two ratios above will indicate how the firm is managing its short-term financing; it may be revealed that the creditors listed amongst current liabilities are forming a larger and larger proportion of the total funding of the company's operations. (A word of warning must be repeated here. Ratios are but demonstrations of matters needing further scrutiny. They rarely give final answers to any problem by themselves alone; it is the ensuing scrutiny of underlying reasons for change which should present management with a plan of action to correct any undesirable developments.)

*Variations in the relationships between outstanding debtors and creditors may well arise from other causes. The income section could be operating more efficiently, thus bringing money in more quickly and reducing balances unpaid. If at the same time a corresponding efficiency in the payments section does not materialise, then debtor balances will fall in relation to creditor balances. The point is that the reason for a change in a ratio must be sought: the ratio itself is but an indication of a need for investigation.

138

By using the figures in Exhibits 57 and 60, the two ratios can now be calculated as shown below:

$$\frac{\text{Debtors}}{\text{Average daily sales}} = \frac{15{,}000^*}{21{,}000 \div 91} = 65 \text{ days}$$

= The average number of days that the debtor accounts remain unpaid

$$\frac{\text{Current level of material purchases per annum}}{\text{Creditors}} = \frac{75{,}000}{13{,}250} = 5.66$$

This figure represents the 'turnover' of creditors in relation to an estimated twelve-month figure of purchases.† To convert this to a statement of the average period, in days, which creditor accounts remain unpaid, we have

$$\frac{365}{5.66} = 65 \text{ days}$$

Review of ratio analysis

The story of ratio analysis of business accounts could continue with other very appropriate comparisons of financial data. However it was not intended to make this chapter into an extensive study of accounts interpretation. Its object is but an introduction to the ease with which a considerable amount of information can be gained from final accounts. The use to which this information is put is far more important than the data itself. The suggested further reading list at the end of this chapter should enable a wider knowledge of the calculation and use of ratios to be obtained together with an appreciation of the ways in which the information should be used. The student is strongly advised to pursue the study of this subject, for the gains available in terms of an ever-growing understanding of financial reports are considerable.

Evaluation of business worth

This section in our studies of the appraisal of corporate worth will view the firm from the standpoint of an investor in the ordinary shares of a company.

---

*The accounts in Exhibits 57 and 60 cover a period of three months. To ascertain the average daily sales, therefore, the actual sales in this period are divided by 91 – the number of days in three months.
†Exhibit 57 shows purchases for the three months planning period as being £18,750. Assuming that this rate of material purchase continues throughout the year, then the annual level of material purchases = £18,750 × 4 = £75,000.

Here we shall see how a company's earning power and dividend record will be expressed in yield percentages, which can be meaningful to investors. To this end the reader will be introduced to the basic elements of calculating investment yields. When that simple exercise has been accomplished we shall examine the effect which current taxation legislation may have on some of these investors' yield percentages. Such taxation implications – arising initially from *The Finance Act, 1973* – are explained on pages 147–50.

The main object in the analysis of business accounts is to be able to reach some assessment of the worth of the firm and the efficiency with which its management uses the corporate assets. Return on capital employed, turnover of stocks and the measurement of costs implicit in the sales mark-up, etc., all have their uses in coming to a decision about the satisfactory conduct of a business. It is pointed out however that the accounts analyst will not always have the same viewpoint towards his analysis: the emphases which he portrays will depend upon the reasons for the investigation. If a company is being scrutinised on behalf of a bank or major financing organisation in response to the firm's request for overdraft or loan, then the sort of information about the firm which would influence the potential lender will be

1 Security in the form of permanent assets, for the loan's liquidation.
2 Security in the form of income to meet loan charges.
3 Security in the form of guaranteed management succession to ensure that the conditions under (1) and (2) continue to be safeguarded.

There are many other matters to consider beyond these but (1) to (3) above reflect an objective approach to a valuation of the firm's worth and viability, in the circumstances postulated.

An examination of the firm, on behalf of a potential creditor for supply of goods, would be greatly concerned with the liquidity state of the company. The trade creditor is worried not so much about the growth, development and continuance of the company over the next ten years as in the company's ability to pay its short-term debts in the next six to twelve months. Therefore whilst return on capital is of minor importance here, the adequacy and soundness of the firm's working capital is a prime factor in deciding whether to do business with the company. (The businessman will always hope for the development and continuance of his customers' business, because such profitability portends further trade for himself in the future. Nevertheless he must look for the security of his own short-term debts.)

Another group of people who may be interested in the status of our company are potential shareholders. Now, in general, shareholders are hopeful of receiving continuing dividends, together with some increase in the rate paid plus a capital growth as shown in the share price quoted on the Stock Exchange. Many investors have little knowledge of company finance or management: the importance of working capital, the influence of depreciation charges upon return on capital employed do not create a financially meaningful impression upon the general body of shareholders. Their main interest is in income received. Therefore an investigation of company accounts which is executed on behalf of a potential investor will be directed to the net *earning* power of the company. An investor's concern with corporate net earning power is really a concern with the value of that earning power to *himself*. Before earnings can be translated into dividends or capital growth for the investor, however, such earnings (profit) must be affected by taxation – corporation tax. It is only after this levy that the residual net profit is available for shareholders' dividends and company growth. Whether retention of profits does in fact contribute to an increase in the value of a company depends on how the retentions are used. It is here that the importance of managerial skill and efficiency comes into the picture. Even so the student of business performance should not forget the influences of the firm's market, its buoyancy and economic development, upon the power of the company to prosper and grow in wealth. To continue the definition of an investor's share of corporate earning power, one does not stop at a consideration of the limiting power of corporation tax; whilst the company suffers a charge called corporation tax, the individual similarly bears a levy upon his income. Thus when a dividend is declared, this total sum is reduced by income tax at the standard rate* before the investor can regard the payment as his own income.

Moreover where retentions are used successfully by the company to promote profitable growth, such growth will result ultimately in an increase in the market value of its shares. Where this new market price rises above that paid by the investor when obtaining his shares, a capital gain is achieved.† Such a gain can be realised only when disposing of the shares – and that realised gain, determined in accordance with tax law and regulations, is taxable in the hands of the recipient, the shareholder. Now the point of this short discourse upon the taxation on investment income is that we all have different amounts and kinds of allowances to set against the final income upon which we pay tax. Many of us pay tax at different rates. For these reasons it is impossible to present a rate of return on income from shares which, net of all income and capital gains taxes, will apply to everyone. Therefore, in assessing the worth of a business, from

---

*This statement must be modified where the investors' own taxation circumstances result in his paying *less than* the standard rate of tax. On the other hand the surtax payer may be even further penalised up to his own higher personal taxation rate.

†In such a limited reference to taxation, particularly of capital gains, the writer does not pretend to offer a complete statement of the taxation problem. The object in tax examples is to show the impact of taxes generally upon an investor's returns and to give some indication of the power of taxation to reduce the monetary value of those returns, before they are received by a shareholder.

the standpoint of a potential shareholder, it is necessary to consider the return on investment:

1 After corporation tax.
2 Before income and capital gains taxes.

Each individual can then apply his own personal taxation conditions to the income thus expressed. This is the approach which is used, by financial analysts and by the financial press, when expressing the dividends and earnings of public companies as a percentage return of the cost of investing in a share of those dividends and earnings.

The value of dividends

It was stated above that '...in general shareholders are hopeful of receiving continuing dividends, together with some increase in the rate paid...'. The reader will remember that dividends are quoted at a percentage rate relating to the paid-up value of shares, as the following example will show:

> One hundred Ordinary shares with a face value of £1 each have a total par, i.e. nominal, value of £100, provided that all of this sum has been demanded by the company, and paid to the firm by the shareholder. If a dividend of 10 per cent is declared, then the shareholder will receive £10 – before deduction of income tax.

In view of the fact that the market price of a share is most often different from its nominal value, any dividend paid on a share needs to be related to its purchase price. In other words the dividend is compared with the current cost of getting that dividend – the price of a share on the Stock Exchange. By this calculation one can show the actual gross (pre-income tax) return on the share's purchase price: this resultant percentage figure is termed the 'Gross Yield Per Cent'. The formula for the calculation is

$$\frac{\text{Dividend per share} \times 100}{\text{Market price per share}}$$

For the 100 shares given in the example above, assuming the share's price to be £2.50 each on the Stock Exchange, the gross yield will be

$$\frac{0.10 \times 100}{2.50} = 4 \text{ per cent}$$

(Care is needed here to ensure that numerator and denominator are both expressed in the same units – in this instance, in decimal currency. The

142

dividend per share is obtained from 10 per cent of £1, the par value of the share.)

It should be remembered that we are, in effect, valuing the company by looking at one aspect of its earning power and seeing how that compares with the market's appraisal of the firm's worth. Now there are many factors which will affect the share's market price. Basically these factors, which will always influence the demand for, and supply of, the shares include

1 The general political and economic climate both for the firm's industry and for the economy as a whole.
2 The firm's prospects as expressed by the size of its order book.
3 The ability of its management to use the corporate assets efficiently.

The importance of earnings

However, dividends are not the sole return to the successful investor. The amount of total profits after tax is a much more valuable indicator of worth for it will reveal the *sum* of profits *available* to the company for expansion and development. To the extent that dividends are paid from this profit, expansion is restricted but from the standpoint of total power to produce a return on investment, the investor must look at the whole corporate post-corporation tax earnings. This is the value he buys when purchasing a share and the index of comparability which expresses the worth of a company's total earnings is called 'Gross Earnings Yield Per Cent'. The formula is

$$\frac{\text{Earnings per share} \times 100}{\text{Market price per share}}$$

These indexes of investment worth refer predominantly to Ordinary shares – the major risk-bearing section of a company's capital. Consequently when earnings after corporation tax have been determined, any sums due for dividends of the preference shareholders must be deducted. The remaining earnings are then divided by the *number* of Ordinary shares *in issue*, to arrive at the available earnings per Ordinary share.

If we now assume that the hypothetical company, whose £1 shares have been discussed, followed a dividend policy of paying out one half of its earnings to its shareholders, then the total post-tax earnings per share would have been 20p. The gross earnings yield per cent, in the circumstances, would be

$$\frac{0.20 \times 100}{2.50} = 8 \text{ per cent}$$

Here we have a means of comparison between different companies. It is a comparison based upon their individual post-tax earnings which is expressed as a percentage of the cost of buying a share of those earnings – the Stock Exchange share price. There is, however, a further point for the student of corporate worth to consider, and this refers to the definition of 'earnings'. In calculating the gross earnings yield per cent, financial analysts refer to '*maintainable* earnings'. In this context they mean the power of the company to continue generating the kind of earnings which are used in the ratio. Thus the earnings yield ratio should not be assessed on a historical basis only: attention should be paid to the firm's order book, its future cost structure and generally its ability to continue achieving its present earnings (at least) in the foreseeable future. Furthermore strict interpretation of maintainability of earnings always refers, as has been noted, to post-corporation tax earnings. It is therefore necessary to appreciate the potential variability of the taxation charge, and the sundry allowances which can operate to reduce that charge. Prominent amongst such tax reductions are capital allowances which are given to a company on the purchase of certain fixed assets. These allowances will vary from year to year according to the size of its expenditure on certain long-term fixed assets: they will also vary as the whims of successive Chancellors of the Exchequer cause changes in the taxation laws of the country. So, to arrive at the true maintainable corporate earnings (the income earned by the company from its own *trading* activities), it is necessary to eliminate non-trading increments from the taxation charge in order to leave an ultimate levy based solely upon the trading results. In this way those factors which tend to distort the year by year, and firm by firm, comparability of profits are removed to give a more reliable appraisal of company worth.

Price/earnings ratio

For many years property valuers have used a method of property valuation which depends upon the earnings which the property can obtain. This method is of importance where the freehold land value portion of a leasehold property is sold. The sale price of the freehold, in these circumstances, is normally based upon an annual ground rent which is payable to the owner of the freehold. To calculate the price at which the freehold may change hands, such ground rent is then multiplied so many times – this multiplier being a specific number of years' expectation of continuance of the ground rent income. Thus, if a ground rent was £20, then a ten years' purchase would amount to a purchase price of £200 and the freehold could be sold, in those circumstances, at that figure. One would not expect that prices would be settled quite as easily as the example shows, for the time pattern for receipt of rent, and the level of current and expected interest rates would have to be taken into account. The reader will encounter the use of interest rates, when evaluating investment spendings, in the subsequent chapters on capital budgeting.

As regards the evaluation of company worth, the price earnings ratio is closely linked with the gross earnings yield. The P/E ratio (as it is termed) is found when the share price quoted on the Stock Exchange is divided by the earnings per share. Therefore, using the figures in the gross earnings yield and applying the formula

$$\frac{\text{Market price per share}}{\text{Earnings per share}}$$

then the P/E ratio of our hypothetical company's shares will be

$$\frac{2.50}{0.20} = 12.5$$

For the mathematically minded, the P/E ratio is but the reciprocal of the gross earnings yield, i.e.

$$\frac{1}{8 \text{ per cent}} = \frac{100}{8} = 12.5$$

The value of the P/E ratio rests on the fact that it specifies the number of years within which a company's earnings per share will repay the present market price of buying that share. It is the time capitalisation of a share's worth. Though it is a close relation to the gross earnings yield, the P/E ratio has an advantage over the yield index. 'Yield' connotes a value being received by the shareholder: but a shareholder does not *receive* the earnings of a company, he receives the dividend only and hopes that the retained earnings will produce eventually some other capital gain for him. Now the P/E ratio indicates the number of years which the shareholder must wait for dividends and growth to repay his capital outlay. It thus gives a value and a time scale to the relationship between earnings and shareprice.

The Standard Plc

The reader is now invited to refer to Exhibit 48 which shows a narrative profit and loss account as it would be affected by various rates of depreciation. Using the figures in the first column of that exhibit, and specifying certain other variable factors, it is now intended to show the relationship of dividend, dividend yield, earnings yield and price earnings ratio for the Standard Plc. The variable items are postulated below:

1 Share price – £3.00.
2 Dividend declared – 10 per cent.
3 Previous highest price in the current year – £3.75.
4 Previous lowest share price in the current year – £2.00.

Dividend yield

This has been shown to be derived from the formula

$$\frac{\text{Dividend per share} \times 100}{\text{Market price per share}}$$

In the circumstances proposed in the previous paragraph, the dividend yield in respect of shares would be

$$\frac{0.10 \times 100}{3.00} = 3.3 \text{ per cent}$$

Here we have the actual percentage revenue return an investor would secure if he bought the company's shares for £3 each, when a dividend of 10 per cent had been declared on the nominal value of those shares. Again, the gross earnings yield, using the formula on page 143, would be

$$\frac{0.1375 \times 100}{3} = 4.58 \text{ per cent}$$

(Exhibit 48 shows the post-tax earnings to be £1,375. As there are 10,000 Ordinary shares of £1 each in issue, the earnings per share are therefore £0.1375. Note carefully that numerator *and* denominator are shown here in decimal units of £1.)

The all important P/E ratio can also be calculated by the method already explained: it shows the number of years necessary for earnings, such as those given in Exhibit 48, to result in each shareholder recovering a capital cost of £3 per share.

$$\text{P/E ratio} = \frac{3}{0.1375} = 21.8$$

Information such as that produced above is given each day in the *Financial Times*. With one final item of dividend appraisal, the student will be able to construct his own *Financial Times* entry for the Standard Plc. The additional item of information refers to dividend cover, which gives an indication of the company's *present* power to repeat the dividends most recently declared.

Dividend cover is quite a valuable index for it tells the investor of the extent to which retained earnings have exceeded the dividend allocation. It can also demonstrate whether the board of directors have had difficulty in declaring a dividend out of (meagre) earnings!

With reference to Exhibit 48, the profit and loss account shows post-tax earnings of £1,375. A 10 per cent dividend would have cost £1,000 and could have been paid 1.37 times: the dividend cover would then be expressed as 1.4 which incidentally is a below average cover when compared with industrial and commercial norms around 1.5 to 2 times.

Post-tax earning under imputation

From 5 April 1973 a new system of dealing with company tax and with tax on shareholders' dividends came into force. It is called the imputation system and its principal features are

1 Company profits will continue to be liable to Corporation Tax.
2 Shareholders' dividends will continue to be liable to Income Tax at the standard rate.
3 The tax deducted from dividends, when the *net* dividends are paid to shareholders, will be treated as an advance payment of the firm's Corporation Tax (ACT).
4 The tax deducted from dividends will be regarded as part of a *gross* sum received by the shareholder.

Clearly the amount of ACT available to meet future corporation tax liabilities will depend upon the amount of dividends being paid. Furthermore, as ACT operates to reduce the amount of corporation tax payable from company funds, then we can say that the post-tax earnings of a company are now available to pay net of tax dividends rather than the gross (pre-tax) dividends as was previously the case.

In this chapter our method of determining earnings for ordinary shares has been based upon

Post-tax profits less other prior dividend, i.e. preference, charges.

We now have to account for the fact that the amount of equity earnings available for paying dividends is dependent upon the dividend itself. It is therefore imperative to adopt some form of calculating equity earnings so that we can continue to appraise the worthwhileness of alternative forms of investment in ordinary shares.

Nil, net and actual earnings

Firstly we can decide that all calculations shall be based upon the assumption

147

that no dividends are being paid. Equity earnings would continue to be calculated as before. This is called the NIL distribution method.

Secondly we can assume that the whole of the post-tax earnings are to be distributed to shareholders. Here the value of the post-tax equity earnings will be increased by the ACT contribution to the corporate tax bill. This is called the FULL distribution method.

The choice between the two methods is not without its complications because ACT must be regarded as an advance of UK Corporation Tax. ACT cannot be used as an advance on account of the taxation liability arising from foreign earnings. In order to deal with those situations where ACT cannot be used, either in part or entirely, to meet a firm's taxation debts, we can calculate equity earnings as though ACT was a cost of paying the dividends. In this case we could justifiably use the nil distribution method for earnings, EPS and P/E ratio calculations.

Alternatively we can regard the unrecovered ACT (that amount which cannot be set off because of the preponderance of foreign earnings) as an additional company tax charge, and reduce the earnings figure by the unrecovered amount. This method is now accepted by the financial press and is termed the NET or ACTUAL method. But we recognise that where a company can recover the whole of its ACT, then there is no difference between the NET and NIL methods so far as earnings based ratios are concerned. Firms for which full recovery of ACT will not be available include those with

1 Large foreign tax liabilities, *and/or*
2 Below average UK tax liabilities due to heavy capital expenditure allowances against tax.

Earnings and dividend rates

One result of the new system is that companies are declaring the percentage rate of their dividends by reference to the net (post-tax) amounts payable. Nevertheless when we calculate dividend yields we shall continue to use the following formula:

$$\frac{\text{Gross dividend per share} \times 100}{\text{Market price per share}}$$

Now dividend cover has been explained as the number of times that a gross dividend could be paid from post-tax equity earnings. Under the new system the cover ratio will be calculated as follows:

$$\frac{\text{Post-tax equity earnings on a full distribution basis}}{\text{Gross dividends declared}}$$

At the same time the earnings yield ratio will be determined by using the full distribution basis as shown below:

Earnings per Ordinary share on the basis of

$$\frac{\text{a full distribution of post-tax earnings}}{\text{Market price per share}} \times 100$$

P/E ratios will be calculated on a NIL basis and, for the special type of company with overseas earnings, a NET basis.

Exhibit 61 shows the effects of the imputation system of taxation upon earnings based ratios. The example presumes a standard rate of income tax of 30 per cent, a company having 5,000 Ordinary shares in issue, and that the market price of the shares is £5 each. Items 6 and 7 in respect of the imputation calculations show that dividend cover and earnings yield are to be based upon full distribution of the profits after tax of £600. In the circumstances £600 would represent the net dividend sum payable to the ordinary shareholders. Therefore the gross dividend belonging to the shareholders will – with the standard rate of income tax of 30 per cent – be

$$\frac{£600 \times 100}{70} = £857$$

ACT therefore would be £257.

There is one final point to note in the relationship between the ratios in the table. In the pre-imputation period, the product of the dividend yield, the dividend cover and the P/E ratio equalled 100, thus:

$$1.8 \times 1.33 \times 41.7 = 100 \text{ (approx. due to decimal points calculation)}$$

This simple relationship no longer applies with the imputation system because dividend cover is based upon a full distribution basis whilst the P/E ratio is derived from a NIL or NET basis,

$$1.8 \times 1.9 \times 41.7 = 143 \text{ (approx.)}$$

The Financial Times

A sample entry in the *Financial Times* (FT) Share Information Service is given below. It incorporates the foregoing imputation related data and the information is shown as it would appear in the FT share columns. To complete the entry it is assumed that

(*a*)   the entry relates to the 'New Company Ltd';

Exhibit 61

Effect of imputation on earnings-based ratios

Details (1)	Pre-imputation (2)	Imputation (3)
1 Post-tax profits	£600	£600
2 Gross dividend	£450	£450
Dividend percentage:		
3 Gross	9%	9%
4 Net	6.3%	6.3%
5 Dividend yield (based on gross dividends, for both systems of taxation)	1.8%	1.8%
6 Dividend cover (on a FULL distribution basis for the imputation system)	1.33 times $\dfrac{600}{450}$	1.9 times $\dfrac{600 + 257}{450}$
7 Earnings yield (on a FULL distribution basis for the imputation system)	2.4% $\dfrac{600 \times 100}{25,000}$	3.43% $\dfrac{(600 + 257) \times 100}{25,000}$
8 EPS ⎰ on a NIL or NET distribution basis for the imputation system	12p	12p
9 P/E ratio ⎱	41.7	41.7

Notes:

1   Where the company has most of its income taxed abroad, the EPS and P/E ratios will be calculated on the NET basis. This recognises ACT as an additional company tax charge, in these special circumstances.

2   Gross dividends are quoted above because the shareholder is deemed to have received the gross sum. Under the imputation system, the dividend shown in the PL account would be recorded as £315 — the amount actually paid. The tax deducted at the time of payment is calculated by taking 30 per cent of £450, i.e. £135. This latter sum is the amount used by the company as an instalment of its liability for Corporation Tax, the ACT referred to in the foregoing pages.

3   In item 7 the denominator of £25,000 derives from 5,000 shares in issue each having a market price of £5.

(b) during the year the price of the company's shares have fluctuated between £3.25 and £5.50 per share;

(c) the market price of the shares fell by 25p on the day prior to publication.

1982					Dividend		Yield	
High	Low	Stock	Price	+ or −	Net	Cover	Gross	P/E
550	325	New Company £1	500	−25	6.3	1.9	1.8	41.7

The high and low values, the price and the net dividend are all quoted in pence. Furthermore the (current) market value of 500p is derived from the middle point between the jobber's buying and selling prices at the close of business on the previous day. The sample entry above states that the New Company's shares have a nominal value of £1; where no value is given here in the FT, then the related shares have a nominal value of 25p.

The reader can verify his own net dividend ratings, in circumstances where the marginal tax rate is higher than the standard, by the following:

$$\text{gross dividend} = \frac{\text{net dividend}}{70 \text{ per cent}} = \frac{6.3p}{0.7} = 9p$$

$$\text{gross dividend yield} = \frac{\text{gross dividend}}{\text{market price}} \times 100 = \frac{0.09}{5.00} \times 100 = 1.8 \text{ per cent}$$

The divisor of 70 per cent given in the gross dividend calculations results from a standard rate of income tax of 30 per cent. For a standard rate of 28 per cent the divisor would be 72 per cent and the net dividend in this example would have been 6.5p. The higher rated tax payer can now determine his own net dividend (achieved at the final year's tax assessment) by multiplying the gross dividend of 9p by his net-of-tax remainder. For example, if an owner of a share in the New Company had a marginal tax rate of 40 per cent then his net dividend would ultimately be 9p × 60 per cent = 5.4p.

Self-examination questions

1 A weakness in ratio analysis of company performance is that it is a study of historical data. How can this weakness be overcome?

2 If a company's current ratio for three successive periods has moved from 1.8 to 1.4 and then to 0.7, how would you explain the

(*a*) significance of the trend

(*b*) possible reasons for the trend

and how would you advise a potential trading creditor of the company?

3 Refer to the published accounts of the companies studied in question 6 of Chapter 7 (page 128), and calculate the current and liquid ratios of the two firms for the past two years. What observations would you now make regarding the solvency status of the two companies?

4 How are (*a*) raw material turnover and (*b*) work-in-progress turnover computed? What would be the significance of a yearly raw material turnover rate of 8 or of 15?

5 What do you understand by the term 'yield' in relation to an Ordinary share of a UK public limited company? What relevance does it have for (*a*) an investor and (*b*) a lender?

6 In what way do the principles of imputation (*a*) tend to an easing of corporate cash flow (*b*) encourage restraint in the size of dividend payments?

7 Certain generally accepted investment practices used to emphasise the value of earnings per share as a principal criterion of the worth of an Ordinary share. Current opinions appear to favour the consideration of dividend yield and dividend cover. What could be the reasons for this change?

Recommended reading

WRIGHT, M.G., *Financial Management*, McGraw-Hill (1970), see chapters 1 to 4 and chapter 10.

ROCKLEY, L.E., *The Meaning of Balance Sheets and Company Reports*, Second Edition, Business Books (1983), see chapters 4, 5, 7 and 9.

HINGLEY, W., and OSBORN, F., *Financial Management,* Allen (1978), see chapters 5 and 10.

JONES, F.H., *Guide to Company Balance Sheets and Profit and Loss Accounts*, Barkley Books (1977).

ROCKLEY, L.E., *Finance for the Purchasing Executive*, Business Books (1978). See case study evaluation in chapters 6 and 12.

9 Accounting for inflation

Introduction

Throughout our studies of the Standard Plc, our analyses of performance and creditworthiness have used profit and loss accounts and balance sheets compiled from historical cost data. The various comparisons of profitability, liquidity and net worth have assumed that the value of the monetary unit remained stable during the years under comparison. But a continuing high level of inflation so reduces the purchasing power of a £ from year to year that the monetary values in successive final accounts do not give realistic data values which are properly comparable, over periods of time, for assessments of net wealth or profitability. Whilst this criticism applies to the content of successive final accounts of a single company or group, it also has a great emphasis when inter-firm comparisons are sought. This is because the consequences of inflation are not felt with equal intensity, nor with the same timing effect, throughout the whole industrial and commercial sphere.

The point is that when we apply monetary values, e.g. past acquisition costs, to items in conventional profit and loss accounts and balance sheets, these statements will give inaccurate pictures of the year-by-year real wealths of a firm and of its operational costs. We know that some firms revalue their fixed assets from time to time, or they make supplementary provisions for asset depreciation. Such adjustments are made in order to give some effect to the extent of the changes in corporate *real* wealth and costs of operations. Indeed the 1981 Act balance sheet formats list a Revaluation Reserve amongst the list of required disclosable reserves – a specific acknowledgement of the fixed asset revaluation practice.

However, adjustments such as these are based upon subjective opinions about the movement in, for example, fixed asset purchase prices just as though exactly the same assets would be available, or desired, for immediate replacement in a continuing business. Clearly we must recognise that the effects of inflation upon statements of income and of net worth will be more far reaching than would be reflected in revaluations of fixed assets and depreciation charges alone. It therefore has become essential that we devise some universally accepted method of adjusting, where relevant, all the data in annual accounts in order to incorporate the effects of an unstable monetary unit. The objective must be the presentation of financial transactions which form the content of successive profit and loss accounts and balance sheets, in constant values. In this way the *real* profitability and wealth of a business will be shown, and the year-by-year comparisons, both for a single firm and taking one firm with another, will be more realistically drawn.

To this end, several methods of bringing to account the impacts of inflation upon the reported performance of business activities, have been promulgated and widely discussed. The object of this chapter will be to examine these various proposals, coming finally to a study of the present recommendations for Current Cost Accounting.

Current purchasing power

In May 1974 the Accounting Standards (Steering) Committee issued its Provisional Statement of Standard Accounting Practice (SSAP) No.7. It recommended that conventional historic cost accounts should be adjusted by a conversion index which reflects measured changes in the value of the monetary unit in which the accounts are expressed. This measured change in the purchasing power of the monetary unit is, from 1962, to be taken from the movements of the Retail Price Index (RPI) which is calculated and published by the Government Statistical Service. As a single annual statement of the RPI would not be adequate for adjusting the accounts of continuing businesses, we have to refer to the monthly statement of the RPI. In this way transactions during the year can be given appropriately adjusted values to take account of the effects of inflation. The data on the month-by-month index are issued by the Department of Employment: the index is also published in the booklet *Price Index Numbers for Current Cost Accounting* issued by the Department of Industry and Trade.*

The aim of using the above indexes is to enable the preparation of supplementary value-adjusted balance sheets and profit and loss accounts, from final accounts based upon historic cost principles. Historic cost annual accounts were, under SSAP7, still to be produced: the separate supplementary statements would then demonstrate the effects of an unstable monetary unit upon those corporate worths and incomes which are recorded in the

*For a comprehensive statement of regularly produced Government Statistics, the reader should obtain *A Brief Guide to Sources* from the Press and Information Service, Central Statistical Office, Great George Street, London SW1P 3AQ.

Exhibit 62

Fixed asset purchases – historical cost

Date of purchases	Costs of fixed assets purchased		Conversion index
	Firm A	*Firm B*	
(1)	(2)	(3)	(4)
	£	£	
1 Jan Year 1	1,000	3,000	100
1 Jan Year 2	2,000	2,000	110
1 Jan Year 3	3,000	1,000	120
31 Dec Year 3	—		130

conventional accounts. Essentially the conversion indexes are derived from movements in the general purchasing power of the monetary unit. By using the appropriate indexes we seek to present a series of balance sheets and income statements which contain realistically comparable monetary values.

The conversion index

An example of the use of a general purchasing power index is given below. Exhibit 62 sets out the fixed asset purchases of two firms, A and B, over a period of three years, during which time the index of purchasing power was as shown in column 4.

In conventional balance sheets the gross costs of the fixed assets would be shown as £6,000 at 31 December Year 3, for both firms. If we now wish to convert the historical cost pounds for the above assets into general purchasing power pounds as at 31 December Year 3, the following calculations will be necessary:

1   Each asset's purchase cost must be multiplied by the index rating at the date of the proposed supplementary statement, i.e. 31 December Year 3.
2   The sum resulting from (1) must be divided by the index rating at the date of the original transaction.

Exhibit 63 gives the appropriate details.

The revised price-adjusted figures show clearly that Firm B possesses assets of a greater real worth than Firm A. This is because more of B's assets were acquired before the monetary unit began to lose its purchasing power. Furthermore if the expected economic lives of the assets were 10 years for

Exhibit 63
Fixed asset purchases, at current purchasing power, at 31 December, Year 3

| Date of purchase | Firm A | | Firm B | |
	Price level adjustments	Revised value, £	Price level adjustments	Revised value, £
1 January Year 1	1,000 × (130/100)	1,300	3,000 × (130/100)	3,900
1 January Year 2	2,000 × (130/110)	2,364	2,000 × (130/110)	2,364
1 January Year 3	3,000 × (130/120)	3,250	1,000 × (130/120)	1,083
Revised totals as at 31 Dec Year 3		£6,914		£7,347

both firms, and each had used the straight-line method of calculating depreciation, then the historical cost depreciation charge would be £600 for each firm (£6,000/10) in Year 3. With a similar depreciation policy, depreciation charges in Year 3 would be

Firm A £691
Firm B £734

in the supplementary statements based upon general purchasing power indexes.

A comparison of the balance sheet entries for these two firms' fixed assets is given in Exhibit 64. The extracts based upon historical cost would result in identical initial cost figures for the stocks of fixed assets in both firms. However, different timings of the various acquisitions must result in different aggregate depreciation amounts at the end of Year 3, in the historical cost accounts. Exhibit 64 shows these impacts upon the net book values of fixed assets and the reader will appreciate their resultant effects upon the book worth of the capital employed sums. The exhibit goes on to show how the accumulation of annual depreciation charges in respect of the several fixed assets:

1   Leads to calculation of the historical total depreciation charges at the end of Year 3 (column 4).
2   Is used to convert the above historical total depreciation charges into pounds of current purchasing power at the end of Year 3 (column 8).

Calculation of the inflation-adjusted annual depreciation charges and aggregate depreciation sums are completed in exactly the same way as inflation adjustment examples in Exhibit 63

These exhibits present simple examples of the application of a conversion index to a single section of a company's balance sheet. In addition to impacts upon quantification of net worth, the consequent changes in annual depreciation charges will affect the profit or loss revealed by the supplementary, price-adjusted, income statement. Furthermore the process of converting historical cost data to their current purchasing power equivalents will involve adjustments to assets of different types as well as to the firm's liabilities also. Here we have to appreciate the varying effects which the possession of (*a*) monetary and (*b*) non-monetary assets and liabilities will generate for corporate wealth and income, in an inflationary environment.

Now monetary items comprise cash, debtors, creditors and loans, whilst non-monetary items include physical assets such as stock, plant, machinery, vehicles, equipment and buildings.

The numerical size of monetary items is fixed in terms of the (historical) pounds in which they were originally expressed. This means that the holder of monetary assets loses purchasing power in a period of inflation.

157

Exhibit 64
Balance sheet data of fixed assets, 31 December Year 3

Details	Historic cost			Index at date of acquisition	Current purchasing power		
	Asset initial cost	Year 3 depreciation charge	Aggregate depreciation at 31 Dec Year 3		Price-level adjusted value (Exh. 63)	Adjusted Year 3 depreciation charge	Adjusted aggregate depreciation at 31 Dec Year 3
	(2)	(3)	(4)	(5)	(6)	(7)	(8)
	£	£	£		£	£	£
Firm A							
Year 1	1,000	100	300	100	1,300	130	390
Year 2	2,000	200	400	110	2,364	236	473
Year 3	3,000	300	300	120	3,250	325	325
	£6,000	£600	£1,000		£6,914	£691	£1,188

Balance sheet book value 31 Dec Year 3 £6,000 – 1,000 = £5,000

Inflation-adjusted balance sheet value 31 Dec Year 3 £6,914 – 1,188 = £5,726

Details	Historic cost			Index at date of acquisition	Current purchasing power		
Firm B							
Year 1	3,000	300	900	100	3,900	390	1,170
Year 2	2,000	200	400	110	2,364	236	473
Year 3	1,000	100	100	120	1,083	108	108
	£6,000	£600	£1,400		£7,347	£734	£1,751

Balance sheet book value 31 Dec Year 3 £6,000 – 1,400 = £4,600

Inflation-adjusted balance sheet value 31 Dec Year 3 £7,347 – 1,751 = £5,596

Conversely those having monetary liabilities will gain purchasing power since delay in settlement of any liability results in payments being made in lower valued pounds.

At the same time we must realise that possession of non-monetary assets during a period of inflation does not earn an inflationary 'profit'. The values given to these assets in the supplementary statements reflect proportionate changes in the monetary worths, consequent upon the rate of inflation operating since the assets were purchased. The possessor of non-monetary assets merely maintains his physical wealth as a result of having exchanged a monetary asset (cash) for a non-monetary asset (plant) before the fall in value of the monetary unit made the asset acquisition more costly in monetary terms.

Practical examples

The next series of exhibits demonstrate the conversion of final accounts data from an historical cost basis to a general purchasing power basis of reporting. Firstly, balance sheets at the beginning and end of a year must be expressed in the general purchasing power values existing at the end of the year, i.e. at the date of the second balance sheet. Secondly, items in the profit and loss account will be similarly adjusted to take note of the changes in the purchasing power index during the year.

Exhibit 65
Consumer price index

Year	At commencement of the year	Average for the year	At commencement of final quarter of the year	Average for the final quarter of the year	At the end of the year
1	100	102.5	103.8	104.4	105
2	105	107.5	108.8	109.4	110
3	110	113.0	114.5	115.2	116
4	116	119.0	120.5	121.2	122
5	122	125.0	126.5	127.2	128
6	128	131.0	132.5	133.2	134

Exhibit 65 details the movements of the index over a six-year period and gives values of the index for certain periods during the year. Appropriate index ratings from this exhibit are used in the conversion process. Exhibits 66 and 67 are directed to a consideration of the firm's position at the end of Year 4

Exhibit 66
The New Values Plc
Balance sheet as at 31 December Year 3

Historic cost details				Price-level adjusted details		
	£	£	×	÷	£	£
Fixed assets at cost		1,000	122	100		1,220
Less depreciation		300	122	100		366
Total fixed assets		700				854
Current assets:						
Stock	330		122	115.2	349	
Debtors	350		122	116	368	
Cash	120		122	116	126	
	800				843	
Less: *Current liabilities*						
Creditors	350		122	116	368	
Net current assets		450				475
Total shareholders' funds		£1,150				£1,329

and explanations of the adjustments are given below, starting with the non-monetary assets.

Fixed assets
It has been assumed that a single fixed asset was acquired by the New Values Plc on 1 January, Year 1. At that time its purchase price was £1,000 and the purchasing power index stood at 100. Because the appraisal relates to the situation at the end of Year 4 when the conversion index had reached 122, the required conversion calculation will be:

£1,000 × (122/100) = £1,220

Now in order to compare the firm's wealth at Year 3 with that at Year 4, both balance sheets must show the purchasing power value of the fixed asset as £1,220. If several assets had been acquired at various times during a year then the appropriate index to be used, in place of 100 in the above equation, would be the *average* index rating for the year in question. For example, if the expenditure of £1,000 related to a number of assets acquired *during* Year 1, the conversion equation would have been:

£1,000 × (122/102.5) = £1,190

Depreciation
Historical cost depreciation is shown as £300 and £400 for Years 3 and 4,

Exhibit 67
The New Values Plc
Balance sheet as at 31 December Year 4

Historic cost details				Price-level adjusted details		
	£	£	×	÷	£	£
Fixed assets at cost		1,000	122	100		1,220
Less depreciation		400	122	100		488
Total fixed assets		600				732
Current assets:						
Stock	440		122	121.2	443	
Debtors	550				550	
Cash	250				250	
	1,240				1,243	
Less: *Current liabilities*						
Creditors	290				290	
Net current assets		950				953
Total shareholders' funds		£1,550				£1,685

respectively. These amounts result from using the straight-line depreciation method in conjunction with an expected 10-year economic life for the asset involved. Conversion of these aggregate depreciation amounts will follow the same principles as those applied to the purchase price of the asset. Therefore to bring data in both balance sheets to a common general purchasing power position at the end of Year 4, our calculations must be:

$$£300 \times (122/100) = £366$$

$$£400 \times (122/100) = £488$$

The first important point for comparative analysis now emerges – the general purchasing power value of the fixed assets declines from £854 to £732, whereas the historic cost data shows a fall from £700 to £600. The percentage fall is the same in both cases *but* the monetary value of the firm's net worth and its capital employed will be more realistically quoted in the supplementary adjusted statement. We shall have to watch the impacts of these (and other) revised figures upon ROC, etc: subsequent exhibits will help us to do this.

In a practical situation, conversion of asset cost prices and their relevant depreciation sums will involve more detailed calculations than above. The simplicity of the basic method remains: but it has to be applied to the year-by-year historic cost data of all the assets presently possessed by the company. Monetary values of yearly acquisitions, disposals and related depreciation sums must be converted to the current general purchasing power index. It is the work involved, not the method, which increases in complexity.

Stock

The stock values in both balance sheets have to be converted to purchasing power equivalents. For this purpose we shall assume that the physical stock on hand at the end of the year was acquired during the last quarter of that year. Consequently the conversion indexes relating to the date of acquisition of these non-monetary assets will be the index's *average* rating during the appropriate final quarter.

Thus the adjustment for Year 3 stock will be

$$£330 \times (122/115.2) = £349$$

and for Year 4

$$£440 \times (122/121.2) = £443$$

Before we leave the subject of current purchasing power values for stock, it must be emphasised that the basic valuation principle of 'lower of cost or net realisable value' is *not* to be ignored. Adjusted purchasing power values for stock will be entered in the supplementary statements just so long as they do *not* exceed the expected net realisable values of that stock. In such an instance (purchasing power values being higher than NRV) the supplementary statements would show stock at its expected net realisable value.

Monetary items

To complete our conversion of the two balance sheets to current purchasing power values, we turn to the monetary items. Now each of these is deemed to have been 'acquired' at the date of the balance sheet in which it is recorded, and consequently no changes to the Year 4 values will be necessary. On the other hand the values of monetary items in the Year 3 balance sheet must be converted by reference to the index obtaining at that date. The calculation applied to the Year 3 debtors is as follows:

$$£350 \times (122/116) = £368$$

Exhibit 66 shows the monetary items being calculated individually. This is not essential, for the same index ratings apply to each of the debtors, cash and creditors. One calculation to convert the *net* monetary assets' value would have sufficed.

Total shareholders' interest

The net effect of the various conversion adjustments to monetary and non-monetary items is now reflected in the book value of the total shareholders' interest (net worth). Here it is vital to note that the constituent parts of net worth – issued shares, reserves and profit and loss account balances – are *not* adjusted by the application of conversion indexes. (It must be pointed out that some authorities do recommend adjustment of, for example, Ordinary share capital by reference to changes in the index since the share issue was made. An evaluation of the current purchasing power of the shareholders' original capital invested is thereby made.)

The figure of net worth shown in a supplementary purchasing power adjusted balance sheet is derived simply by deducting the other liabilities from the assets when those other liabilities and assets have been converted to general purchasing power pounds, at the date of the statement. The published accounts booklets of the New Values Plc at the end of Year 4 would show the historical cost balance sheet as at that date together with the comparable historical cost figures relating to the previous year. At the same time, if CPP was the accepted method of accounting for inflation, supplementary value-adjusted statements would also be given for the two years. Exhibit 68 below presents the relevant data which the annual accounts booklets would contain. The exhibit gives the information in adjoining columns, in order to enable the reader to see the effects of the indexed changes with some emphasis. The company would not be required

Exhibit 68
The New Values Plc
Balance sheets at years ended …

Historic cost statement				*Supplementary value-adjusted statement*			
		Year 3 £	*Year 4* £			*Year 3* £	*Year 4* £
Fixed assets		1,000	1,000	Fixed assets		1,220	1,220
Less: Depreciation		300	400	*Less:* Depreciation		366	488
		700	600			854	732
Current assets:				*Current assets:*			
Stock	330		440	Stock	349		443
Debtors	350		550	Debtors	368		550
Cash	120		250	Cash	126		250
	800		1,240		843		1,243
Less: *Current liabilities*				Less: *Current liabilities*			
Creditors	350		290	Creditors	368		290
Net current assets		450	950	*Net current assets*		475	953
Total shareholders' funds		£1,150	£1,550	Total shareholders' funds		£1,329	£1,685

Exhibit 69
The New Values Plc
Profit and loss account for Year 4

	£	£	×	÷	£	£
Sales		3,150	122	119		3,229
Stock on 1 January	330		122	115.2	349	
Purchases	2,000		122	119	2,050	
	2,330				2,399	
Less: Stock on 31 Dec	440		122	121.2	443	
Costs of goods sold		1,890				1,956
Gross profit		1,260				1,273
Less:						
Admin. and selling expenses	760		122	119	779	
Depreciation	100		(10% × £1,220)		122	
Monetary items	—	860			16	917
NET PROFIT		£400				£356

to locate these statements side by side, as in the exhibit, but the data would be adequately disclosed in appropriate sections of the accounts booklet.

Profit and loss account
The final stages in the conversion process are recorded in Exhibits 69 and 70. Again we have as our objective the conversion of each group of historic costs, in the profit and loss account, into their year end equivalent purchasing power values. Thus if we start with sales, and assume that the transactions had occurred evenly throughout the year, then the 'time of transaction' index to be used would be the average rating for the year. In such circumstances the conversion calculation will be, as is given in Exhibit 69:

$$£3,150 \times (122/119) = £3,229$$

If we can identify a spasmodic sales pattern, it would be better to deal with the sales, quarter by quarter, in our conversion calculations. Here we would have to determine an average rating of the purchasing power index for each of the separate quarters. All that this means is that there would be four computations for the year's sales, instead of the one given above.

Gain or loss on monetary items
One item in the supplementary profit and loss account requires further examination. It is the charge of £16 being 'borne' by the New Values Plc, and

Exhibit 70
The New Values Plc
Loss of purchasing power during Year 4 from holding net monetary assets

	Historic cost details	Adjusted for price level changes
	£	£
1 January		
Debtors	350	368
Cash	120	126
	470	494
Less: Creditors	350	368
Net monetary assets	120	126
Receipts		
Sales	3,150	3,229
	£3,270	£3,355
Less: *Payments*		
Purchases	2,000	2,050
Expenses	760	779
	£2,760	£2,829
Difference	£510	£526
31 December		
Debtors	550	550
Cash	250	250
	800	800
Creditors	290	290
	£510	£510
LOSS OF PURCHASING POWER		16

which results from holding monetary items during a year when the purchasing power of the monetary unit was declining. Clearly a holder of cash loses wealth in a period of inflation: his money possessions will buy less and less as inflation continues. For the same reasons granting credit to customers results in a loss of purchasing power, whilst the amounts due remain unpaid. Conversely, the receipt of credit facility from a supplier will act to the benefit of the recipient, when inflation is rife.

Thus we have to measure the costs of being a holder of net monetary assets and Exhibit 70 details the calculations necessary for this purpose. This exhibit shows that the New Values Plc started the year with net monetary assets of £120, and to this extent the firm was liable to lose purchasing power in the inflationary environment. During the year, monetary assets flowed to the company from the sales of £3,150. At the same time the outflow of monetary assets to meet costs of operations were £2,760. The arithmetical results of the opening state of £120, adjusted for subsequent inflows and outflows, indicates a net monetary asset position at the end of Year 4 of £510. This is confirmed by the debtors, cash and creditor amounts recorded in Year 4 balance sheet.

Now, when the historical cost data are converted to pounds of current purchasing power at 31 December, Year 4, we find that the net monetary asset position *ought* to be £526 if no loss of purchasing power was to be suffered. But since the net monetary assets state at the year end is shown to be £510, then a loss of purchasing power of £16 is established. This is the amount recorded in the supplementary profit and loss statement given in Exhibit 69.

Performance appraisal

If we use the figures given in Exhibits 68 and 69 we can compare returns on capital employed, as reported in the two accounting statements for Year 4. Exhibit 71 shows the results.

Clearly the effectiveness of the company's manufacturing and trading operations has been given a lower rating under CPP accounting than by conventional historic cost principles. It is most likely that year by year comparisons of performance, for such a company, would show more marked falls in the returns to investment when CPP accounting is used than by conventional accounting. Furthermore it is important to recognise that the extent of the difference in returns as shown by comparisons such as those above, will be affected by the nature of the business of the many different types of company which we may encounter. A highly capitalised company engaged in manufacturing operations, perhaps, with a lengthy production cycle, will tend to experience lower CPP rates of return percentages – in periods of high inflation – than those firms, such as major retailing organisations, which do not have considerable fixed asset possessions or lengthy production and stock turnover cycles.

Future years

The above exhibits give an introduction to a recommended method of accounting for inflation, though more detailed matters of practice have been omitted in order to give emphasis and reason to the relatively simply principles involved. The next stage examines the preparation of supplementary statements in the years ahead after the major tasks, involved in the first of such statements, have been completed. Clearly, when the first

Exhibit 71
The New Values Plc
Return on capital employed

| *Details* | *Profit as a percentage of* | | *Sales per £ of capital employed* |
	Capital employed	*Sales*	
Historic cost accounting	(400 × 100)/1,550 = 25.8%	(400 × 100)/3,150 = 12.7%	3,150/1,550 = £2.03
Current purchasing power accounting	(356 × 100)/1,685 = 21.1%	(356 × 100)/3,229 = 11.03%	3,229/1,685 = £1.92

167

inflation-adjusted statements are being prepared a considerable amount of 'once only' research and analysis will be necessary. Past records of fixed asset acquisitions and disposals have to be scrutinised in order to determine the current purchasing power equivalents of the existing fixed asset stock. In a subsequent year these purchasing power equivalent values will be merely updated by relevant conversion indexes applicable to the year-end accounting date of the later statement. In addition, continuing programmes of asset acquisitions and disposals will have to be recorded in working papers which support the inflation-adjusted accounts. The data will be stored in readily usable form and further time consuming research will not be necessary.

Balance sheets

To instance the updating of supplementary statements, we now return to Exhibit 63. Purchasing power equivalent values were given to the fixed assets of two firms: these values were £6,914 and £7,347 for Firms A and B, respectively, at the end of Year 3. Therefore if we prepared inflation-adjusted statements for 31 December, Year 4, taking the index at that date to be 140 and assuming no changes in the physical assets the inflation-adjusted asset values would be:

Firm A   £6,914 × (140/130) = £7,446
Firm B   £7,347 × (140/130) = £7,912

Furthermore, the depreciation charges in the adjusted Year 4 profit and loss accounts would be £745 and £791 for A and B, respectively. The reader must recognise that, in assessing the effects of inflation during Year 4, the balance sheets at the beginning and at the end of the year will *both* be expressed in the purchasing power values obtaining at the end of Year 4.

We can pursue the example further by assuming that the following fixed asset purchases were made, by the two firms, on 1 July, Year 4, when the conversion index stood at 135

Firm A   £1,500
Firm B   £1,000

These additions to the fixed asset stock will be included in the supplementary statements at the end of Year 4 at the values shown below:

Firm A   £1,500 × (140/135) = £1,556
Firm B   £1,000 × (140/135) = £1,037

and the new inflation-adjusted figures for fixed assets as at 31 December, Year 4, would be

Firm A £9,002
Firm B £8,949

Depreciation charges for Year 4 will depend upon the firm's policy towards

1   Not charging depreciation in the year of acquisition of an asset.
2   Charging depreciation for the proportion of a full year that the assets were available for use.

We can apply the above principles to the accounts of the New Values Plc as shown in Exhibits 67 and 69. All of the items in the next (Year 5) historical cost balance sheet would have to be adjusted to their purchasing power equivalents as at 31 December. Appropriate conversion indexes must be used for this purpose. Now, just as we have a series of historic cost balance sheets which purport to show the variations in corporate wealth over the years, so we can present a series of supplementary statements based upon a common general purchasing power index. (In practice the published accounts of companies will show supplementary statements for the two most recent years only.) The point to note about a series of current purchasing power statements is that the historical cost data for each year's balance sheet must be expressed in the pounds of current purchasing power obtaining at the end of the last account period. For the New Values Plc this means that the supplementary balance sheets for Years 4 and 5 will have their figures adjusted by reference to the purchasing power index of the monetary unit, as at the end of Year 5. Comparisons can then be made between two statements of corporate net wealth, in the knowledge that both statements report the situations in terms of a monetary unit with a common purchasing power rating.

Profit and loss accounts

A profit and loss account for the operations of the New Values Plc during Year 5 should be converted by the same methods as those displayed for the Year 4 account. Furthermore the net gain or net loss arising during Year 5 from the effects of inflation on the firm, due to its holdings of net monetary liabilities or net monetary assets, must also be calculated.

When this is done a series of general purchasing power adjusted profit and loss accounts can be presented. They will show the impact of inflation upon the firm's reported incomes, over a period of years. It is emphasised that, as with supplementary balance sheets, the series of supplementary profit and loss accounts must have their data expressed in pounds of current purchasing power relating to the last account in the series. In other words the inflation-adjusted profit in the supplementary statement for Year 4 will be updated by reference to the general purchasing power of the monetary unit at the end of Year 5.

Conclusions

Many criticisms of the CPP proposals were voiced and the accounting standard was withdrawn. Such adverse views arose from the opinions exemplified below:

1 In the CPP balance sheet, equity capital was not amended, it emerged merely as a balancing figure after all the other adjustments had been made: this criticism is unfair for it has already been stated that the shareholders' section of the balance sheet can also be adjusted to pounds of a constant value
2 A CPP balance sheet does not show the real value of the company's possessions: when historical costs are varied by reference to retail price indexes, the resultant figures do not offer any measure of the cost of replacing the related assets – their so-called 'business deprival value': consequently depreciation amounts, balance sheet totals and profit and loss accounts are affected unrealistically.
3 Stock values are adjusted in accordance with movements in the retail price index: this may not reflect either the direction (up or down), or the extent, of price changes in the market: again the profit and loss account and balance sheets are affected.

Nevertheless the CPP methods did result in the real value of the shareholders' investment being shown: it was either being maintained or it was being eroded. Subjective judgement played no part in the preparation of supplementary CPP statements: the adjustment of historic cost values was completed by reference to RPI movements.

Current cost accounting

In September 1975 the Sandilands Committee on inflation accounting issued its report. It proposed a complete change of approach from the current purchasing power system to one which, in essence, uses replacement costs for measuring the value of resources consumed in business operations. We have seen above that the CPP method of inflation accounting entails the continued use of historic cost accounts, the financial data in which are then adjusted by reference to movements in the Consumer or Retail Price Indexes. Moreover the CPP system demands that variations in these indexes are applied uniformly to the accounting data of *all* businesses, whatever their nature. This feature is the most prominent weakness of CPP

170

accounting: inflation does not affect every industrial and commercial undertaking to the same extent, or in the same way.

Now the Sandilands Report envisages basic changes in the accounting principles upon which annual reports of corporate wealth and profitability are based. This approach to an acceptable system of accounting for inflation identified three main groups of gains (or losses) which may accrue to a firm in consequence of operating in an inflationary environment. These three groups are discussed below.

Holding gains (or losses)

This term is defined as the difference between the depreciated initial acquisition cost of an asset which is actively retained in a firm's possession, and its current value to that business. Under historic cost accounting, fixed assets are shown in the balance sheet at cost less depreciation, where depreciation has been calculated with the object of spreading the net initial acquisition cost over the asset's economic life. Clearly where the monetary values of assets increase after their original purchase, normal historic cost depreciation amounts remain as proportions of the outdated historic acquisition cost. Thus profit and loss accounts do not reflect realistic values of the costs of asset consumption appropriate to the period of the account in which that consumption took place. Though some firms have revalued certain assets from time to time, and consequently reassessed their depreciation charges, such actions have not been universally or consistently applied. The problems of performance evaluation and comparison have been exacerbated rather than eased.

Now the 'value to a business' of an asset is defined, by the terms of the Sandilands Report, as the loss which a firm would suffer if it were deprived of the asset's use. In general an asset's business value will be represented by the current replacement cost – after allowing for depreciation. At this point in the valuation procedure the holding gain (or loss) which results from replacing the net initial acquisition cost of an asset by its current value, would be credited (or debited) to a Fixed Asset Revaluation Reserve. In this way the asset worth of the firm would be increased as would the book value of the total shareholders' interest.

In order to aid objective reporting of corporate asset values, it is proposed that the Government Statistical Service will make available a series of price indexes for various categories of plant and equipment and other capital expenditures. Such independent criteria for determining current (replacement) values will remove a major criticism of previous replacement cost proposals which were also designed to account for the cost effects of inflation. This is because the use of an independent index for fixed asset revaluation would remove the possibility of an interested party's subjective judgement being able to influence unduly the balance sheet data. The likelihood of balance sheet window dressing by a member of the firm would be minimised. By transferring the holding gains to a reserve account the Current Cost Accounting recommendations aim to show fixed assets and stocks at their current values to the business. Any emergent gains or losses from holding such assets should not form part of the profit and loss account. They are to be shown as part of the net invested capital (amongst the reserves) of a continuing business. Moreover they indicate the financial sums necessary to keep the firm in business, and they show more clearly than CPP the potential *cash* needs of a firm intending to stay in business. Clearly if such gains were passed to the profit and loss account, the payment of improper dividends or over-large wage increases might be encouraged. The special nature of property assets is given some prominence in that their values are not to be determined by reference to some specific indexes. The report suggests that property assets should be independently valued at regular intervals.

Such an orderly system of restating the values of all fixed assets and the transfer of consequent gains or losses to a reserve account, located within the sum of the total shareholders' interest, will present a more realistic view of the asset worth of the firm and of the value of the shareholders' net investment in the firm.

Operating gains

The term operating gains is defined as the difference between (*a*) the realised value of a firm's output (sales of goods and services) and (*b*) the current values of the resources consumed in generating those sales. Here again the current value of resources consumed is measured by the 'current value to the business' of all the inputs which were necessary to achieve the related outputs. When calculating the operating gains for a period of account, the amount of the depreciation charge will be derived by taking a proportion of the asset's value to the business, as shown in the balance sheet at the commencement of the year. Furthermore, any appreciation in the value of stocks* must be included in the cost of sales shown in the profit and loss account. (At present such increases in the year-end stock values are deducted from the cost of sales in the income accounts.) Stock appreciation amounts should be shown as a special adjustment to the cost of sales and transferred to a reserve in the same way as holding gains on fixed assets.

*This refers to an inflationary rise in the value of any quantity of stocks: it does not refer to an increased *volume* of stocks except in so far as such increased volume has suffered an inflationary rise in its replacement cost.

It must be appreciated that historic cost accounting coupled with the use of FIFO results in stock appreciations acting to increase a firm's accounting profit. This occurs even though such higher valued stocks have not been sold during the period of the account.

Thus such stock appreciations, when forming part of the accounting profit, become subject to company taxation. Current Cost Accounting would remove this unreasoned burden from the cash and financial planning activities of business managers. There may be difficulties, however, in the determination of the current value of the stock consumed. It is expected that the Government Statistical Service will be able to provide indexes of price movements for the principal stock items purchased by specific industries.

By identifying holding and operating gains, the income account will be charged with the year's proportion of its current replacement costs of fixed assets *and* by an amount relating to the current replacement cost of stocks used during the accounting period. In a time of falling money values, therefore, the book profit would be reduced. At the same time the book value of the total shareholders' interest could be increased markedly by these two classes of gains and consequently the percentage return on capital invested would in these circumstances fall. The accounts should enable a more realistic return, on a real-worth invested sum, to be calculated. Such lower real returns should lead to a restructuring of sales prices for the firm's output, or to the production of completely fresh products, or to expanding abroad rather than at home. The possibility of a re-direction of some aspects of industrial and commercial effort, or some reappraisals of present activities, could lead to an improved gross output from business activities in this country.

Extraordinary gains

Here the report specifies those types of gain (or loss) which do not form part of the firm's normal trading activities. Whilst these gains or losses may be shown in the profit and loss account, because they will have been *realised* as a result of completed disposal transactions, the gains or losses must be shown separately from the operating gains.

Additional information

The report went on to recommend that the information published with the final accounts of companies should be supplemented by

'...a summary of the total gains for the year of the accounts: the summary should show separately
 (i)   operating gains (net profit under current cost accounting),

173

Exhibit 72
The Operating Plc
Balance sheets as at 1 January 19 ..

	Historic cost accounting		Current cost accounting	
	£	£	£	£
Employment of funds				
Fixed assets				
Land, buildings, plant, etc.		700		1,000
Current assets				
Stock	300		300	
Less: *Net current liabilities*	250		250	
Working capital		50		50
Net capital employed		£750		£1,050
Funds employed				
Share capital and reserves				
500 Ordinary shares of £1 each		500		500
Reserves		250		550
Total shareholders' interest		£750		£1,050

(ii)   extraordinary gains, and

(iii)   holding gains from revaluing fixed assets and gains arising from stock appreciations'.

Furthermore it is suggested that the directors' report which accompanied the final accounts should include a statement on the adequacy of the cash resources expected to be available to the firm in the forthcoming year.

Practical example of Sandilands proposals

The following series of exhibits will enable the reader to study the effects of applying the principles of Current Cost Accounting to the accounts of any company. Exhibit 72 shows the asset/liability state of the Operating Plc at the commencement of the year: the balance sheets have been prepared for both historic cost and current cost accounting conventions. Exhibit 73 sets out profit and loss accounts for the ensuing year, again in historic cost and current cost terms. Now there are two items of importance for the reader to

Exhibit 73
The Operating Plc
Profit and loss accounts for the year ended 31 December 19 ..

	Historic cost accounting		Current cost accounting	
	£	£	£	£
Sales		1,500		1,500
Less: *Materials consumed*				
Opening stocks	300		300	
Purchases	1,000		1,000	
	1,300		1,300	
Less: Closing stocks	500		500	
		800	800	
Adjustment for stock appreciation			200	1,000
Gross profit		700		500
Administrative expenses	300		300	
Depreciation	70	370	100	400
NET PROFIT		£330		£100

note in that income account which shows data in current cost values. These are:

1 The closing stocks have increased in value over the opening stock values by £200 and it is assumed for the purpose of the example that this is the result of inflationary price rises. The historic cost accounts have deducted the past cost of the closing stock (£500) in arriving at the gross profit of £700. On the other hand the current cost accounts have charged the profit and loss account with an inflationary price rise of £200 as a separate 'cost of sales' adjustment. Thus the gross profit in current cost terms is shown as £500.

2 Depreciation has been calculated in both accounts by the reference to the fixed asset values given in the 1 January balance sheet. The straight-line method of depreciation has been used upon expected future lives, for the assets, of ten years. Consequently the depreciation charge in the historic cost profit and loss account is £70 whereas the current cost account bears a higher 'cost of use' charge of £100.

The effect of aggregating these two current cost adjustments with other operational costs, is to reduce the pre-tax profit from £330 to £100. The *operational gain* is therefore £100.

Exhibit 74
The Operating Plc
Balance sheets as at 31 December 19 ..

	Historic cost accounting		Current cost accounting	
	£	£	£	£
Employment of funds				
Fixed assets				
Land, buildings, plant, etc.		630		1,500
Current assets				
Stock	500		500	
Less: *Net current liabilities*	50		50	
Working capital		450		450
Net capital employed		£1,080		£1,950
Funds employed				
Share capital and reserves				
500 Ordinary shares of £1 each		500		500
Reserves		580		1,450
Total shareholders' interest		£1,080		£1,950

We now turn to Exhibit 74 which presents balance sheets at the end of the trading period covered by the above profit and loss accounts. Fixed assets have been revalued to £1,500 in the current cost accounts but the historic cost data merely shows the commencing book value of £700, reduced by the year's depreciation charge of £70. The 'current value' of the stocks in hand appears at the same amount in both balance sheets.

There remains only to account for the changes in the amounts of reserves and consequently of the total shareholders' interests. Clearly the total value of the reserves shown in the historic cost accounts consists of (*a*) the sum of £250 in the 1 January balance sheet plus (*b*) the year's retained pre-tax profit of £330. The much greater variation in reserves such as is given in the current cost balance sheet is derived as follows:

	£	£
Balance of reserves, 1 Jan.		550
Add:		
Operating gains for the year	100	
Holding gains during the year:		
Stocks	200	
Fixed assets	600	900
Balance of reserves, 31 Dec.		£1,450

176

Exhibit 75

Funds flow statements for the year ended ...

Historic cost			Current cost*		
	£	£		£	£
Sources of funds			*Sources of funds*		
Profit	330		Operating gains	100	
Add depreciation	70	400	Add depreciation	100	200
			Increase in reserves (holding gains on fixed assets and stock)		800
					£1,000
Application of funds			*Application of funds*		
Increase in working capital		400	Fixed asset revaluations		600
			Increase in working capital		400
					£1,000

*Not strictly a funds flow statement because it contains non-funds items as fixed asset revaluations and the related holding gains. However it is desired to show the complete picture for comparison with the historical cost statement.

The fixed asset holding gains are calculated by deducting, from the year end values of £1,500, the fixed asset book values at 1 January, as reduced by the year's depreciation, i.e. £1,000 − £100 = £900.

Appraisal of the data

The Sandilands Report came out strongly in favour of requiring companies to provide Funds Flow Statements with their annual published accounts. Exhibit 75 shows how the requirement could be met in relation to the current cost accounting example given in Exhibits 72-74. At the same time a Funds Flow Statement based upon the historic cost accounts is presented for comparison purposes.

If we now consider the impact of current cost accounting on the Operating Plc's reported profitability, the effect of showing the real asset values needed to achieve the more realistically calculated profit, is startling (see Exhibit 76). It becomes evident how industrial and commercial effort can be misrepresented by historic cost accounting. The real returns for business activities are being wrongly stated. More importantly new investment and the consumption of human and physical resources will be uneconomically directed.

Conclusions

The foregoing examples demonstrate some of the calculations involved in preparing accounts based upon the current cost criteria: they formed the bases for discussions (Exposure Draft 18*) throughout the profession, in the search for a realistic method of accounting for inflation. Under these CCA proposals, comparisons of returns being achieved by different companies during similar time periods were expected to be more sensibly and usefully appraised than is the case under historical cost accounting (HCA). But, in a serious deficiency, the CCA recommendations of Sandilands did *not* enable the results of successive accounting periods to be compared with one another in any acceptable way. This was because CCA did not incorporate any adjustments for changes in the value of the monetary unit, from one year to another. On the other hand CPP accounting *does* attempt to measure movements in the value of the unit of account over time; moreover it does envisage the preparation of index adjusted balance sheet and profit and loss accounts for the current and immediately previous years.

There were no similar provisions, under CCA proposals by Sandilands, for publishing successive years' final accounts in a way which would have the objective of showing changes in the real worth or the real returns of business activity. Comparisons from *one time period to another* were not better based under CCA, if the aim is to eliminate the effects of inflation from the two sets of data. CCA deals with the fluctuations of market prices, which will happen whether inflation persists or not.

Nevertheless under CCA, corporate management would have its gainful activities displayed in two meaningful ways, the operating gains would show management's skill in using its net assets in the pursuit of profit. At the same time holding gains, which could arise from the wise purchase of fixed assets and stocks, would be separately stated. This means that the whole gains of a business unit would not be hidden or aggregated within unrealistic data values of conventional accounting practices. In other words, gains which were due to the productive efforts of management and staff would be prominently displayed. Gains due to the good fortunes or to the skills of management would also be clearly identified and quantified. CPP and HCA

*Issued in December 1976.

Exhibit 76
Performance appraisal

Details	Profit as a percentage of		Sales per £ of capital employed
	Capital employed	Sales	
Historic cost accounting	(330 × 100)/1,080 = 30.5%	(330 × 100)/1,500 = 22%	1,500/1,080 = £1.39
Current cost accounting	(100 × 100)/1,950 = 5.13%	(100 × 100)/1,500 = 6.67%	1,500/1,950 = £0.77

179

methods do not provide automatically for this kind of control information, though *ad hoc* studies completed by internal managements of companies can – and do – provide the data required.

Finally we must consider the treatment of monetary items, as specified by CCP accounting. Broadly these proposals deal with advantages which arise from being a borrower, rather than a lender, during a period of inflation. We have seen earlier how the gains or losses arising from being a net holder of monetary liabilities, or a net holder of monetary assets, should be accounted for. Sandilands did not envisage such treatment, nor did it recommend that any special regard should be given to the inflationary aspects of dealing in monetary items.

Now the basic CPP philosophy which has led to recommending a special treatment for monetary items is based upon an expectation of purchasing power benefits or losses. Such benefits or losses would stem from holding monetary liabilities or assets whilst the purchasing power of the related money was falling. Any gains or losses from such transactions would impact upon the total shareholders' interest, as shown in Exhibits 69 and 70. On the other hand CCA recognised that the possession of certain monetary liabilities, e.g. long-term loans, would enable fixed assets to be bought earlier rather than later. It was in this way that any consequential benefits or losses would have been brought to account within the total shareholders' interest. Similar considerations would have applied to the use of current liabilities to finance the acquisition of stocks.

The Sandilands recommendations for CCA suggested that its proposals should ultimately be a requirement for

1 Companies listed by a recognised stock exchange.
2 Companies not listed by a recognised stock exchange, but showing in their published accounts for the previous period:
   (*a*) turnover in excess of £10 million, *or*
   (*b*) total assets in excess of £10 million.
3 Nationalised industries.

The Hyde report adjustments

In view of the intensity of the debate, and the existence of serious divisions of opinion regarding the most appropriate method of accounting for inflation, interim recommendations were published in November 1977. Entitled the Hyde Report, these recommendations superseded the previous proposals for an interim period. The contents of the report were to be regarded as giving provisional guidance on the preparation of profit and loss accounts so far as to reflect some of the impacts of inflation upon reported profits. The report's suggestions were to be implemented until such times as

180

a satisfactory and workable whole system of accounting for inflation would be promulgated.

The recommendations of the Hyde Report were an important step along the road. They envisaged three adjustments to profit and loss accounts which had been prepared under historic cost principles. Details of these adjustments are given below.

Cost of sales

The object of this adjustment is to amend the cost of stocks, as shown in conventional profit and loss accounts, from their historic cost valuations to relevant current costs existing at the date of sales. It represents a specific application of the matching principle which is already being implemented where firms employ

1 The last in, first out (LIFO), system of stock cost flows. *Or*
2 A standard costing system which envisages regular revisions of standard costs in the event of regularly rising prices.

In other circumstances, it is recommended that the cost of sales adjustment is calculated by using an average method where appropriate indexes of stock price changes are applied to historic cost values used in the conventional accounts. The mechanics of the adjustment to accounting profit are shown in Exhibit 77.

Depreciation

In order to give a similarly current valuation to the cost of having fixed assets available – the annual depreciation charges – we have to recalculate these charges by reference to a current acquisition cost of the related fixed assets.

The initial impacts of this operation may be time-consuming because the assets' historic acquisition costs and dates of purchase must be discovered from company records. When this is done, their historic costs and depreciation charges must be revised, again by using relevant indexes showing the movement of prices over the years for such corporate assets. Thus the depreciation adjustment recommended in the Hyde Report is derived from:

the revised current cost depreciation charges
less
the historic depreciation charges.

An example of the calculations required is given in Exhibit 78.

Exhibit 77

Cost of sales adjustment using the averaging method

			£000	£000
A	*Historic cost trading account*			
	Opening stock		500	
	Purchases		4,500	
				5,000
	Less: Closing stock			800
	Cost of sales (historic cost basis)			£4,200
	Relevant index numbers:			
	1 January	100		
	31 December	120		
	Average for year	110		
B	*Revise Opening and Closing Stock to*			
	Average Current Cost for the Year			
	Opening stock: $500 \times (110/100) =$			550
	Closing stock: $800 \times (110/120) =$			733
C	*Compute current cost of sales using*			
	the revised figures			
	Opening stock		550	
	Purchases		4,500	
				5,050
	Less: Closing stock			733
	Cost of sales (current cost basis)			£4,317
D	*Calculated cost of sales adjustment*			
	Cost of sales (current cost basis)			4,317
	Less: Cost of sales (historic cost basis)			4,200
	Increased cost of sales			£117
	This reduction in profit is accounted for by:			
	(*a*) Increase in opening stock and therefore a decrease in profit			50
	(*b*) Decrease in closing stock and therefore a decrease in profit			67
	Total decrease in reported profit			£117

Exhibit 78

The depreciation adjustment

	£000
Value of assets at year end	6,000
Annual depreciation rate = 5%	
Therefore, revised current cost depreciation charge	300
Assume that historic cost depreciation charge is	200
Depreciation adjustment for year	£100

The gearing adjustment

When the foregoing two adjustments are deducted from a conventionally determined accounting profit, the resultant lower figure is deemed to reflect a real profit, i.e. the net gain achieved after taking into account those specific cost increases relating to fixed assets and stocks alone. The next stage in the amendments to accounting profit is designed broadly to segregate those price rises which stem from expenditure financed by:

1 The equity investment in the company, i.e. issued Ordinary shares plus reserves, *and*
2 Other sources such as preference shares plus debentures plus current liabilities as *reduced* by the firm's own monetary assets.

This adjustment, termed the gearing adjustment, is demonstrated in Exhibit 79. It is based upon an average of the opening and closing balance sheets in any year after updating by the respective current valuations of stock and fixed assets. To the extent that the adjustments for cost of sales and depreciation are deemed to be financed by (2) above, then that proportion of the inflationary cost increases (for stock and fixed assets) is added back to the profit and loss account.

The exhibit at item B describes the net monetary liabilities of the firm whose *average* balance sheet is given at item A. This is the evaluation of the financing of the firm's operational facilities by the net monetary liabilities – the net funds provided by sources other than the total equity interest [see (1) and (2) above]. When the net monetary liabilities are expressed as a percentage proportion of the whole net monetary financing, as at item D in

Exhibit 79

The gearing adjustment

		£000
A	*Average balance sheet*	
	Ordinary share capital and reserves	2,000
	Preference shares	750
	Long-term liabilities	1,000
	Current liabilities	850
		4,600
	Fixed assets	3,000
	Stocks	640
	Monetary assets	960
		4,600
B	*Calculation of net monetary liabilities*	
	Preference shares plus long-term liabilities plus current liabilities	2,600
	Less: Monetary assets	960
	Net monetary liabilities	1,640
C	*Calculation of net monetary liabilities plus equity interest*	3,640
D	*Calculation of gearing proportion*	
	Net monetary liabilities plus Ordinary share capital and reserves, all divided into net monetary liabilities to determine percentage relationship:	
	$(1,640/3,640) \times 100 = 45\%$	
E	*Application of the gearing proportion*	
	Depreciation adjustment	100
	Cost of sales adjustment	117
		217
	Gearing adjustment, i.e. the proportion of the increased costs of sales and depreciation which is added back to the operating profit: $£217 \times 45\% =$	98

the exhibit, we arrive at the gearing ratio. Finally item E demonstrates application of the gearing percentage to the adjustments for depreciation and stocks. Here we identify the amount of the inflationary cost increases which does not need to be provided from current business incomes in determining the profit available for equity shareholders.

In the event that calculations shown in Exhibit 79 produced a balance of net monetary *assets*, a further *deduction* from profit will ensue. This would therefore reduce profit whilst the gearing adjustment in Exhibit 79 results in an increase in profit – the consequences of net monetary liabilities situation. The adjustment to be made to account for the net monetary assets state will be determined by the formula

Net monetary assets total × An appropriate index of the value of money

Clearly the 'appropriate index' is vital to the calculation: as the adjustment should reflect the cost of holding money rather than assets, the multiplying index should be some yearly average of the Retail Price Index.

The published accounts

Exhibit 80
Current cost statement for year ended 31 December …

	£000	£000
Turnover		7,500
Profit: as per historic cost profit and loss		
account, before interest charges and taxation		600
Less: adjustments for:		
Cost of sales	117	
Depreciation	100	217
Operating profit		383
Gearing adjustment: add		98
Adjusted profit before interest charges		—
and taxation, etc.		£481

Exhibit 80 now shows a profit and loss account such as might be published by the company whose balance sheet is given in Exhibit 79 and where adjustments, similar to those exemplified above, should be brought to account.

SSAP16 – current cost accounting*

In March 1980 the Accounting Standards Committee issued its Statement of

---

*Before this accounting standard was published a period of debate and appraisal thereof was encouraged by the issue of Exposure Draft 24 (a draft of the then forthcoming standard) in April 1979.

Standard Accounting Practice No. 16. It sets out to be a distillation of the results of the debates which had followed upon CPP, Sandilands, Hyde, their various explanatory drafts and – in the case of CPP – SSAP7.

The accounting practices specified in SSAP16 were put forward as required forms for annual financial statements (balance sheets and profit and loss accounts) which cover accounting periods starting on or after 1 January 1980. For the moment (1982) the standard is not mandatory: a three-year trial period is envisaged with progress to a compulsory standard, in due course and after due debate. During this period the standard applies to businesses listed on a recognised stock exchange and those which satisfy at least two of the following specifications:

1 A turnover not less than £5 million per annum.
2 A balance sheet total*, at the commencement of the relevant accounting period, of not less than £2.5 million, as shown in the historical cost account.
3 Have not less than 250 employees on average.

The standard, which does not apply to insurance companies, property investment and other 'dealing companies', clearly recognises two important matters, namely that

1 Historical cost accounting will continue.
2 CCA is not a method of accounting for general inflation, in that it does not purport to measure changes in the general value of money from one period to another.

However it is pointed out that the supplementary statements, prepared under CCA rules, *do* now envisage the presentation of the current year's and the immediately prior year's current cost profit and loss accounts and balance sheets. Nevertheless they are not being put forward as inflation-adjusted statements of corporate wealth and profitability. This has been recognised by the ASC in their considerations of the importance of publishing 5 and 10 year statements of corporate progress. The committee proposes that a year by year sequence of CCA statements should be adjusted by related movements in the RPI, in order to give some effect to the inflationary impacts of changes in the value of the currency unit, during the 5 and 10 year periods.†

But the problems inherent in the revaluation of fixed assets for a CCA balance sheet‡ derive from the availability of objective criteria upon which

*Comprised of the net book value (HCA) of the fixed assets, plus investments, plus current assets (before deduction of current liabilities).
†The ASC's discussion paper issued subsequently to SSAP16.
‡'... the value to a business of the existing asset is the net current cost of a replacement asset which has a similar output or service capacity.' (CCA guidance notes.)

to base the revaluation adjustments. For UK assets we have the industry based indexes issued by the Department of Industry: for overseas assets we have no such continuous data and here subjectivity will replace objectivity.

Finally it is noted that the new standard contains directions for computing (similar to those recorded earlier in this chapter):

1   Hyde gearing adjustments (except for nationalised industries).
2   A cost of sales adjustment.
3   Monetary working capital adjustments.

A new reserve, called a 'current cost reserve', will be shown in CCA balance sheets: it will include, where appropriate,

1   Unrealised revaluation surpluses on fixed assets, stocks and investments.
2   The realised equivalents of the current cost adjustments for (*a*) depreciation, (*b*) working capital and (*c*) gearing.

Self-examination questions

1   If the accounts of all UK companies are prepared in terms of a common unit of currency – the £ sterling – how can the effects of inflation render comparisons of corporate profitability and wealth unreliable?

2   Current purchasing power accounting differentiates between monetary and non-monetary items. Why?

3   When adjustments to accounting data are based upon general price level indexes, the value of the outcome depends upon the reliability of the indexes used. Discuss.

4   What is the difference between an operating gain and the conventional accounting profit?

5   How valid is the Hyde gearing adjustment in its impact upon historic cost profit/loss reporting?

6   Refer to the published accounts of the companies studied in question 6 of Chapter 7 (see page 128) and compare their current cost profit and loss accounts with the conventional historic cost accounts. How do you account for the different effects which CCA has upon the two companies' reported (HCA) profit/loss statements?

Recommended reading

'Inflation Accounting is not Economic Valuation', *Journal of Business Finance*, Spring 176, Volume 3, Number 1.

BIRD, P., *Accountability: Standards in Financial Reporting*, Accountancy Age Books (1973), see chapters 4, 5 and 6.

CUTLER, R.S., and WESTWICK, C.A., 'The Impact of Inflation on Share Values', *Accountancy*, March 1973, see page 15 on.

PIZZEY, A., *Accounting and Finance*, Holt, Rinehart and Winston (1980), see chapters 16 and 17.

SSAP16, The Accounting Standards Committee, published by ICAEW.

BAXTER, W.T., 'The Sandilands Report'; *Journal of Business Finance and Accounting*, Spring 1976, Volume 3, Number 1.

WILSON, J.P., *Inflation, Deflation, Reflation: Management and Accounting in Economic Uncertainty*, Business Books (1980).

10　The statement of value added

Introduction

A predominant feature of our earlier studies has been the measurement and appraisal of business profitability, the effectiveness with which the firm has used its net assets to create wealth. Here the created wealth has been expressed in the form of accounting profit, and the monetary value of profit has been used in the return on capital employed equation. Return on capital employed enables comparisons of corporate profitability over time; it also enables profitability comparisons to be made between different firms operating in similar or diverse trades. Now the monetary value of that created wealth which is stored in the business – retained profits – is recorded in the balance sheet as a part of the Total Shareholders' Interest. Thus the treatment of accounting profit tends to emphasise a role of wealth created for the firm's proprietors, the shareholders.

The function of value added

Value added is also a measure of wealth creation. It is very similar to accounting profit in that both profit and value added measure a firm's performance over a specific period: their calculations are each derived from incomes and expenditures arising from the firm's trading activities and shown in the conventional profit and loss statements of the whole corporate body. The distinctions between profit and value added are shown in the analyses of those incomes and expenditures, when value added is seen to emphasise

1　The *increases* in wealth created by the firm *itself*, and
2　The appropriation or sharing out of that additional wealth created.

Clearly the amount of sales reported by a firm denotes the value of its output, the wealth it has passed to its customers or clients. But the wealth represented by a firm's sales does not measure the value *added* by that firm's operations. The value of sales shown in any profit and loss account will include materials and services consumed by the firm and purchased from its suppliers. Therefore we recognise value added as the additional wealth which a firm creates over and above the cost of those bought-in materials and services which are used in its own manufacturing and trading activities.

For example, the assembly and sale of a motor car for £5000 does not mean that the car assembly firm has itself added £5000 of value to the resources consumed in the manufacturing process. If the materials, components and other services bought by the firm had cost £4000, then the value *added* by car manufacture would be £1000 only. Those firms who supplied the car manufacturer had themselves created value added in their consumption of steel, rubber and plastics, etc., in order to provide the materials and components for the car manufacturer. Somewhere along the chain of manufacture and supply of goods and services, other firms had added up to £4000 of value by their various operating activities.

Definition of value added

Therefore we will state that the ultimate sales value of a firm's output is not created entirely by the firm itself. Some of the total growth in wealth came in the goods and services bought-in from the firm's suppliers and incorporated in its own final product. Hence the definition and quantification of the value *added by a business* as a result of its trading activites will be given by

The value of its sales LESS the cost of bought-in goods and services

Now the second distinction between profit and value added concerns their different objectives. It has been suggested that the accounting treatment of profit implies a role of wealth created for the firm's proprietors, the shareholders. On the other hand the concept of value added measures the wealth created by a partnership – a partnership of

1　The firm, with its various assets.
2　The employees, using their diverse skills.
3　The providers of capital funds (shareholders and lenders).
4　The government, which provides the environment within which the firm operates and its employees have their living.

Exhibit 81 displays, in part A, an abridged form of profit and loss account. It shows the calculation of accounting profit after tax, from which shareholder dividends are derived: the resultant total, being profits retained by the firm, would be shown in the balance sheet as a part of the shareholders' total investment in the company. Thus the amounts of

Exhibit 81

Value added and accounting profit compared: I

A   Profit and loss statement for the year ended …

	£	£
Sales		500
Less expenditure:		
Materials consumed	250	
Wages and salaries	120	
Services purchased (light, heat, insurance, etc.)	50	
Interest payable	10	
Depreciation	20	
		450
Profit before tax		50
Corporation tax		25
Profit after tax		25
Less dividends payable		10
Retained profits, transferred to balance sheet		£15

B   Value added statement for the year ended …

	£	£
Sales		500
Less bought-in materials and services		300
Gross value added		£200
Application of gross value added:		
To employees		120
To providers of capital funds:		
Interest	10	
Dividends	10	
		20
To Government in taxes		25
To the company for maintenance and growth of assets:		
Depreciation	20	
Retained profits	15	
		35
Gross value added		£200

Government taxation, shareholders' dividends and company retentions are prominently displayed.

Part B of the exhibit uses the same data in the preparation of a value added statement. The vital difference in objectives of the two concepts – profit and value added – is shown in the appropriation of the total value added between the members of the partnership team. Here the employees join with the Government, the providers of capital and the firm, when the value added wealth created by their joint activities is shared amongst them in varying proportions.

The relevance of the value added statement

The relevance of any form of information depends upon its value to a potential user – does it provide a sound base for more realistic decision-making? The value added statement emphasises the partnership's performance in creating wealth: it does not treat the shareholder with the exclusive status afforded by conventional profit and loss accounting. Yet existing and prospective shareholders (and lenders) may gain benefit from studies of company value added disclosures. They can see how the available wealth is being appropriated and they should note the percentage proportions of the value added which has gone, for example, to employees and the government. Thus the potential effects of high wage and low company allocations on the company's future prospects for growth and further wealth creation can be realistically assessed. Upon such assessments, appraisals of continued investment in companies can be realistically established.

Lenders of long-term finance and trade suppliers are more likely to be interested in the solvency and continuance of the business entity. In this context regular prompt payments of

Annual interest charges *and* Suppliers' accounts for goods delivered

may well be their prime considerations. Conventional balance sheets, rather than a value added statement, will provide much of the relevant appraisal data. However, as with shareholders, the various apportionments of corporate wealth which are shown in value added reports should give additional means for corporate appraisals. The potential for future business stability and operations can be considered in a more practical sense.

One of the greatest advantages to be gained from the use of value added statements rests with the firm's employees and their trades union representatives. On the one hand, the employees' part in wealth creation is given some pride of place in the value added statement. On the other hand, a limit to the size of employees' total wage and salary bill must be seen to be determined by the value added sum itself. Nevertheless trends in the proportion of total value added which are being paid to employees can be studied. These trends and their comparison with apportionments found in other companies may well generate effective debate on corporate efficiencies, and may stimulate interest in increased productivity.

Excessive added value apportionments

An example of the consequences of apparently excessive wage (e.g.) costs can be given by revising the content of Exhibit 81 to show a wage and salary bill of £275, instead of £120. Exhibit 82 presents the results.

There is an answer to the paradox of an accounting loss which is nevertheless linked with a positive value added sum. Here we have to remember that the *team* of employees, capital providers, government and firm, bring about the creation of value added. Their joint efforts create wealth, but the sharing out of that wealth shows the effects of an excessive appropriation – by any single member of the team – of the total wealth jointly created.

Exhibit 82 emphasises that £200 of value was added by the corporate efforts of making and selling goods and services. The applications of gross value added show that whilst the employees have gained value to the amount of £275

1 The government has received no allocation.
2 Shareholders have received no allocation.
3 The company has *lost* value to the total of £85.

Depreciation and value added

The preparation of value added statements in the business world reveals some remarkable misunderstandings about the nature and purpose of the value added concept. It shows clearly that a standard accounting practice needs to be specified in order to render the value added statements – important indicators of corporate performance – properly comparable between diverse firms and industries. The treatment of depreciation in value added calculations provides a controversial issue for the value added compiler. Exhibit 83 below sets out the relevant considerations. The arguments given in the exhibit should lead the reader to an acceptance of depreciation as a bought-in item. Consistency demands this because a capital asset is bought-in by a firm in just the same way as a supply of raw materials. Thus they must be treated each in the same way when value added statements are drawn up.

Exhibit 82

Value added and accounting profit compared: II

A *Profit and loss statement for the year ended …*

	£	£
Sales		500
Less expenditure:		
Materials consumed	250	
Wages and salaries	275	
Services purchased (light, heat, insurance, etc.)	50	
Interest payable	10	
Depreciation	20	
		605
Loss – pre-tax		105
Tax		—
Loss – post-tax (deducted from total shareholders' interest in the balance sheet)		£105

B *Value added statement for the year ended …*

	£	£
Sales		500
Less bought-in materials and services		300
Gross value added		200
Application of gross value added:		
To employees		275
To providers of capital funds:		
Interest		10
To the company for maintenance and growth of assets:		
Depreciation	20	
Loss	(105)	(85)
Gross value added		£200

The case for including depreciation charges within the sum of bought-in goods and services becomes overwhelming when we consider an engineering firm buying

1 Steel plating materials for embodying in the firm's products, and
2 A steel press or cutting machine which is to be used in preparing the raw material – steel – for its inclusion in a finished product.

Now if only half of the steel plating is used in the firm's manufacturing activities, during an annual accounting period, then only one half of the cost

Exhibit 83
Depreciation and value added

Gross value added (excluding depreciation sums from total of bought-in items)	Net value added (including depreciation sums within the total of bought-in items)
1 Depreciation sums derive from methods of calculation influenced by opinion. The group of bought-in items is based on verifiable facts of expenditure. Value added should reflect the consequences of goods and services bought-in AND consumed during the period.	Depreciation cannot be regarded as a part of wealth created by the partnership. Its value stems from bought-in assets which are used in the creation of wealth.
2 To exclude depreciation from the total of bought-in items would result in double counting. This would arise when the seller of a fixed asset showed its value in his value added calculation, whilst a purchaser of the fixed asset would not. The combination of values added by separate firms would not display the TOTAL creation of wealth.	By including depreciation sums in the bought-in section of corporate value added statements, we do achieve the principal objective of identifying and locating the sources of wealth creation.
3 Excluding depreciation from the bought-in items and joining it with retained profits in the appropriations of value added emphasises the CASH FLOW concept. This is a valuable appraisal tool for use as a measure of corporate efficiency.	The prime object of the value added statement is not the measurement of cash flow. Value added must represent the wealth created and available for division between the groups forming the partnership team – AFTER ALL bought-in items are brought to account.
4 When depreciation is excluded from bought-in items, the sum of value added thus determined would imply a distribution of capital assets, for consumption by all partnership team members. The ultimate wearing out or obsolescence of the fixed assets would occur with no provisions for its replacement.	Inclusion as a bought-in item is technically and realistically correct. It represents the year's 'apportioned cost' of that item – the related capital cost. Where plant and equipment is replaced, modernised or expanded, the power to create wealth is thus enhanced. This must be recognised by the partnership team by a deduction from sales income, BEFORE showing divisible value added.

of the total purchase will be charged against the period's sales in the profit and loss account *and* the value added statement. The remainder will form part of the raw material stocks on hand. Similarly if the steel press or cutting machine is deemed to have a twenty-year life, it follows that only one twentieth of its value will have been 'consumed' during that same accounting

Exhibit 84

Gross and net value added compared

Details	Gross value added			Net value added		
	£	£	%	£	£	%
Sales		500	100		500	100
Less bought-in materials and						
services		300	60		320	64
Value added		200	40		180	36
Applications of value added						
To employees		120	60		120	66.7
To providers of capital funds:						
Interest	10			10		
Dividends	10			10		
		20	10		20	11.1
To Government in taxes		25	12.5		25	13.9
To the company for maintenance						
and growth of assets:						
Depreciation	20			—		
Retained profits	15	35	17.5	15	15	8.3
		£200	100.0		£180	100.0

period. Both items have contributed to the output during the specified accounting period. If we propose to carry forward one half of the year's raw material purchases to a subsequent period's value added calculation, there is an equally sound case for carrying forward 19/20ths of the capital asset purchase to subsequent value added calculations. The accounting conventions of matching, materiality and consistency are thereby observed.

Referring back to Exhibit 81 the reader will note that part B of the exhibit had been calculated on the *gross* value added principle. If we now apply the more realistic principles of *net* value added to our calculations, the results will emerge as given in Exhibit 84. Clearly the amount of Net Value Added gives a true and fair view of the surplus which arises when the consumption of bought-in *values* is set against the output of *values* represented by the turnover. Moreover a more relevant piece of management and industrial relations information is presented in the appropriation section of a value added statement if we show the percentage proportions, of total value added, which are taken by member groups of the partnership team.

It has been shown (Exhibit 82) that member group(s) of the team cannot take more than 100 per cent of the value added sum without other member

196

group(s) suffering a real loss. Because it is wholly reasonable for the employee group to be rewarded by a specific (or growing) percentage of the total value added to which they have actively contributed, it is even more reasonable that the sum of value added itself should be realistically computed on a *net* value added basis. Exhibit 84 shows the percentage apportionments to the team members of the related value added sum.

Treatment of stocks

The foregoing sections have examined the addition of values stemming from a consumption of matching values. In the exhibits which demonstrated the arithmetical calculations of value added, details of sales and purchases were used in the determination of a value added total. But the concepts of consumption and creation of values are not confined to purchases and sales alone, because some value changes will be contained in the stocks of raw materials, work-in-progress and finished goods. Their financial valuation must be brought into comparisons of

1 The net values consumed, with
2 The matching values produced.

To demonstrate the impacts of stocks, Exhibit 81 will now be adjusted to take note of

(*a*) Opening stocks of finished goods and work-in-progress valued at £120.
(*b*) Closing stocks of finished goods and work-in-progress valued at £150.
(*c*) Opening stocks of raw materials valued at £75.
(*d*) Closing stocks of raw materials valued at £85.

An amended profit and loss account and a *net* value added statement, which takes these facts into account, are shown in Exhibits 85 and 86.

The introduction of adjustments for stocks of finished goods and work-in-progress gives rise to a technical problem of interpretation in value added calculations. Valuations of finished goods and work-in-progress generally contain an element of the (direct) labour cost involved in their production. Now such labour costs cannot be regarded as a bought-in item and it would appear that they must be excluded from determination of the value added sum. If this is done but the wages total in the appropriation section is left unadjusted, then the value added sum and the sum of the appropriations will not agree.

Clearly we can eliminate the wages element from stock valuations and at the same time reduce the wages sum in the appropriations section of the value added statement. In such an adjustment the employees' share of the total value added would be related to 'wages caused by sales' rather than the

Exhibit 85
Value added and accounting profit compared: III

Profit and Loss Statement for the year ended ...

	£	£
Value of goods sold (net amount receivable by the company, after trade discounts)		500
Opening stocks of finished goods and work-in-progress	120	
Closing stocks of finished goods and work-in-progress	150	
Increase in finished goods and work-in-progress		30
Value of output		£530
Expenditures:		
Purchases of raw materials (net amount payable by the company, after trade discounts)		250
Opening stocks of raw materials	75	
Closing stocks of raw materials	85	
Increase in raw material stocks		10
Materials consumed in the trading operations		240
Wages and salaries		120
Services purchased		50
Interest payable		10
Depreciation		20
Total expenditure		£440
Profit before tax		90
Taxation		25
Profit after tax		65
Less dividends payable		10
Retained profits, transferred to balance sheet		£55

total of 'wages payable during the period'. Even these adjustments should relate to the changes only in the levels of stocks valuations, but it would nevertheless result in the value added calculations being divorced from the data given in the profit and loss account. It is probable that it would lead to a lack of confidence in the validity of the whole value added concept. It is suggested therefore, and in view of its marginal impact on value added, that no such adjustments are made in any value added calculations.

There are other problems of technical interpretation of net value added which the reader should study in his pursuit of the subject. The reading list at the end of this chapter will enable a more detailed knowledge to be

Exhibit 86
Value added and accounting profit compared: IV

Value added statement for the year ended ...

	£	£
Value of output		530
Less value of bought-in materials and services consumed		
(materials £240, services £50, depreciation £20)		310
Net value added		£220
Application of net value added:		
To employees		120
To providers of capital funds:		
Interest	10	
Dividends	10	
	—	20
To Government in taxes		25
To the company for maintenance and growth of assets:		
Retained profits		55
Net value added		£220

obtained. However the basic principle remains – a bought-in item is included in net value added calculations. If this bought-in item is used in conjunction with an employee input, the two items will normally be separated. An example of such a situation is best seen in the operation of a transport pool. The maintenance and running cost materials must be brought within the bought-in totals for value added calculations whilst the wages of drivers, maintenance engineers and administrators will be recorded in the employees group in the value added appropriations section.

Inflation, the Hyde Report and value added

The power of the value added concept for identifying the sources of corporate wealth creation, and its sharing out, have been demonstrated in the context of a conventionally prepared profit and loss account. Yet we must concern ourselves with the *real* wealth which the partnership team produces, not the unreal monetary values of wealth which derive from the data given in historic cost accounts.

Therefore Exhibit 87 has been prepared to show the effects upon the sum of net value added and its appropriations, when the following Hyde adjustments are applied to the figures in Exhibit 84:

Exhibit 87
Net value added and the Hyde adjustments

Details	Historic costs (Exhibit 84)		Current costs	
	£000	£000	£000	£000
Profit and Loss Account				
Sales		500		500
Less bought-in materials and services		320		320
Historic cost net value added		£180		£180
Less adjustments for:				
Cost of sales			25	
Depreciation			10	
				35
Current cost net value added				145
Gearing adjustment (40%)				14
Hyde Report net value added				£159
Appropriated as follows:				
To employees		120		120
To providers of capital		20		20
To Government in taxes		25		25
To the company for maintenance and growth of assets:				
Retained profits		15		(6)
TOTALS		£180		£159

1   Cost of sales adjustment, £25,000.
2   Depreciation adjustment, £10,000.
3   Gearing proportion, 40 per cent.

It is clear that the full effects of the inflationary rise in the costs of operations have reduced the sum of net value added. At the same time the appropriations to the first three members of the partnership team remain – in money terms – unchanged. A loss in value of £6,000 is now shown to be suffered by the firm, instead of an apportionment of £15,000.

Uses of value added ratios

As in all of our appraisals the *relationship* between two variables, rather than a consideration of their individual absolute sizes, is a more effective measure of judging the results of business activities. Thus it is with value added. Here the following paragraphs will give examples of appraisal ratios which can be used in the overall management of corporate affairs.

Perhaps the most easily understood and widely used of the value added ratios are concerned with labour productivity. They emphasise the importance to be attached to this vital member of the wealth creating partnership team. The first ratios examined in this context are:

1 Wages per £ of value added: the wages/value added ratio.
2 Value added per £ of wages: the value added/wages ratio.

The intention behind the publication of these ratios must be clearly explained to the partnership team. Furthermore the data used in value added statements must be freely revealed to employees. The relevance of the second ratio depends upon employee confidence in the value added concept: consequently exhortations to raise value added per £ of wages will be better understood when employees see their own welfare being enhanced by

(a) The same percentage of a larger total, or
(b) A growing percentage of a larger total.

I would not recommend the application of suggestions which may be implied by ratio 1 – the reduction of the wages element in value added. Yet both ratios are useful measures of productivity appraisal albeit giving emphasis to *labour* productivity.

Other value added ratios which reflect the impact of employee contribution to corporate well-being will include

3 Value added per employee.
4 Value added per employee-hours worked.

Ratio 3 will be affected by numbers of part-time or casual employees. Therefore the 'per employee' secton of the calculation would have to refer to 'full-time equivalent' employees. Alternatively, this difficulty is overcome by showing the amount of value added in relation to hours worked. In connection with labour productivity ratios, the value added/wages ratio has the greatest merit in that both arms of the ratio are quoted in money terms. Ratio 3, with its denominator being stated in human rather than money terms, will suffer some distortion in trend comparisons because of the effects of inflation upon the quantification of value added.

In seeking out appraisal of capital productivity we should use

5 Value added/capital employed.

In a progressive, efficient company one would expect the assessed ratio to be rising, though this effect could be achieved by a falling value of capital employed where old assets were depreciated but not modernised or replaced. A careful examination of the year-by-year growth through acquisition of new capital assets should therefore accompany the use of this ratio.

Finally the reader will be aware of the proportionate appropriations of value added, as demonstrated in Exhibit 84. Here we can see clearly the influences of government taxation upon the power of the business to generate and *keep* some of its own wealth creation for corporate growth purposes and for the benefit of those who have contributed to the creation of wealth – the members of the partnership team.

Company accounts and value added

In the annual accounts booklets published by UK companies, we find but a few instances only where value added statements form a part of the general data disclosures. An example of such a statement, together with notes regarding its compilation, is given below; it refers to Courtaulds Plc. It is pointed out however that most company value added statements show the year's depreciation sum as a part of the corporate retained earnings in the *disposal* section, rather than as an essential part of the *calculation* of the value added.

The company's published statements have therefore been amended by bringing the annual depreciation sums within the section which determines the size of the total corporate value added. Thus the amount of the year's depreciation becomes a part of the bought-in goods and services, demonstrating the total cost of bought-in items being consumed in the process of creating the value added surplus. No criticism of the company concerned is intended; the adjustments reflect the views of the author and are his responsibility.

Courtauld's published profit and loss accounts for 1982 and 1981 are given in Exhibit 88 below, whilst the related value added statements are shown in Exhibit 89.

Before appraising the value added statements, the reader should note the marked change in Courtaulds' profitability in 1982, as compared with 1981. The improvement shown in the 1982 account must redound to the credit of the company's board and its management during a period of recession and difficult trading conditions.

Exhibit 89 records the calculation and disposal of Courtaulds' total value added sums. All the data used in the statements – except the cost of employees and the bought-in items* – can be verified from the profit and

*The 1981 Act prescribed formats for profit and loss accounts (see Appendix A, page 339) show that the cost of bought-in items will be largely ascertainable from the disclosures of data, such as cost of sales, raw material and consumables and other external charges etc., which are required in the new accounts layouts.

Exhibit 88

Group profit and loss accounts – Courtaulds Plc

	1982 £m	1981 £m
Sales to external customers	1,789.4	1,709.9
Trading profit	69.6	29.8
Associated companies	3.5	4.8
	73.1	34.6
Interest payable net of investment income	(22.0)	(29.5)
Profit before tax	51.1	5.1
Taxation	(21.4)	(12.1)
Profit after tax (1981 Loss)	29.7	(7.0)
Minority interests	(10.8)	(9.5)
	18.9	(16.5)
Extraordinary items	(5.0)	(97.6)
Release of deferred taxation	4.0	
Attributable to Courtaulds Plc	17.9	(114.1)
Preference dividends	(0.1)	(0.1)
Attributable to Ordinaries	17.8	(114.2)
Ordinary dividends	(8.2)	(2.7)
Profit transferred to reserves (1981 Loss)	£9.6	£(116.9)

loss accounts in Exhibit 88 or from explanatory notes accompanying those accounts. (Prior to the 1981 Companies Act the requirement to disclose information regarding employees was limited to data relating to UK employees only. In future, data regarding *all* of the employees of a company or a group will have to be published and thus be available for use by analysts – *Schedule 1, 1981 Act.*)

In each of the value added statements the retained *earnings* items shown in the disposals section of the statement are derived as follows:

	1982 £m	1981 £m
Profit after tax and minorities	18.9	(16.5)
Less dividends to shareholders	8.3	(2.8)
	£10.6	£19.3

Exhibit 89

Statements of value added – Courtaulds Plc

	1982		1981	
	£m	£m	£m	£m
Sales		1,789.4		1,709.9
Less:				
Bought-in materials and services	1,169.1		1,103.4	
Depreciation	55.3	1,224.4	58.6	1,162.0
		£565.0		£547.9
Disposal of total value added:				
Employees (wages, pensions, social security costs)		495.4		518.1
Taxation		21.4		12.1
Capital:				
Net interest after associate companies' profits	18.5		24.7	
Minority interests	10.8		9.5	
Dividends to shareholders	8.3	37.6	2.8	37.0
Retained earnings (loss)		10.6		(19.3)
(excluding extraordinary items)		£565.0		£547.9

Clearly profit and loss account entries described as

> extraordinary items
> transfer from reserves
> associated companies' profits

have no part in a year's value added assessement; they do not describe the company's generation of value added from its own *trading* operations for the year in question.

Exhibit 90 below now shows the percentage apportionments of total value added to the four 'partnership teams' which have contributed to the years' outcomes. The exhibit introduces information about Simon Engineering Plc – another reputable UK company. The reader should study the progress of these two companies in the coming years. Calculations of value added per £ of capital employed, per £ of wages, per employee etc., can be prepared year by year. Here it should be noted that any manufacturing company needs to retain a meaningful proportion (10 per cent) of its value added in order to finance its own modernisation and growth.

Exhibit 90

Distributions of value added

	Courtaulds		Simon Engineering	
	1982	1981	1981	1980
	%	%	%	%
Employees	87.7	94.6	77.6	77.3
Taxation	3.8	2.2	5.7	7.0
Capital	6.6	6.7	5.0	5.1
Retained earnings	1.9	(3.5)	11.7	10.6
	100.0	100.0	100.0	100.0

Self-examination questions

1 State clearly how value added differs from accounting profit.
2 What is the case for placing the year's depreciation charge within the cost of bought-in items? Does this adjustment affect materially any appraisals of the disposal of the total sum of value added?

3 The absolute total of a company's value added can be increased without any improvements in productivity. How?

4 Using the data in Exhibits 88 and 89 calculate for each year:
  (*a*) value added per £ of capital employed (capital employed in *each* year was £647.4m)
  (*b*) value added per £ of sales
  (*c*) value added per £ of cash flow
  (*d*) value added per £ of employee costs.
What do you conclude from the trends of your ratios over the two year period?

5 How would you deal with year end stocks of raw materials, work-in-progress and finished goods in a value added statement?

6 How would a state of excessively high gearing be reflected in a company's value added statement?

7 Do the disposal apportionments in value added statements have any relevance in the appraisals of
  (*a*) potential investors in the related company's shares,
  (*b*) corporate solvency by the company's trade suppliers?

Recommended reading

BROSTER, E.J., 'Measuring productivity: the delusion of value added', *Certified Accountants Journal*, pp. 73–80 (February 1971).

MORLEY, M.F., *The Value Added Statement – A Review of its use in Corporate Reports*, Institute of Chartered Accountants of Scotland (1978).

WOOD, E.G., 'How to add value', *Management Today*, pp. 73–7 (May 1974).

WOOD, E.G., *Added Value – the Key to Prosperity*, Business Books (1978).

COX, B., *Value Added: An Appreciation for the Accountant Concerned with Industry*, Heinemann (1979).

Part 2

Cost analysis

11 Break-even analysis

Introduction

An analysis of the composition of product cost is a study of prime importance. Its conclusions can affect pricing policies, production and production mix policies and all decisions concerning capacity planning. Even before determining the cost of a product or service, the term 'cost' must itself be defined. To the accountant, cost represents the expenditure incurred on the goods and services which are consumed in producing an output of other goods or services. This output aims to meet the needs of the firm's forecast sales demand. Now the accountant's figures of expenditure (cost) will be found in the ledgers and other books of account which record the business' dealings: details of the sales will also be found there. Each of these recorded expenditures and incomes can be traced to a commercial transaction, which was completed at some point in the firm's history and inevitably resulted in a transfer of cash, to or from the firm. (Notional charges, such as interest, made for the purposes of a theoretical total cost comparison have been ignored here.)

The economist, on the other hand, regards cost as meaning *opportunity* cost. Opportunity cost refers to the gain, benefit or return which is given up when the decision-maker elects to make product A rather than product B. In this context the opportunity cost of product A would be the gains which could have been obtained by making product B. This is not to imply that product B's rejected gains are the only costs in the economist's eyes: it is the fundamental addition to all other output costs of goods and services which are used to achieve an output – the turnover. The whole idea therefore adds to what may be termed the market cost of inputs, the net incomes which are surrendered when deciding to manufacture product A instead of B.* The

*The economist's costs therefore are not all traceable to ultimate cash transactions in the books of the firm under examination. The services of an 'unpaid' manager or proprietor would not necessarily appear in the accountant's assessment of cost. However the economist *would* include, at an appropriate market price, the value of such a proprietor's services in the total input cost of obtaining the corresponding output.

concept of opportunity cost can be applied to doing certain things at different times, e.g. the opportunity cost of postponing a venture to next year will be those gains which could have been achieved by doing that particular thing today.

Cost groups

It is intended that we should concern ourselves with accounting cost, at this stage. Now the total accounting costs of an operation or business can be divided into as many different groupings as the managers wish to have. By these means it is expected that an exact cost of some process or component can be found. Whatever the variety of cost groups which may be used, they each fall within three main categories. The common terminology for the main divisions of accounting cost comprises:

> Variable cost.
> Semi-variable cost.
> Fixed cost.

Not all of these descriptive titles are going to be accepted here. Before criticising the rigid group definitions, let the reader consider the cost sequence of engaging in manufacture, for example. As soon as production commences, some goods and services must be employed. A man working upon raw materials or components, and the material itself, are examples of input costs which must be incurred as soon as production is engaged. To this type of expense is given the name 'variable cost'; it describes those expenditures which must change in monetary size, whenever the level of production changes. Frequently called direct, or marginal costs, they are those costs of operation which cannot be avoided once production is engaged.

The 'fixed' group of costs concerns the environment within which production is undertaken. The machine operator is located within a factory building: his machine is ready and available for use: the business also provides services of administration and transport, etc. Now within the limits of a certain level of capacity, these buildings, machines and administrative services are needed to enable the firm to carry on its business. The expenditures which were incurred on setting up the firm's factory and administration, were incurred in consequence of a management decision which was taken sometime in the past. The *cash* was spent some time ago to provide a capacity structure. Most of capacity structure costs such as:

> Administrative salaries,
> Buildings, plant and machinery depreciation,
> Works salaries,
> Rent, rates and insurance,

are accumulated as time passes, *not* because production is engaged. For this reason therefore, the term fixed cost is inappropriate. Other more meaningful descriptions would be

1 *Capacity costs* – the cost of establishing the particular capacity for the firm.
2 *Period costs* – relating to a specific period, and it is the passage of time which largely determines their monetary cost.
3 *Decision costs* – incurred because of some past management decision to enter into a business at a certain level of output.

One can of course insist that, however we may describe the above costs, they *are* fixed in fact. They are fixed in relation to a particular size of firm. Nevertheless, and this is vital, as soon as the firm changes its capacity size, then the so-called fixed costs must change to reflect the level of decisional costs implicit in the new physical capacity of the company. The so-called fixed costs will change, *not* in consequence of a change in the quantity of goods being produced, but because of a change in the power or capacity to produce.

The final category of costs, the semi-variable cost, relates to those goods and services whose market price is not linked solely to the consumption of individual items. The telephone bill consists of a standard quarterly expense plus a charge for each call that is made: power supplies may well consist of a standing charge relating to the potential demand of the firm's power load plus a sliding scale of charges for units of power consumed. Thus it can be said that such a kind of cost is not wholly fixed, nor is it wholly variable. It is therefore regarded as a semi-variable expense. One of the most important and time consuming tasks in the sphere of management accounting is the location of any item of cost into one of the three main divisions of cost. A careful precise analysis must be carried out in practical circumstances, of the effect upon individual expenditures, of changes in the level of production before cost data can be used in intelligent planning. Here the semi-variable expense must be dissected into its fixed and variable elements in order to enable a meaningful analysis of the incremental costs of engaging in business activity. In the long run, when variations in capacity occur, ALL costs will be seen to be variable!

Break-even point

A most useful managerial planning tool which stems from an appreciation of the nature of variable and capacity costs, is the break-even chart shown in Exhibit 91. The chart displays on its horizontal axis various levels of output up to the total capacity, whilst the vertical axis shows sizes of costs and incomes in units of £1. Capacity or decision costs for the firm are

Exhibit 91

Break-even chart 1

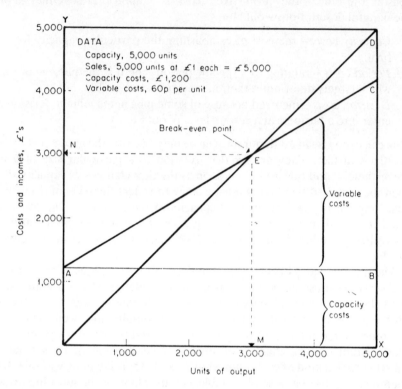

DATA

Capacity, 5,000 units
Sales, 5,000 units at £1 each = £5,000
Capacity costs, £1,200
Variable costs, 60p per unit

Break-even point

Variable costs

Capacity costs

Units of output

represented by the straight line AB: these costs apply to the maximum capacity of 5,000 units of output and are constantly up to that level of production.* Those additions (to capacity costs) which we have called variable costs are shown by the area CAB. The reader will notice that these expenditures increase as the level of output in units increases. Therefore the *total* costs of producing the firm's output is represented by the line AC. Now any level of output on the horizontal axis can be related to a point on the total cost line AC: then this point on AC can be compared with the relevant level of cost as shown on the axis OY. Thus we can ascertain the costs of specific levels of output, up to 5,000 units.

If the line of expected sales income, OD, is then superimposed upon the graph, the reader will see that the point E gives the level of output/cost at

*Here the analysis excludes rises in prices of capacity costs which may result from inflation or revaluation of capacity assets. In such circumstances the break-even graph would be redrawn to portray the new cost levels for the whole output potential. Furthermore the chart has excluded semi-variable costs, so as to present a relatively simple study of the break-even concept.

212

which the expected sales income first equals, and then begins to exceed, the total cost of output. This is the break-even (B/E) point: it is the output level at which the firm makes no loss or profit but just *breaks even*. It is important for the reader to realise that the B/E graph is a series of static points – it is *not* a progress chart of a company's developing performance. The graph shows the expected cost/income situation of the firm *at each possible level of output*: it does not show the firm first making a loss, then making a profit as *it proceeds through the year*. Each example of output on the horizontal axis is a single static exposition of a possible production level: the lines on the graph can then show the firm's expected net income position should that level of output be achieved during the accounting period of the company.* When this precise function of the B/E graph is accepted, it can be seen that the area AEO enables the determination of operating loss for any output level up to OM. Similarly DEC indicates the area of profit for any output level from M up to maximum capacity.

Contribution

Previously the nature of variable and capacity costs have been shown to be closely connected with their response to variations in output. For profitable business operations, sale price must be in excess of variable costs at least. Therefore the extent to which sales price exceeds variable cost will measure the amount earned, by each unit produced and sold, towards meeting the capacity costs of the firm. This amount earned in excess of variable cost is termed the product's 'Contribution' to the total capacity costs. Exhibit 92 which is based upon the same data as that used in Exhibit 91, is redrawn in order to emphasise the concept of 'Contribution'. In this instance the total variable cost line OC compares with line AC in the previous chart, and the area COX represents the area of variable expenditures up to the total capacity of 5,000 units. Capacity costs are again portrayed by the line AB, so that the area of total capacity cost BAOC is equivalent to BAOX in Exhibit 91. The total cost, in Exhibit 92, is represented by the line AB. Now it must be observed that the total sales indicator OD again cuts the total cost line *at the same B/E point*, E. The important feature in presenting B/E analysis in this way concerns the line OE, and the shaded area EOF. This section shows the amount earned towards the total capacity costs, by each unit produced and sold at the various levels of output up to OM. At the output level OM, enough has been produced and sold so that the total earnings of

---

*The level of capacity costs have been quoted at £1,200 and this figure relates to a specified period, i.e. the accounting period of the company. Therefore the cost/income relationships revealed by the B/E graph must refer to the firm's accounting period.

Exhibit 92

Break-even chart 2

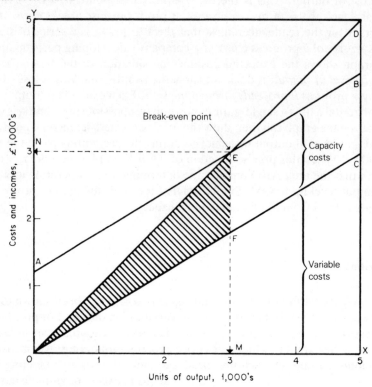

Units of output, 1,000's

the output will meet the expenses of:

1   The variable cost of each item.
2   The total capacity costs of the firm which is geared to a maximum output of 5,000 units.

For output performance above OM, therefore, the firm is in the profit making area. Now the situation of M on the axis OX is of material importance to the company's power to withstand a falling off in business. MX is termed the 'Margin of Safety'. In the instance shown in Exhibits 91 and 92, the saleable output of the company can fall from a maximum of 5,000 units to 3,000 units before the business begins to make a loss. The margin of safety is 40 per cent of total capacity.

Multiple break-even points

So far the graph has shown one simple break-even situation – a factor which can be calculated from the following formula:

214

$$B/E = \frac{C}{S - V} = \text{Units of output at B/E point}$$

where C is the total capacity costs, S the sale price per unit and V the variable cost per unit. Using the data given in Exhibit 91, the formula confirms the B/E point as shown in Exhibits 91 and 92:

$$B/E = \frac{1{,}200}{1 - 0.6} = \frac{1{,}200}{0.4}$$

$$= 3{,}000 \text{ units}$$

Thus an output of 3,000 units is the company's break-even production level: at a sales price of £1 per unit the sales value at B/E is £3,000. The concept of a single break-even point represented in precise, linear graphical form must now be contested. Firstly the reader must consider the effect of a decision to double the capacity of the firm, and the impact of this decision upon the firm's capacity costs. This is shown in Exhibit 93.

In drawing this chart it is assumed that doubling the capacity of the company will double the capacity costs. In practice this ratio may not apply since costs of administration, for example, have a considerable elasticity in meeting changes in output. However, for purposes of emphasis, the variation in capacity costs from £1,200 to £2,400 is depicted in a sharp outline. The addition of variable costs at a constant 60 pence per unit portrays in a similar outline the consequent changes in total costs.

(It will be said that if the company doubles its capacity from 5,000 units to 10,000 units, then the capacity costs will be £2,400 for *all* levels of output up to 10,000 units. The reason here for showing a level of capacity costs of £1,200 up to 5,000 units and then another level of £2,400 for output levels from 5,000 to 10,000 units, is to bring out clearly the effect on B/E of decisional costs. The firm does not have, in perpetuity, *one* break-even point.)

Now if the line of total income is once more superimposed upon the graph, *two* B/E points emerge. The essential feature which is brought out in Exhibit 93 is that a business is not a rigid association: changes in the conditions of demand, or in the nature of costs, will produce new cost/profit situations for management to consider. In this instance the question to be asked is whether doubling the capacity of the firm will increase its net returns. Problems such as these are of frequent occurrence in dynamic business and the effects of the expansion upon earnings per ordinary share and upon the ordinary share's P/E ratio (see pages 143–5) are examples of the approach of modern managements to the impact of profit/capacity relationships.

Returning to a study of Exhibits 92 and 93 the reader can see that the net profit at the maximum output of 5,000 units is £800. If capacity is doubled, the

Exhibit 93

Break-even chart 3

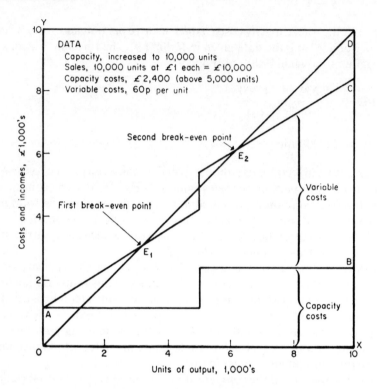

DATA
Capacity, increased to 10,000 units
Sales, 10,000 units at £1 each = £10,000
Capacity costs, £2,400 (above 5,000 units)
Variable costs, 60p per unit

Second break-even point

First break-even point

Variable costs

Capacity costs

Costs and incomes, £1,000's

Units of output, 1,000's

company's sales must reach 8,000 units before any extra gain from the expansion can be expected. Above 8,000 units, provided that no additional ordinary share capital has to be issued to finance the expansion, earnings per ordinary share should increase. Consequently either the P/E ratio will be reduced or the market price of the company's shares will rise – the latter feature being very acceptable to the company's top management. *All* of the above factors must be considered by the Board before it authorises any expenditure on capacity increases. Thus can capacity costs be truly called 'decision' costs.

Criticisms of the orthodox break-even chart

A vital deficiency in the normal method of B/E presentation must now be discussed. In each of the Exhibits 91–93, the sales income line shows a progression which, after B/E point has been passed, portrays an ever widening gap between total cost and total income. As a demonstration of

216

a perpetual relationship between total cost and total income, the hypothesis is fanciful. To maintain an ever growing sales volume requires, at the higher ranges of sales, additional expenses such as:

1　Incentive commissions to salesmen.
2　Extra discounts to tradesmen.
3　Eventually, price reductions to the buying public.
4　Possibly higher wage costs through overtime working or employment of less efficient labour (engaged to meet the need of increased production programmes).

The operation of any of the above constraints will result in a narrowing of the margin between total cost and total income: for these reasons the hypothetical chart's ever widening profit gap can be seen to be unrealistic. Even those products which are a household name must eventually reach a plateau of sales income, at and beyond which net income will always have a tendency to decrease due to the costs of maintaining sales/production activity. The results of the effect of the limitations on an ever-growing margin are shown in Exhibit 94. Here the impacts of the various cost increases and net sales decreases have been shown in a falling off in the income line OD_1. This has been done in order to present a graph which is as closely comparable as possible with Exhibit 93. The main outlines of total cost and total income in this next exhibit are the same as those in the third break-even chart. The effect of the constraints, on both cost and income, which make it more and more difficult for the firm to obtain additional sales, is shown by the broken line D_2. The falling off of income thus can be seen to produce a potential third B/E point. The chart shows the possibility of a loss at a production level of 9,400 units. Nowhere does the increased capacity produce profits similar to those which were experienced when the firm's maximum output was limited to 5,000 units. However, good management would not allow this situation to persist to the detriment of corporate profitability. Cost reduction exercises, improvements in factory outputs, 'new' product promotions would be undertaken in order to secure the firm's stability and its ultimate growth.

Alternative formula

The calculations shown earlier have arrived at the number of *units* of output which need to be produced in order to achieve B/E point. Where unit costs and unit sales prices are not known, however, B/E point can still be found by using the alternative formula*

*The formula assumes – in the normal situation of a multi-product company – that the product mix remains the same.

Exhibit 94

Break-even chart 4

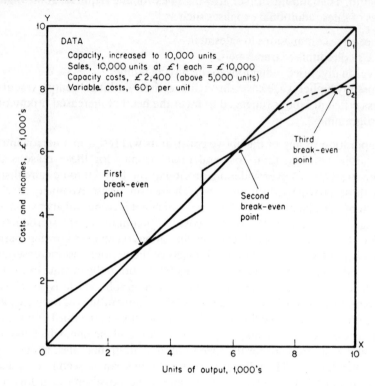

DATA

Capacity, increased to 10,000 units
Sales, 10,000 units at £1 each = £10,000
Capacity costs, £2,400 (above 5,000 units)
Variable costs, 60p per unit

First break-even point

Second break-even point

Third break-even point

Costs and incomes, £1,000's

Units of output, 1,000's

$$\text{B/E} = \frac{C}{1 - (V_t/S_t)}$$

where V_t are the *total* variable costs and S_t the *total* sales income, both at the current maximum output level. The reader must observe that this second formula will indicate the total sales value of the output at B/E point, NOT the number of units of output.

By transferring data from Exhibit 91 to the second formula, we have

$$\text{B/E} = £\frac{1,200}{1 - (3,000/5,000)}$$

$$= £\frac{1,200}{0.4}$$

$$= £3,000, \text{ i.e. } 3,000 \text{ units of } £1$$

218

Both formulae produce the same answer, as they should. Now the calculated B/E point can be verified by showing a statement of costs and incomes at an output of 3,000 units.

	£	£
Sales: 3,000 units at £1 each		3,000
Less:		
Variable costs: 3,000 units		
at 60p per unit	1,800	
Fixed costs	1,200	3,000
PROFIT/LOSS		Nil

The profit/volume ratio

Contribution – the difference between sales price per unit and variable cost per unit – can be effectively used to locate the potentially most profitable lines of a product mix. Clearly the B/E calculations given above would be applicable only to a single product firm. When a total output consists of more than one product, the location of a B/E point is a complicated task involving the arbitrary allocation of fixed costs to the various products being manufactured. In these circumstances a more factual basis for judging product profitability entails a use of the profit/volume (P/V) ratio. The ratio is calculated as follows:

$$\text{P/V ratio} = \frac{S - V}{S} \times 100$$

$$= \frac{\text{Contribution} \times 100}{S}$$

where S is the sales value per unit, or in total amount, and V the variable cost per unit, or in total amount.

Again, by transferring the data from Exhibit 91, we have in total value terms

$$\text{P/V ratio} = \frac{5,000 - 3,000}{5,000} \times 100$$

$$= \frac{2,000}{5,000} \times 100$$

$$= 40\%$$

In the unit cost terms the calculations would show

$$\frac{S - V}{S} \times 100 = \frac{1.0 - 0.60}{1.0} \times 100$$

$$= \frac{0.4}{1.0} \times 100$$

$$= 40\%$$

The P/V ratio states that 40 per cent of the product's sales income will contribute to fixed costs and profit. Thus with several products to be manufactured, their respective P/V ratios will indicate a potentially most profitable manufacturing mix policy. BUT it must be emphasised that the ratio should not be used by itself. Other considerations need to be examined in relation to each product, for example:

1 The effect on working capital requirements may vary widely from product to product: a high P/V ratio may conceal a lower return on capital due to greater working capital needs.
2 Availability of materials supplies to support a larger output.
3 Availability of appropriate work force skills to attain a larger output.
4 The manufacturing plant and related factory space necessary to produce the product: fixed costs may increase for a high P/V product.

The answer to these and other constraints on corporate profitability will be revealed if the P/V ratios or product contributions are expressed in relation to the limiting factor of production. Thus we may need to ascertain

Contribution per £ of working capital.
Contribution per £ of direct labour cost.
Contribution per £ of materials cost.
Contribution per square foot of operating space.
Etc.

The following examples will show the limitations of contribution analysis and of the profit/volume ratio when they are used without reference to other vital features of the firm's output capabilities. The object of the exercises is to show how the best choice of a manufacturing/selling mix can be revealed.

Example A

The XYZ Manufacturing Plc makes three products. Product A sells for £19, product B for £24 and C for £40. Variable costs for each unit of sales are calculated at £7, £12 and £28 respectively. The company's total machining capacity available for production purposes is 20,000 hours whilst the necessary machine time to manufacture each unit is

A = 3 hr; B = 2 hr; C = 1 hr

The firm's attainable market share for each product has been determined by market research to be

A = 10,000 units; B = 2,000 units; C = 1,000 units

What would be the best manufacturing mix of these products for the most profitable operations?

Suggested solution

A logical solution to this problem will involve an appraisal of the relative contributions and P/V ratios for the three products:

Product	A	B	C
	£	£	£
Selling price per unit	19	24	40
Variable costs per unit	7	12	28
Contribution per unit	£12	£12	£12

Therefore it appears that, from the standpoint of contribution, there would be no benefit from concentrating production on one specific product in preference to the others. A study of profit/volume ratios shows the following:

$$\text{Product A} \quad \frac{12}{19} \times 100 = 63\%$$

$$\text{Product B} \quad \frac{12}{24} \times 100 = 50\%$$

$$\text{Product C} \quad \frac{12}{40} \times 100 = 30\%$$

The P/V ratios indicate that Product A will be more profitable to produce than B, and B more profitable than C. But when we express the several contributions and P/V ratios in relation to the machining time required by each product (machine time is the scarce resource) we are led to a different ranking of potential product profitabilities.

Product	A	B	C
Necessary machining hours per unit	3	2	1
Contribution per unit	£12	£12	£12
Contribution per machine hour therefore is	£4	£6	£12
P/V ratio	63%	50%	30%
P/V ratio adjusted for machining hours	21%	25%	30%

The above data must have an influence upon manufacturing mix decisions. Here the order of preference is completely reversed as a result of a comparative analysis of contribution and P/V ratio, for C is better than B which is better than A. If the business manager now proceeds to plan his production programme, the following combination of outputs of A, B and C should be envisaged, bearing in mind the constraints of the attainable product markets:

				£
C	1,000 units × 1 hr = 1,000	machine-hours × £12 =	12,000
B	2,000 units × 2 hr = 4,000	machine-hours × £6 =	24,000
A	5,000 units × 3 hr = 15,000	machine-hours × £4 =	60,000
	TOTAL MACHINE-HOURS = 20,000	TOTAL CONTRIBUTION =	96,000

Clearly an *analysis* of the circumstances surrounding product P/V ratios and contributions will be a valuable exercise leading to more profitable operating decisions in such areas as

Manufacturing methods.
Manufacturing mixes.
Sales and marketing methods.
Locations of production units, etc.

Example B

The valves and springs division of the Component Manufacturing Plc has four main products which it makes and sells in the UK. The marketing and financial details of these products are given below.

Product	A	B	C	D
Prospective market (in units):	10,000	8,000	6,000	4,000
	£	£	£	£
Unit selling price:	48	50	38	34
Unit variable costs:				
materials	20	18	16	12
labour	11	10	8	3
expenses	2	2	1	1
Total variable costs	33	30	25	16

In its plan for next year's operations, head office has allocated to the valves and springs division a sum of £300,000 as its maximum materials purchase budget for that forthcoming period. With no similar limitations on the variable labour and expense items, the divisional managing director has

222

requested that a manufacturing mix of items A to D be prepared, so as to achieve maximum profit for the division. The related fixed costs are stated to be £250,000.

Suggested solution

Initial investigations will show that unit contributions and P/V ratios emerge as follows:

Product	A	B	C	D
Contribution	£15	£20	£13	£18
P/V ratio	31.25%	40%	34.21%	52.94%

This reveals a disparity in the sequencing of the best profit earning products. Here it is emphasised that a product's contribution identifies its absolute profit earning capability whilst the P/V ratio will locate the product's profitability rate, i.e. it demonstrates, for each product, that proportion of total sales income which is available to meet fixed costs and give a best return on sales.

The constraint upon the division's materials budget now requires that the above unit contributions and P/V ratios be compared with each product's materials cost:

Product	A	B	C	D
Contribution per £ of materials $\left(\frac{c}{m}\right)$	£0.75	£1.11	£0.81	£1.5
PV ratio per £ of materials $\left(\frac{Pr}{m}\right)$	1.56%	2.22%	2.14%	4.41%
Order of preference for best profitability	4th	2nd	3rd	1st

The above order of preference – in terms of contribution and P/V ratio – should be used to establish the division's production programme as presented below.

Product	Maximum output in units	Materials cost per unit	Total materials cost
		£	£
D	4,000	12	48,000
B	8,000	18	144,000
C	6,000	16	96,000
			£288,000

Clearly the programme will leave £12,000 for the purchase of materials necessary for the manufacture of the fourth choice, product A. As each unit of A consumes £20 worth of materials, the production schedule for this item will be limited to 600 units. Thus divisional total profit is now determined as:

Product	Output in units	Contribution per unit	Total contribution
		£	£
D	4,000	18	72,000
B	8,000	20	160,000
C	6,000	13	78,000
A	600	15	9,000
			319,000
		Total fixed costs	250,000
		Profit	£69,000

giving a return on total sales of 8.7 per cent.

Example C

A persistent theme throughout the earlier chapters has been a watchful concern for the return on capital employed which a business achieves. Now business budgets are frequently compiled on the basis of a required level of future profit. This requirement may arise from a strategic planning exercise completed by top management. It may develop from a desire to achieve a specific return on capital employed, or it may reflect corporate cash flow problems. When that profit target has been settled we can use our B/E formulae to identify the sales target which will enable the profit target to be met.

If we assume the following data about a firm

Fixed costs	£50,000
Profit target	£40,000
Product sales price per unit	£14
Product variable costs per unit	£5

we can proceed to calculate the required turnover as shown below:

Sales target in units of sales

$$= \frac{\text{Fixed costs} + \text{Profit target}}{\text{Product contribution per unit}}$$

$$= \frac{50{,}000 + 40{,}000}{14 - 5} = \frac{90{,}000}{9}$$

= 10,000 units at £14 each

= £140,000 sales value

The profit/volume ratio could have been used to ascertain the required sales value in the above problem, as is shown below

Sales target in total sales value

$$= \frac{\text{Fixed costs} + \text{Profit target}}{\text{P/V ratio}}$$

$$= £\frac{90{,}000}{64.285\%} = £\frac{90{,}000 \times 100}{64.285}$$

= £140,000

Example D

Again the P/V ratio or unit contribution can show management the potential consequences of proposed actions. The following example deals with the effects of a proposed reduction in the current selling price of a product:

Fixed costs	£50,000
Product selling price per unit	£14
Product variable costs per unit	£5
Current sales, 9,000 units at £14	= £126,000

In view of some strong competition from other firms it is suggested that the selling price be reduced to £10 per unit. How many units would the firm have to sell to maintain its existing profit level?

Suggested solution
Present profit level

= Current sales – (Fixed costs + Variable costs)

= £126,000 – (£50,000 + £45,000)

= £31,000

Now if the P/V ratio is reduced from its existing 64.285 per cent to 50 per cent (the result of reducing the selling price to £10), then the sales necessary to maintain the present level of profits will be calculated as shown below:

Sales target in total sales volume

$$= \frac{\text{Fixed costs} + \text{Required profit}}{\text{New P/V ratio}}$$

$$= £ \frac{50,000 + 31,000}{50\%}$$

$$= £ \frac{81,000 \times 100}{50}$$

$$= £162,000 \ (16,200 \text{ units at } £10)$$

The reader can prepare an abridged revenue account to prove the accuracy of the above figures (see page 219).

Profit/volume graph

The B/E graph is basically the chart of a company's profitability path. The reader has seen the effect of the different cost groups upon profit, and upon the margin of safety relevant to a particular cost/volume relationship. Now a principal objective of business operations must be profit and many different techniques are employed in the search for improved profitability. Some of these techniques and methods, such as plant modernisation, will result in increased capacity costs. Such expenditures are incurred in the expectation that greater efficiency, better quality and more reliability will result in increased sales and increased net profit. Exhibit 95 demonstrates the profit/loss implications of a (hypothetical) production-flow re-organisation, carried out in pursuit of greater efficiency and greater profit.

Here the chart is concerned only with profit or loss (shown on axis AB) at the various levels of output given on AX. The continuous line P_1P_1 repeats the profit expectation revealed in Exhibits 91 and 92. At this stage it is to be assumed that wage increases are negotiated to stimulate greater productivity. These productivity agreements, together with other cost reduction studies, are planned to give an expected profit of £1,600 at maximum output. This profit potential is indicated by point P_2 on the chart.

Now, many of the increased costs which accrue from greater productivity policies have a rigidity which reacts unfavourably upon the company when production falls. Increased expenditure, such as higher *levels* of wages rates, sales commissions, distribution costs, etc., will remain with the company

Exhibit 95
Profit/volume chart

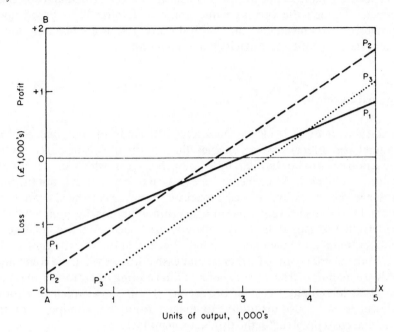

Units of output, 1,000's

even though the demand for its products falls off. Therefore the impact upon the firm's profitability, as a result of the wage negotiations and cost-reduction studies, will be demonstrated by the broken line P_2P_2. It can be seen that whilst profit can be considerably increased at an output of 5,000 units, a corresponding increase in the loss incurred at an output of 1,000 units is to be expected – even though break-even point has been reduced.

A further hypothesis can now be introduced. Assume that management decides to replace old plant and machinery with more sophisticated equipment. The object of the exercise would be, for example, the production of better goods, a more reliable production flow with less wastage. It is furthermore assumed that, in consequence of the re-equipment, the expected profit at maximum output ought to be increased to £1,000. This amount is represented on the graph at P_3. Increased costs of plant will result in a higher B/E point, because capacity costs will be higher (assuming that the company has always calculated its depreciation charges on a historical, rather than a replacement basis). However the expected profit increase of £300 at maximum output is judged to be worth the risk of the re-equipment capacity costs. The essential point here is that increased capacity costs are a feature of the firm's costing at *all* levels of output. Therefore whilst higher profits are possible beyond the higher B/E point, *greater losses* are just as possible below that new B/E point. The decision

227

for management, in these cases of whether to modernise or not, must be influenced by their expectations of the future level of demand for their products. Though the profit/volume graph in Exhibit 95 is based upon hypothetical circumstances, the graph does represent a commonly found situation when profit and capacity planning is undertaken.

Marginal costing

Break-even analysis leads on naturally to a study of marginal costing. Marginal (or direct) costing enables the impact of business activity on production costs to be clarified, by locating those costs which are sensitive to production changes. While income in excess of *marginal* cost is not the final net gain to the company, because capacity costs have yet to be allocated, the marginal return can reveal areas of true profitability for the company. This arises from the fact that many capacity costs such as those relating to buildings, plant and machinery will have been paid for at some time in the past. They do not result in further similar cash outflows when the company's goods are manufactured. A study of marginal costing, therefore, will reveal the actual incremental cost of producing: it will show which of various products is the most profitable to make* from the standpoint of the *additional* costs involved in the product's manufacture.

Exhibit 96 compares the reporting of cost information under a marginal cost system with that obtained with full-absorption costing. The latter system involves the aggregation of all costs of specific types, whether they be of a variable or capacity nature. Marginal cost reporting demonstrates the amount of additional expenditure, termed the 'variable cost of sales', which must be incurred when production is engaged. The marginal return, therefore, is the profit in terms of current cost accounting. It is applied in Exhibit 96 to the whole cost complex of a company's operations. Its relevance to product mix planning can be appreciated by studying Exhibit 97. In this exhibit the company has made an operating profit £10,000 and a net profit of £6,000. The whole direct and indirect (capacity costs) cost of keeping the company in business was £94,000: it is this sum which has reduced the sales income of £100,000 to the net profit of £6,000. Information of this kind gives a hazy, over-all picture of the company's activities, whereas the marginal cost analysis, into groups of costs which are *caused by the manufacture* of each of the three products, provides more useful data for profit planning. The table shows that £11,500 of the total indirect decision, i.e. capacity,

---

*Other factors such as the marginal contribution per hour or per day are pertinent to this statement. Again the company's objectives in the field of business, such as growth of sales, may affect the decision. Whatever is decided, marginal costing can be of assistance in revealing the direct cost of the decision.

Exhibit 96

Schematic diagram of differences between full-absorption and direct-marginal costing

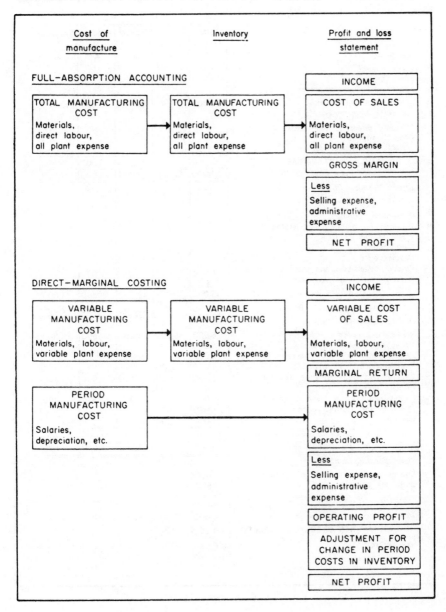

Exhibit 97

Analysis of income statement by product group

	Total	Common	Product A	Product B	Product C
Net Sales.	£	£	£	£	£
Home market					
Inter–Company					
Export and direct shipment					
TOTAL NET SALES	100,000		80,000	10,000	10,000
Direct Variable Costs					
Standard direct variable costs					
Cost allowances					
Freight, duty, insurance					
TOTAL DIRECT VARIABLE COSTS	60,000		48,000	6,000	6,000
DIRECT VARIABLE PROFIT	40,000		32,000	4,000	4,000
Direct Decision Costs					
Decision factory costs					
Production tooling					
Warehousing and machine storage					
Warranty and policy					
Rectification					
Obsolescence					
Product advertising and sales promotion					
Direct engineering expense					
TOTAL DIRECT DECISION COSTS	15,000		12,000	1,500	1,500
DIRECT PRODUCT PROFIT	25,000		20,000	2,500	2,500
Indirect Decision Costs					
Marketing expense	6,000	4,000	1,000	500	500
Marketing expense, Export	1,000	1,000			
General manufacturing administration	1,000	1,000			
Engineering administration	1,000	1,000			
General and administrative expense	2,000	1,000	500	400	100
Finance fees	1,000	1,000			
Miscellaneous income and expense	1,000	500	300	100	100
Provision for doubtful accounts	1,000	1,000			
Interest	1,000	1,000			
TOTAL INDIRECT DECISION COSTS	15,000	11,500	1,800	1,000	700
OPERATING PROFIT	10,000		18,200	1,500	1,800
Non-operating Impacts					
Change in decision costs in inventory	(500)				
Corporate expense	500				
Taxes	4,000				
TOTAL NON–OPERATING IMPACTS	4,000				
NET INCOME	£6,000				

costs are not influenced by the manufacture of any particular product. These expenditures have to be met whether the company is in business or not. Therefore, after recognising that some portion of the total capacity cost will be affected by engaging in operations, the reader can see the true total variation in the cost of manufacture of each of the three products. This variation in cost is shown by the line 'operating profit'. When operating profit is expressed as a percentage return on sales, i.e. the P/V ratio, it can be seen that:

Product A gives a 22.8 per cent return.
Product B gives a 15 per cent return.
Product C gives an 18 per cent return.

This kind of information, coupled with data on market size for each product, will assist in the profitable planning of a manufacturing mix of products. Exhibit 98 presents a similar situation where no variation in any of the period costs is envisaged as being caused by varying levels of productions.

Self-examination questions

1 Fixed costs per unit tend to vary with output changes, whilst variable costs per unit tend to be fixed. Explain this apparent paradox.

2 Why are 'fixed costs' so called? What other definitions would you suggest as better descriptions of this class of cost, and why?

3 What are the principal assumptions on which the conventional break-even chart is based?

4 Explain the meaning of contribution analysis. Discuss its uses and examine the validity of the assumptions on which the technique is based.

5 Give examples of factors which may cause (a) increases in break-even points and (b) decreases in break-even points. Do such effects necessarily reflect unfavourable/favourable conditions for the related business unit?

6 What is the 'margin of safety'? How important is this factor for a highly capitalised manufacturing company in a period of trade recession?

7 How does the application of marginal costing assist management in its product mix planning? What factors, other than production *cost*, should be examined by corporate management in planning its future operations?

Exhibit 98

Analysis of income statement by product group

Details	Totals	Product		
		A	B	C
	£	£	£	£
Sales				
Home				
Intercompany				
Export				
TOTAL NET SALES	100,000	75,000	10,000	15,000
Variable Cost of Sales				
Materials				
Labour				
Expenses				
TOTAL VARIABLE COSTS	60,000	50,000	5,000	5,000
MARGINAL RETURN	40,000	25,000	5,000	10,000
MARGINAL RETURN AS % OF SALES	40.0	33.3	50.0	66.6
Period or Capacity Costs				
Salaries	8,000			
General Administration	3,000			
Engineering Administration	2,000			
Financing Costs	1,000			
Bad Debts	1,000			
Depreciation	15,000			
TOTAL CAPACITY COSTS	30,000			
OPERATING PROFIT	10,000			
Non-operating Costs				
Corporate expense	1,000			
Taxation	3,000			
TOTAL NON-OPERATING COSTS	4,000			
NET INCOME	£6,000			

Recommended reading

BAGGOT, J., *Cost and Management Accounting*, W.H. Allen (1977), see chapters 1, 3 and 19.

HORNGREN, C.T., *Cost Accounting: A Managerial Emphasis*, Prentice Hall (1972).

ROCKLEY, L.E., *Finance for the Purchasing Executive*, Business Books (1978), see chapters 7 and 8.

SIZER, J., 'The Development of Marginal Costing' *Accountants Magazine* (1968).

SOLOMONS, D. (ed.), *Studies in Cost Analysis*, Sweet and Maxwell (1968).

12 Cost analyses and management decisions

Introduction

Our analyses of break-even and of marginal costing have placed emphasis upon the importance of the variable cost element of a total production cost. At no time has it been suggested that the whole costs of production are irrelevant to business pricing policies or to the firm's continued existence. The emphasis has been placed on our need to appreciate that variable costs, by their nature, are immediately affected by management's operating decisions. Thus the effects of changes in corporate operations are reflected promptly in the total amount of the variable costs incurred. It is vital to recognise this feature because we need a reliable, ready means of analysing the impacts of change upon corporate well-being. At the same time we cannot ignore the fact that – in the long run – the so-called fixed costs will have to be recouped by the firm's total income. But an informed plan for total cost recovery requires an understanding of the causal relationship between the existing cost structure and current business activities.

Therefore this chapter will show some of the criteria by which fixed costs are customarily allocated to a variety of product lines. It will be noted that much of the resultant fixed cost apportionments will be influenced by tradition and by subjective opinions. Really we need a more factual statement of costs actually incurred by a specific business activity than would be provided by arbitrary cost allocations alone. To some extent marginal costing will highlight this factual element of activity costs and will aid sound decision making. Nevertheless, we still need to test the validity of fixed cost allocations to separate parts of a multi-product manufacturing mix.

Overhead costs – allocations and apportionments

The first stage in an ordered programme of fixed cost recovery relates to the specification of those overhead (fixed) costs which are actually involved in the particular outputs being costed. Clearly when product A is examined we should be concerned with the overhead costs of only those machines which are part of that particular product line. The same comment refers to the related costs of the buildings in which production is carried on, to supervisory wages and salaries, etc. The vital notion in overhead cost recovery is the identification of those overhead costs which are caused by, are relevant to, the specific output being costed. It is these overhead costs which should be charged to that item of output.

Where production programmes change over the years without a matching re-examination of fixed cost allocations, then the assessed total costs of the various products may well be wrong and totally misleading for pricing and production policies. Once the total sum of overhead costs is determined, its allocation to product lines or to particular areas of activity is accomplished by methods such as those outlined below.

Rent or rates Apportioned on the floor space occupied by the relevant factors of production: together with allowances for corridors and gangways, this system links the firm's total cost with those areas of activity which contribute to the total cost.

Depreciation The actual depreciation on those buildings, vehicles and machines involved in the specific output, forms a principal fixed cost item. The calculation of the depreciation sum is a critical factor: a realistic cost item must consider replacement rather than simply historic acquisition cost.

Repairs and maintenance Apportionment of these costs may follow the allocations established for depreciation. In many cases however, the total amount will be an estimate based upon past experience.

Power May be allocated by metered supplies: again it is more likely that the apportionments will be estimated, though the power loading of the various machines would be taken into account.

The reader will be acquainted with other categories of fixed costs or general overhead expenses and the (arbitrary) way in which they are apportioned to the several outputs or production areas of a firm. But it is when we consider such overhead expenses as management salaries, and the concomitant costs, that customary apportionments are most suspect. These types of cost are apportioned by the accountant perhaps, according to his opinion about the areas of business activity to which the specific managers give their time and attention. Probably the only precise way would be for the relevant officers to keep a diary showing the time they spend on the various aspects of the firm's business. It is doubtful whether diaries would be realistically maintained: furthermore it is doubtful whether they would be comprehensive enough to aid sensible cost allocations.

So we have to admit that certain costs, e.g. management salaries, are part of the essential expenses of having a firm in existence at all. If we accept that such costs will be incurred, irrespective of the level of activity which the firm is undertaking, then apportionments of such expenses will be recognised as a questionable piece of spurious accuracy. Marginal costing implies that it is impossible to allocate accurately *all* of these costs (and other similar items), so limited benefits will accrue from such suspect apportionments, and will add to the unreliability of fixed cost allocation generally.

Overhead costs – absorptions

When we have calculated the sum of fixed costs belonging to a product line or area of activity, the next stage involves the method of charging the various units of outputs with their share of the total. The methods used vary, depending on whether the manufacturing processes are machine or labour intensive, for example. The mechanics of the various bases of overhead cost allocation to units of output are simple. Consequently they may lead to inaccurate costing, even though great care be taken during the earlier stages of fixed cost allocations and apportionments. A review of some of the methods of charging corporate outputs with a portion of the fixed cost sums, is given below.

Percentage on direct materials cost
This can be easily calculated and reliably applied where output consists of one product only: when the type and cost of diverse materials varies from product to product, a percentage on direct materials will give unrealistic manufacturing cost totals: similar comments apply where several products use varying grades of labour skills.

Percentage on direct wages cost
The method is suitable where the nature of the work performed by all the work force is similar, or where the mix of skilled and unskilled labour is constant for each item of production: if wage payments are related to time spent on the manufacturing process, the method will have some realism because most fixed costs accrue as time passes.

Percentage on prime costs
Suitable for firms which manufacture a 'standard' article, and where uniform costs for material and labour are to be expected: if the mix of labour

236

and materials cost is subject to variation, the system will not produce reliably comparable unit manufacturing costs.

An over-riding consideration in allocating a sum of fixed costs to units of output must be the time pattern of fixed cost accrual. Totals of depreciation, rent, rates, salaries, insurance, and many other expenses, are influenced by the passage of time: they aggregate as one month succeeds another. A realistic passing of these types of cost to product lines must therefore attempt to match the feature of time/cost aggregation with the time element in producing output. Here we are led to a study of the *machine-hour rate* and some form of (direct) *labour-hour rate*.

The machine-hour method involves sharing the overhead expenses of a production department amongst the various machines or banks of machines. The objective is to present a total overhead cost portion per manufacturing unit(s). Dividing this total cost by the expected operating hours per machine(s) in the period, a machine-hour rate is produced, e.g.

$$\frac{\text{Total overhead costs}}{\text{Total forecast operating hours}} = \frac{£4,950}{1,800 \text{ hrs}}$$

$$= £2.75 \text{ per hour}$$

This amount is multiplied by the operating hours necessary to produce each item or batch of items, and the resulting sum added to the direct costs of manufacture. Forecasting the expected operating hours per machine(s) is a critical feature: it involves market forecasts for the firm's products, estimates of machine idle times (for whatever cause) and eventually leads on to a study of standard costing. Clearly a machine-hour rate should be used only for those sections of the firm's manufacturing processes where machines are the predominant factor.

The (direct) labour-hour rate has similar characteristics to the machine-hour rate. But as the description implies, an allocation of fixed costs to units of output is based upon labour time spent in producing the good, or devoted to some stage of manufacture. The prime requirement must be that the manufacturing process involved is predominantly labour intensive. For situations employing differing classes of workforce – skilled and semi-skilled – it may be necessary to establish different hourly rates for the several grades of employee. In most manufacturing businesses both the machine-hour rate and a labour-rate will be used in separate parts of the whole concern. Nevertheless the decision to employ a machine-hour rate or a labour hour rate must involve an appraisal of the extent to which machinery or labour is able to *control* the output of a manufacturing unit. Thus if labour does effectively control the rate and volume of output – even when using expensive machinery – a labour-hour rate may well be the more appropriate apportionment routine to adopt.

After the above extensive fixed cost allocations have been established as part of the system for determining an ex-works cost, certain other costs will remain to be apportioned. Here we refer to costs which cannot be identified, with complete certainty, with any single area of activity. Promotion, general advertising, exhibitions and showroom etc. expenses are cases in point. To deal with these and other extra non-manufacturing expenses, allocations of total cost to units of output (in a pricing policy) are frequently based upon some percentage rate which is then loaded on to the assessed ex-works cost. An example of the calculations involved is given below:

$$\frac{\text{Total forecast (selling e.g.) expenses}}{\text{Total forecast value of manufacturing output}} \times 100$$

   = Percentage proportion of ex-works cost

   = Sum added to ex-works cost to recoup overhead cost

There are other formulae used for this transaction and for other non-manufacturing overheads. They will depend on the significance of the particular overhead cost in relation to the sums of other such costs. We shall meet allocations based upon:
1   An estimate amount per unit of production.
2   A percentage of each article's selling price.

Overhead costs analysis

The several stages in a procedure for determining the overhead costs to be borne by outputs of several separate production areas are described in Exhibit 99. Here the foregoing explanations of overhead recovery methods are correlated within an overall corporate programme. At the same time the exhibit gives indications of the types of overhead costs being encountered at each step in the whole process.

Example A demonstrates these stages of cost allocation, apportionment and absorption as they will be found to operate in a practical situation.

Example A
The Machine Tool Manufacturing Plc is organised with three operational areas:

Machine shop
Finishing department
Assembly and packing department

together with two service departments which operate for the benefit of the whole firm:

238

Exhibit 99
Determination of product total cost

Stage	Examples of overhead costs involved and their allocation	Production areas/Cost centres (e.g. factory, division, machine group, manufacturing process) A B C D	Service departments — Canteen E, Mainte-nance F, Welfare and Medical G, Transport H
A	Management salaries Supervisory salaries and wages Depreciation Rent, rates and insurance, etc.	Allocation to the separate production areas/cost centres of the sum of those overhead costs which are *specifically identified* with that production area/cost centre only.	Allocation to each service department of the sum of those overhead costs which *are specifically identified* with that service only.
B	Head office expenses Directors' fees Management salaries Corporate policy and planning Depreciation Administration etc.	Apportioned to the separate production areas/ cost centres of a share of the total corporate overhead costs, i.e. those costs NOT specifically identifiable with any single product – incurred on behalf of the whole firm rather than for one single product.	Apportioned to each service department of a share of the total corporate overhead costs, i.e. those NOT specifically identifiable with any single service department.
C	Apportioned on bases of the benefits or services given to production areas.	Add to each separate total for A, B, C and D, its related apportionment of the total service departments' costs, thus absorbing the whole costs of the service departments.	Each service department's total cost comprising (a) allocations and apportionments of fixed costs plus (b) the service department's own variable costs all apportioned to production areas/cost centres.
D	Absorption of total overheads by units of output by ratios of (a) direct labour cost (b) direct labour hours (c) machine hour rates, etc.	Each unit or product in the total output of the various production areas to absorb its assessed portion of the total overheads. When the related overhead cost absorption is added to product variable cost, the total cost of each item is achieved.	

Canteen
Administration

The budget for the forthcoming year has been based upon a planned output of 5,000 units, when the overhead cost totals were expected to be:

	£
Machine shop	56,000
Finishing department	20,000
Assembly and packing department	15,000
Canteen	8,000
Administration	15,000

At the same time, direct (i.e. variable) cost totals in respect of the canteen and administration sections have been estimated at £8,000 and £25,000 respectively. In the production areas, standard variable costs per unit have been set at:

	£
Labour:	
manufacturing	8
finishing	5
assembly and packing	4
total per unit	£17
Materials:	
manufacturing	15
finishing	2.40
assembly and packing	6
total per unit	£23.40

The total costs of the service departments are to be appointed to the production areas in the following proportions

Administration:	
manufacturing	50%
finishing	20%
assembly	15%
canteen	15%
Canteen:	
manufacturing	25%
finishing	40%
assembly	35%

The whole of the corporate overhead costs should then be absorbed into the cost of the products passing through the three production areas on the bases noted below

Machining: machine hour rate – 25,000 hours budgeted

Finishing: direct labour hour rate – 12,500 hours budgeted

Assembly etc.: direct labour hour rate – 10,000 hours budgeted

Suggested solution

Distribution of overhead costs

Details	Manufac-turing £	Finishing £	Assembly £	Canteen £	Adminis-tration £
Overhead cost allocations	56,000	20,000	15,000	8,000	15,000
Service departments' direct costs	—	—	—	8,000	25,000
Service departments' total costs	—	—	—	16,000	40,000
Apportionment of administration costs	20,000	8,000	6,000	6,000	(40,000)
Canteen department's total costs				22,000	
Apportionment of canteen costs	5,500	8,800	7,700	(22,000)	
Total overhead costs of production areas	£81,500	£36,800	£28,700		

Consequently the overhead recovery rates to be used by the separate production areas in absorbing fixed costs into the total costs of individual units of output, will be calculated as follows:

Machining department: $\dfrac{\text{total overheads}}{\text{machining hours}} = \dfrac{£81,500}{25,000}$

= £3.26 per machine hour

$$\text{Finishing department:} \quad \frac{\text{total overheads}}{\text{direct labour hours}} = \frac{£36,800}{12,500}$$

$$= £2.944 \text{ per direct labour hour}$$

$$\text{Assembly department:} \quad \frac{\text{total overheads}}{\text{direct labour hours}} = \frac{£28,700}{10,000}$$

$$= £2.87 \text{ per direct labour hour}$$

If we now suggest that the manufacture of a particular machine tool involved 8 hours of machining time, 5 direct labour hours in the finishing department and 3 direct hours in the assembly and packing department, the total company cost will be determined by:

	£	£
Variable costs:		
materials	23.40	
labour	17.00	40.40
Overhead absorptions:		
machining		
(8 × £3.26)	26.08	
finishing		
(5 × £2.944)	14.72	
assembly		
(3 × £2.87)	8.61	49.41
Total cost		£89.81

Thus if a desirable profit of 10 per cent on total cost was the company's aim, the selling price would be £98.79 (£89.81 × 1.1).

Overhead costs – misconceptions

The whole process of fixed costs allocation is based upon estimates of future events. Too frequently past operating and selling performances are analysed in order to allocate data relating to future actions. Moreover, proportions and/or percentage rates of recovery which were used in the past are arbitrarily varied in readiness for product cost calculations relating to a future period. Clearly such inadequate methods not only compound past errors but also do not recognise that the incidence of individual cost groups can vary markedly. Two examples of possible misdirections of corporate effort, arising from relying too greatly on a total cost concept, are now presented.

Absorption and marginal costs

Example B

Exhibit 100 shows in columnar form the profit and loss accounts for three products A, B and C. It is assumed that the goods are produced in factories operating within a division of a larger manufacturing group. After apportionment of the various overhead expense totals, the final profit from the three items is shown to be £86,000.

Exhibit 100
Total cost appraisals

Details	Product A	Product B	Product C	Totals
	£	£	£	£
Direct materials	10,500	12,000	15,000	37,500
Direct labour	1,500	6,000	14,000	21,500
Direct expenses	500	3,000	2,000	5,500
PRIME COST	12,500	21,000	31,000	64,500
Factory overheads	11,000	25,000	30,000	66,000
MANUFACTURING COST	23,500	46,000	61,000	130,500
Divisional admin. costs	3,500	6,000	14,000	23,500
TOTAL DIVISIONAL COST	27,000	52,000	75,000	154,000
Head office selling & distribution costs	£10,000	5,000	50,000	65,000
COST OF SALES	37,000	57,000	125,000	219,000
Profit	8,000	18,000	60,000	86,000
SALES	£45,000	£75,000	£185,000	£305,000

Now the system of total cost allocation (also called absorption costing) shows the following return on sales ratings:

$$Product\ C \quad \frac{60,000}{185,000} \times 100 = 32.4\%$$

$$Product\ B \quad \frac{18,000}{75,000} \times 100 = 24.0\%$$

$$Product\ A \quad \frac{8,000}{45,000} \times 100 = 17.8\%$$

Exhibit 101
Marginal cost appraisal

Details	Product A		Product B		Product C		Totals	
	£	£	£	£	£	£	£	£
Sales		45,000		75,000		185,000		305,000
Direct materials	10,500		12,000		15,000		37,500	
Direct labour	1,500		6,000		14,000		21,500	
Direct expenses	500		3,000		2,000		5,500	
PRIME COST		12,500		21,000		31,000		64,500
Variable factory overhead		2,000		10,000		25,000		37,000
Factory marginal cost	14,500		31,000		56,000		101,500	
Variable admin. costs			5,000		10,000		15,000	
Variable head office	14,500		36,000		66,000		116,500	
selling costs		3,500		2,500		35,000		41,000
Marginal costs	18,000		38,500		101,000		157,500	
Contribution		27,000		36,500		84,000		147,500

These results suggest that any expansion plans would be directed first to product C, before B and A. Other related matters would have to be taken into account before the final decision was made however. These other factors have been discussed on pages 221–22 and they will involve studies of

1 The working capital requirements for each product
2 The impact of sales of one product upon the sales of the other products

A different picture of the products' contributions to corporate profitability is given in Exhibit 101. The presumption in this exhibit is that the analysis of total costs has identified areas of variable costs at factory, division and head office levels of the group. When each product is then charged with the related amounts of those expenses upon which its *production has a regular direct impact*, then we arrive at the marginal costs of manufacturing. It is these costs which must be incurred when production activity is undertaken: in general other costs reflect the costs of having a production organisation in being, ready to operate at a specific capacity level.

The aggregate product contributions to corporate profit is shown to be £147,500. By deducting the remaining actual fixed costs from the contribution total we shall arrive at the net operating profit. The actual fixed costs are therefore found as given below:

	Exhibit 100 Totals	Exhibit 101 Variable elements	Fixed elements
	£	£	£
Factory overheads	66,000	37,000	29,000
Divisional admin.	23,500	15,000	8,500
Head office	65,000	41,000	24,000
TOTALS	£154,500	£93,000	£61,500

The net profit is then calculated by

	£
Product contribution total	147,500
Less: Fixed costs	61,500
PROFIT	£86,000

which agrees with the total profit amount reported in the end column of Exhibit 100.

But the results deriving from the marginal costing approach provide data which is more relevant to cost/profit comparisons of alternative choices of action. Exhibit 101 enables our calculation of profit/volume ratios, and thus suggests a different ranking of product profitabilities from that shown by absorption costing:

$$\text{Product } A: \text{P/V ratio} = \frac{27{,}000 \times 100}{45{,}000} = 60.0\%$$

$$\text{Product } B: \text{P/V ratio} = \frac{36{,}500 \times 100}{75{,}000} = 48.7\%$$

$$\text{Product } C: \text{P/V ratio} = \frac{84{,}000 \times 100}{185{,}000} = 45.4\%$$

Clearly product A must now be regarded as the most likely candidate for any extension programme. Again however, one must emphasise the need for further comparative studies of other factors affecting the whole of the company's financial/asset structure. Nevertheless, marginal cost analysis does show the immediate costs of change, within the parameters of an existing organisation.

Example C
The decision to adopt a marginal costing approach to the appraisal of business activity will be reflected in the stock valuations reported in the year-end accounts. Previous chapters have dealt with the impact of stock valuations upon the corporate wealth and profitability. Now we shall study how marginal costing will affect those stock valuations, demonstrating a particular view of a firm's progress over a period. The reader will see that absorption costing would produce a totally different progress picture. It is important to realise that the consequences of business decisions – to operate at one level of activity or another – are being reported.

Management must have the results of its decisions reported in a realistic way. The accounts must show the results of change in clear outline

Exhibit 102 presents a three-year series of profit and loss accounts for a firm. Each of the year-end stock values has been calculated on a (total) absorption cost basis. Thus the values of each of the units of stock have been derived from the total fixed and variable costs of manufacturing the output of the factory for the related accounting period. The firm is shown to be suffering a decline in its sales during the three year period. From year to year the directorate have reduced the firm's manufacturing overheads (retiring plant and equipment) from £2,200 to £1,750. Nevertheless the managerial decisions on these contractions of manufacturing capacity have not brought much encouragement in the pattern of year-by-year net profit figures. Profits have fallen from £1,100, through £450 to £100 in year three.

But when the year-end stock values reflect the actual additional costs of deciding to have or make that stock, and when other *variable* costs are identified, a more meaningful series of profit statements is produced (see Exhibit 103).

The true impact of management's action on the fixed costs is revealed.

Exhibit 102

Stock valuation and profit trends: I – Absorption costing

	Year 1	£	£	Year 2	£	£	Year 3	£	£
	Sales: 1,000 units at £10 each		10,000	Sales: 800 units at £11 each		8,800	Sales: 700 units at £12 each		8,400
	Cost of goods sold:			Cost of goods sold:			Cost of goods sold:		
	Variable mfg costs 1,100 at £6 each	6,600		Variable mfg costs 900 at £7 each	6,300		Variable mfg costs 500 at £7.5 each	3,750	
	Fixed mfg costs 1,100 at £2 each	2,200		Fixed mfg costs 900 at £2.5 each	2,250		Fixed mfg costs 500 at £3.5 each	1,750	
		8,800			8,550			5,500	
				Add opening stock	800		Add opening stock	1,900	
	Less stock at year end: 100 units at £8 each	800			9,350				7,400
			8,000	Less stock at year end: 200 at £9.5	1,900				
	Gross margin		2,000			7,450	Gross margin		1,000
				Gross margin		1,350			
	Administration, selling and distribution expenses (including £400 of variable expenses)		900	Admin., S&D exp. (including £400 of variable exp.)		900	Admin., S&D exp. (including £400 of variable exp.)		900
	Profit		£1,100	Profit		£450	Profit		£100

Note: total profit over the three years: £1,100 + £450 + £100 = £1,650

247

Exhibit 103

Stock valuation and profit trends: II – marginal costing

	Year 1			Year 2			Year 3		
		£	£		£	£		£	£
Sales: 1,000 units at £10 each			10,000	Sales: 800 units at £11 each		8,800	Sales: 700 units at £12 each		8,400
Cost of goods sold:				Cost of goods sold:			Cost of goods sold:		
Variable mfg costs 1,100 at £6 each		6,600		Variable mfg costs 900 at £7 each	6,300		Variable mfg costs 500 at £7.5 each	3,750	
Less stock at year end: 100 units at £6 each	600			Add opening stock	600		Add opening stock	1,400	
		6,000			6,900			5,150	
				Less stock at year end: 200 units at £7 each	1,400				
					5,500				
Plus variable admin., S&D exp.	400			Plus variable admin. etc. exp.	400		Plus variable admin. etc. exp.	400	
		6,400				5,900			5,550
Contribution margin			3,600	Contrib. margin		2,900	Contribut. margin		2,850
Less:				Less:			Less:		
Fixed costs	2,200			Fixed costs	2,250		Fixed costs	1,750	
Fixed admin., S&D exp.	500			Fixed admin., etc. exp.	500		Fixed admin., etc. exp.	500	
		2,700				2,750			2,250
Profit			£900	Profit		£150	Profit		£600

Note: total profit over the three years: £900 + £150 + £600 = £1,650

248

The sale of assets and other fixed cost reduction activities are separated from the operating activities. It is the changing income/expenditure situations reported by the profit and loss accounts which are of material importance to an evaluation of the firm's development.

In the marginal costing statement the firm is shown to have adopted sound operating and capacity policies in that its profit trend shows an upturn in year three. In fact the P/V ratios are relatively stable as the following figures show:

Year 1	36%
Year 2	32.95%
Year 3	33.92%

Again a marginal costing technique has been able to give management a much more pertinent statement of profitability by recognising that it is only the variable element of a cost structure which can show the effect of varying levels, or mixes, of output.

Standard costing

Our study of the use of cost analysis as a management tool must now embrace systems of standard costing. Whilst a comprehensive view of the subject is beyond the scope and size of this volume, the basic philosophy and techniques of standard costing can be demonstrated.

Earlier chapters on break-even and marginal costing have shown how the future well-being of a company can be appraised We have not concerned ourselves with detailed examinations of past costs. This is not to say that historic cost results are not relevant to future corporate profitability. They certainly are. They can show the manager where past performance was weak, why and where profitability could have been better. But an effective business manager must plan for the future, plotting the firm's survival/ profit pathways for the forthcoming years.

Standard costing recognises this need. It is concerned with making detailed assessments of the various elements of total cost of a product *before* it is actually manufactured. Predetermined total costs of production are established: these total cost estimates also show the detailed expected cost impacts of the various factors involved in production – wages, materials, capacity, etc. Then as the future plan unfolds in the form of current operating activities, the forecasts can be compared with the actual costs experienced in the week by week workings of the firm. In these ways standard costing combines the better elements of two systems of cost control. First, it looks forward into the future and establishes acceptable cost structures for varying levels of output. Second, it tests frequently and promptly the *recent* past actual costs against those embodied in the standard.

Here it is the promptness with which actual and forecast costs are compared which is vital to the success of systems of standard costing. Normal historic cost analysis involves appraisals of data long after the actual event, thus giving little opportunity for effective remedial action. Standard costing provides up-to-date information for cost control which, being based upon accepted yardsticks, enables a cost conscious management to improve profitability.

Clearly a standard costing system has certain minimum requirements for its operation. These are

1   An orderly aggregation of costs of operations so as to enable the comparisons of actual with forecast costs: this is accomplished by specifying 'cost centres' – stages in the operations (for example) for which actual costs are identified and gathered together.
2   Codification of expenses so that they can be almost automatically directed to their appropriate cost centres.
3   A consideration of the *type* of standard to be applied to the forecasting of cost structures.
4   The setting of the standard costs for the various factors of production.

Types of standard

The choice of type of standard is important because it is against its consequent yardsticks that future operations will be judged. The need for management's remedial action will be conditioned by the extent to which future actual costs succeed, or fail, to match the forecast cost structures deriving from the type of standard used. Various conceptions of the standard are given below.

The ideal standard
As the term indicates, it describes a level of operating performance and efficiency which would be experienced if ideal conditions for the firm's activities were to be available: no allowances are made for production stoppages or other adverse cost/price/economic circumstances: in reality, such a standard represents the unattainable goal and its resultant cost comparisons offer discouragement to the firm's staffs.

The expected standard
The level of operating performance and cost efficiency which is expected will be attained in the planning period – the forthcoming budget period – within the context of the trading conditions expected to prevail during that period.

The normal standard
Similar to the expected standard but relating to a period longer than the

250

immediate budget: it is applied to a time period which would be long enough to cover a trade cycle: more precisely the normal standard is based upon an average expected level of operations, for the available asset capacity, over a period of *years* rather than just one year.

Other definitions are found such as the 'basic' standard which really constitutes a statistical index of the movement of costs over a period of years. In an age of inflation, with constantly changing costs of the various factors of production, fluctuating exchange rates for the £, it is clear that revisions of our chosen standard will be more frequently necessary than was historically the case.

Variances

When the actual operating costs are compared with those in the (forecast) standard, differences will occur. These differences are called 'variances'. If the actual costs experienced in manufacturing are lower than those expected by the standard cost structure, the variance is termed a 'favourable' one. In this sense variance is a measure of profit, for the reduced costs which give rise to the favourable variance indicate a potential profit increase. Nevertheless we do not use the description profit, as many other factors must be taken into account before the profit/loss state of the firm can be quantified.

Should the actual costs turn out to be greater than those envisaged by the standard, an unfavourable variance will arise. Again, when we call the variance 'unfavourable', we recognise that a tendency to a lower profit, or even a loss, is present. Now unstable cost conditions can lead to large unfavourable variances, when the trend of cost is upward, unless standards are revised at least annually. Determination of the number and size of favourable and unfavourable variances is essential if management is to have firm control over the direction of corporate profitability. Reasons must be sought for significant variances so that adverse tendencies, which threaten corporate profitability, can be corrected.

Where standards are not revised periodically, and in consequence numerous (for example) unfavourable variances occur, then the essential corrective effort may be

1 Dissipated over too many investigations.
2 Blunted through loss of faith in the system.

The result is that effective cost control is not achieved. Nevertheless the reporting of cost variances, followed by prompt management action where loss tendencies are apparent, enables the directing managers' time to be used in a most effective manner. Responsibility for the loss tendencies can be quickly and firmly located and the major proportion of management time can then be devoted to those aspects of the firm's business which appear to be deteriorating. We thus encounter the notion of 'management by exception' because the satisfactory aspects of the firm's affairs may be left to continue without major investigations: they are 'excepted' from an immediate, searching management enquiry.

The following pages now give examples of variance analysis when, firstly, we shall examine the costs of material and labour consumed in manufacturing a saleable product. Clearly the materials cost of a product might vary as a result of

1   *Price* increases or decreases for the material to be used.
2   Economy or waste in the *amount* of material used.

Both of these features may be present during a manufacturing cycle. But normal historic cost reporting would not automatically identify the separate extents to which the two sets of circumstances had influenced the total cost. On the other hand, standard costing will show readily

3   The material price variance – reflecting the impact of (1) above.
4   The material usage variance – reflecting the impact of (2) above.

Again the labour cost of the product can change because of

5   Variations in the wage rate being paid to the operatives.
6   Variations in the efficiency of working by the operatives.

Once more we can see that the total labour cost of manufacturing a product may be affected by one or both of the features noted at (5) and (6): the effectiveness of standard costing will be further endorsed when we see that variance analysis will report

7   The labour rate variance – reflecting the impact of (5) above.
8   The labour efficiency variance – reflecting the impact of (6) above.

Now historic reports about the total direct labour and direct materials costs of a product would conceal the features of material price usage changes, as well as those for labour rate and efficiency: standard costing brings them to light.

Example

The ABC Company make a product for which the standard direct costs per unit were expected to be

Raw materials – 2 metres at £1 per metre.
Labour – 4 hours at £1.25 per hour.

The actual production in the recent operating period was 250 units. In this period the costs actually experienced were

Raw materials – 480 metres at 94p per metre.
Labour – 1,100 hours at £1.20 per hour.

Standard cost variance analysis

		£
1	*Total variance:*	
	(*a*) Actual production at actual cost	
	Materials: 480 metres at 94p per metre	451.2
	Labour: 1,100 hours at £1.20 per hour	1,320.0
	TOTAL ACTUAL COST	£1,771.2
	(*b*) Standard costs of production	
	Materials: 500 meters at £1 per meter	500
	Labour: 1,000 hours at £1.25 per hour	1,250
	TOTAL STANDARD COST	£1,750

Thus it is shown that an overall unfavourable variance of £21.2 resulted from the operations just completed. We need to know exactly how this has arisen, and the following variances will show this.

		£
2	*Total materials variance:*	
	(*a*) Actual material usage at actual cost	451.2
	Standard material cost of production	
	(500 metres at £1 per metre)	500.0
	FAVOURABLE TOTAL VARIANCE FROM MATERIALS	£48.8
	Materials price variance:	
	(*b*) Actual material usage at actual cost	451.2
	Actual material usage at standard cost	
	(480 metres at £1 per metre)	480.0
	FAVOURABLE MATERIAL PRICE VARIANCE	£28.8

The calculations at (*b*) above highlight the impact on total cost of a *price* variation from the expected per unit standard cost. In this section of the analysis the amount of materials consumption is uniformly quoted as the actual usage in order to emphasise the precise effect of the *price* change:

		£
	Materials usage variance:	
	(*c*) Actual materials used at standard cost	480.0
	Standard material cost of production	500.0
	FAVOURABLE MATERIALS USAGE VARIANCE	£20.0

Therefore the total favourable materials variance is shown to derive from price effectiveness (good buying?), £28.8, and from economic usage, £20. The control data becoming available to management are more informative than was shown in (1) above. Yet we have not located the vital loss area.

		£
3	Total labour variance:	
(a)	Actual labour hours at actual cost	1,320
	Standard labour cost of production	
	(1,000 hours at £1.25 per hour)	1,250
	UNFAVOURABLE TOTAL VARIANCE FROM LABOUR	£70

		£
	Labour rate variance:	
(b)	Actual labour hours at actual cost	1,320
	Actual labour hours at standard cost	
	(1,100 hours at £1.25 per hour)	1,375
	FAVOURABLE LABOUR RATE VARIANCE	£55

Here the variance calculations are designed to show the effects of a change in labour rate: the actual hours employed remain the same in each of the calculations at (b). Thus whilst we have located the cause of the overall unfavourable variance of £21.2 [see (1) above] to belong to labour, we cannot yet specify the precise cause.

		£
	Labour efficiency variance	
(c)	Actual labour hours at standard cost	1,375
	Standard labour cost of production	1,250
	UNFAVOURABLE LABOUR EFFICIENCY VARIANCE	£125

The final variance calculation reveals the cause of the firm's loss tendencies which were first expressed in the overall unfavourable variance of £21.2. Management must apply itself to the problem of labour efficiency to find out why the labour outturn of production is so unsatisfactory. The inter-relationship of these cost variances can be displayed diagramatically as shown in Exhibit 104.

Budget comparisons

The results of the foregoing, and other, analyses of the firm's progress should be reported regularly to the directing management. Such management information reports will compare actual current performance with the expectations of the budget. Exhibit 105 below exemplifies a typical comparative cost/profit statement. The statement takes into account

254

Exhibit 104

Direct cost variances

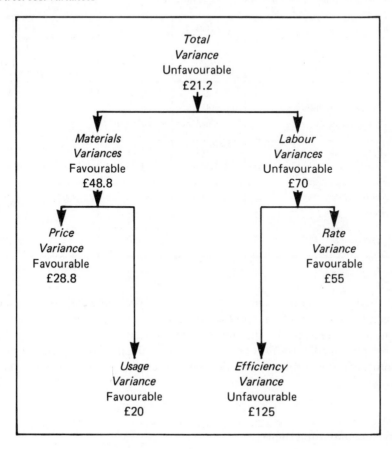

1 The direct cost variances calculated in the previous pages.
2 An assumption that fixed costs were expected to be £2,100 whereas the actual fixed costs were £2,000. The reasons for the difference may be (*a*) actual price changes, (*b*) changes in output leading to low recovery of fixed costs.
3 An assumption that the firm's sales would be £4,200 whereas they were only £4,000 in fact. Here the difference may have arisen from sales price changes, sales mixture changes or sales volume changes.

Items (2) and (3) can be explored by appropriate variance analysis such as that demonstrated for the elements of direct cost.

The statement of Exhibit 105, albeit a brief example, shows in broad outline why the actual profit achieved in the periods is £121.2 less than

Exhibit 105

Budgeted Profit and Loss Statement for the period

Details	Budgeted	Actual	Variances	
			Fav.	Unfav.
(1)	(2)	(3)	(4)	(5)
	£	£	£	£
(a) Direct materials	500.0	451.2	48.8	—
(b) Direct labour	1,250.0	1,320.0	—	70
(c) Prime cost	1,750.0	1,771.2	—	21.2
(d) Fixed costs	2,100.0	2,000.0	100	—
(e) Total cost	3,850.0	3,771.2	78.8	—
(f) Sales	4,200.0	4,000.0	—	200.0
(g) Profit	350.0	228.8	—	121.2

that budgeted. Four main areas of difference between actual and expectations are specified, and they should lead management to searching enquiries for reasons for the unfavourable variances. Finally though the exhibit presents the results of one recent operating period (say a week or a month), additional columns should contain the aggregate totals for the year thus far.

Self-examination questions

1 Define and appraise at least three methods by which overhead costs are absorbed into the total cost of a product.

2 Analyse and distinguish between (a) absorption costing and (b) marginal costing. How do these two techniques affect periodic stock valuations and corporate profits?

3 Should those overhead costs which will be incurred whether the business is working or not (e.g. depreciation, insurance, management salaries) be apportioned to product and stock items, OR should they be regarded as period costs and charged wholly to the revenue accounts of the related periods?

4 Define 'normal activity', 'expected activity' and 'ideal activity', in relation to the standards used in standard costing.

5 What do you understand by the 'materials price' and 'materials usage' variances? List those factors which bring about (*a*) favourable and (*b*) unfavourable variances from the standard values expected.

6 How does variance analysis aid 'management by exception'?

Recommended reading

DEARDEN, J., *Cost Accounting and Financial Control Systems*, Addison-Wesley (1973) see chapters 1 to 4.

HARPER, W., 'Thou Shalt Not Apportion for Control', *Accountancy*, January 1980, pp. 85–7.

HARPER, W., 'Profit Control and the Non-Apportionment Rule', *Accountancy*, April 1980, pp. 70–4.

HART, H., *Overhead Costs*, Heinemann (1973).

SSAP9, 'Stock and Work-in-progress', Accounting Standards Committee, May 1975 and August 1980.

Part 3
Investment analysis

13   Capital expenditure evaluation

Introduction

The reader has seen how a company's accounts can reveal information on a business's performance. Furthermore it has been shown how forecasting and a study of the relationships between specific groups of *operating* costs can aid the planner to guide and control performance in the future. At this point it becomes necessary to consider how the business manager can improve his decisions concerning expenditure on long terms assets – the *capacity* costs of break-even analysis. Capital expenditure concerns money spent with the knowledge that the gain therefrom will not accrue immediately or even within a few months. More often it implies that such expenditure is buying a stake in the future and, as capital assets are usually of limited specific use,* the needs of the future must be carefully assessed. Once capital expenditure is engaged, it is most difficult to change the course of the firm spending the money – at least without considerable cost. This considerable cost could stem from having to sell the capital assets at unfavourable prices, or from having to spend further sums on altering and modifying the assets retained. Either of which happenings would mean a loss which could have been avoided if the original capital expenditure proposal had been properly assessed and the decision thus taken on better informed bases.

Business management is concerned with decision making. In the capital asset sphere it frequently involves the making of a choice between several possible alternatives. There may be different ways in which a company can proceed to manufacture a particular commodity. Various types of machinery are available: such choices of machines could be influenced by their

---

*If a shoe-making plant is set up, the machinery involved could not be used to manufacture motor cars, or shirts, or bearings. It is vital therefore that the correct choice is made before expenditure is incurred.

running costs, their purchase costs, the quality of work produced and so on. Again there are various commodities that a company might decide to produce: it could buy, lease or rent the equipment and buildings which it would need to complete its manufacturing programme. The extent of the possible alternative opportunities open to a dynamic business are much wider in scope and greater in number than those instanced above. Therefore it becomes essential to be sure about the means of measurement of the worth of alternatives, when a manager is planning his firm's capital expenditures. These plans will determine the future direction, profitability and growth of his business. Finally, the concept of choice between available alternative investments in capital assets must always consider the consequences of *not* investing at all. In this way a complete picture of the consequences of a decision-maker's actions is obtained, and the future of his company is the better evaluated and influenced.

Techniques of appraisal

Now the choice criterion, the yardstick by which investment in capital assets is assessed, involves measuring future incomes which will arise from operating an asset, against its purchase and installation costs. In all cases this is a calculation of the effects of change; thus it is the costs and incomes relating from change which are relevant, and these are termed incremental costs and incomes.* Any yardstick of measurement must present a means of identifying acceptable and unacceptable investment proposals. It must also be a means of choosing between alternatives, and this is of utmost importance where there are two ways of achieving one end. Furthermore the capital planner will find it helpful if the criterion of choice gives not only a 'go' or 'no go' answer, but also presents a ranking of projects in an order of desirability. This latter quality in the evaluation technique is not easy to achieve and the examples given below show why the business planner should approach with care his selection of a criterion of investment choice.

Payback

The most widely used method of investment evaluation is payback. Its popularity derives from its simplicity and cheapness of operation. This technique gives forth a ratio which is a simple expression of the length of

---

*The notion of incremental costs and incomes refers to those costs and incomes which arise as a result of doing something, e.g. of capital investment. It has its comparisons with the variable costs in break-even analysis and is frequently referred to as the marginal cost of doing something or the marginal saving from *not* doing that something.

Exhibit 106
Evaluation of investments by payback

Details	Project A		Project B		Project C	
Cost of investment	£5,000		£7,500		£10,000	
Cash flows	£	Percentage of original cost	£	Percentage of original cost	£	Percentage of original cost
Year 1	2,000	40	5,000	66.7	6,000	60
Year 2	3,000	60	2,500	33.3	4,000	40
Year 3	1,000	20	1,500	20.0	2,000	20
TOTAL CASH FLOWS	6,000	120	9,000	120.0	12,000	120
PAYBACK	2 years		2 years		2 years	

time it takes for a project to return to a firm the cash outlays involved in the original investment. It indicates the speed with which the corporate treasury is replenished by the incomes generated from the activity of the capital expenditure. Payback looks no further than the time necessary for a project to re-finance its initial cost, and therefore has no regard for subsequent receipts, or for the length of economic life of the investment.

Exhibit 106 demonstrates three different investments and their related annual cash flows and costs. Each investment has the same grade in the payback index – two years, i.e. it takes exactly two years for the several projects to return the cash cost of the original capital investment to the investor.* No regard is paid to the varying distributions of cash flows, although the time of receipt could well be of importance to the firm's liquidity position. To emphasise the time factor of cash flowback, the percentage column in the table indicates the proportion of the original cost represented by each separate year's net cash flows. These cash flow comparisons tend to emphasise the inequality of the three investments, at least from the liquidity point of view. The use of payback therefore should be questioned as to its reliability and this specific point will be exemplified below.

In Exhibit 106 it should be noted that when comparing alternative prospects of A and B, the *additional* capital cost of B, £2,500, returns *additional* cash to the corporate funds of £3,000 in the first year alone. This first year incremental receipt gives a payback of 5/6ths of a year to the incremental capital cost. So though the calculation of payback is simple, easy to understand and its costs of calculation are inexpensive in operation, its use poses problems of choice. It does not solve problems of choice in a reliable fashion. Nevertheless it can be seen that, for a company which is short of liquid funds, payback may have some usefulness. Doubtless, the liquidity problems which have faced many companies in the recession have given an added emphasis to the apparent effectiveness of payback as an evaluating device. Such a policy, used in isolation, would be unwise: industry's liquidity problems have arisen from many factors such as

Trade recession.
High costs of operation coupled with controls on selling prices.
Bad capital investment in the past.

---

*The reader will have noticed that comparisons of *profit* with investment cost are not being made in these appraisals of the worth of capital expenditure proposals. In earlier chapters the impact of asset valuation upon profit calculation has been examined, and the potential distortion of the profit figure has been clearly shown. In capital investment analysis we must compare like with like – cash going out upon payment of investment cost is compared with the cash flow return resulting from the operation of the investment. To refresh the mind upon cash flow, it would be useful to refer to pages 99–104.

We cannot expect that the adoption of payback as a criterion will solve industry's present cash shortages or avoid future similar crises.

However, payback can be used as an initial screening device in a comprehensive programme for evaluating large cash spendings, such as capital goods purchases. In this situation a maximum payback would be specified as a first requirement for all capital expenditure proposals to satisfy before passing on to more stringent tests. The payback screening device is widely used in industry: it may seem a shortsighted policy to adopt when we should be appraising all of the expected-life factors of an investment proposal, not just the first 2 or 3 years' cash flows only. Yet we cannot dismiss the demands of immediate-cash-flow management, and in the short period some firms may well be compelled to an acceptance of payback, in selecting their projects for approval. In this case, a realistic method of establishing a maximum payback index has to be examined. Many firms have ruled that the required payback period should not exceed a half or a third of the project's expected economic life.

Decisions such as these do not appear to have been scientifically calculated however. But such an index (half or third of life) does envisage the allowance of a substantial margin for error. After all, payback does indicate a kind of 'risk period' for the funds invested, i.e. the time during which at least some of the funds invested will remain unrecovered. On the other hand it can be shown that, with uniform net cash flows from year to year, a maximum payback of two-thirds of the expected economic life will give a satisfactory rate of return from the project provided

1   The life expectation is achieved in practice.
2   The life expectation does not exceed 12 years.

Rates of return on book cost

There are several expressions of the simple rate of return method of investment evaluation. When formulating this rate of return index therefore, it is necessary to be precise in the descriptions of the data to be used in the evaluation. The ratio or percentage of return figure which is intended to be a demonstration of an investment's profitability should be used consistently to enable effective comparison of alternative proposals to be made. That the rate of return should also indicate a preferential ranking of those alternatives is also desirable. Now the simple criteria are to be criticised for ignoring the importance of the yearly flow of cash receipts. In general, early replenishment of investment outgoings is to be preferred to a later recoupment, if only because it may enable advantage to be taken of possible opportunities for re-investment. In favour of the various returns on book cost is the fact that a projection of earnings *over investment* life should be calculated,* whereas payback is concerned with those years of life up to the time of capital cost replenishment only. Simple book rates of return are as easy to calculate as payback: they are equally popular because of this, but their effectiveness in locating the profitable investment, in presenting a ranking of investments in order of profitability, is dubious.

Return per £ invested

This variant of ROR (rate of return) gives a desirability index by dividing the cost of the investment into the total net cash flows. The resulting factor, while ignoring the time period of the receipts, purports to give a measure of investment assessment. Lack of consideration for the timing of the proceeds is however a major fault in this measure of investment worth. Applying the return per £ invested criterion to the investments shown in Exhibit 106 will produce the indexes of investment worth shown in Exhibit 107. By this method also each of the proposed capital spendings appear to be of equal worth. Yet the analyst must wonder how this can be so, especially when project B returns 66.7 per cent of its capital cost in *the first year of its life*.

Exhibit 107

Evaluation of investments by return per £ invested

Details	Project A	Project B	Project C
Total cash flows	£6,000	£9,000	£12,000
Investment cost	£5,000	£7,500	£10,000
Desirability index	1.2	1.2	1.2

Average annual income per £ invested

Here an assessment is made by calculating the annual average of the total net cash flows and dividing that sum by the initial cost of the investment. *Some* credit must be given to these evaluating criteria because they are concerned with the whole life of the project. Applying this method to the proposals in Exhibit 106 demonstrates desirability indexes for each of the proposals (see Exhibit 108). Similar doubts (to those already quoted for payback and return per £ invested) arise concerning the acceptability of this criterion as an indicator of investment worth. Each project still has a common appraisal of desirability.

*My examination of business practices has shown that many companies express the first full year's net receipts *only* as a percentage of capital investment cost. This may be acceptable if the yearly gains from the investment are expected to be constant. In other cases forecasts are made for the first 4 years of a project's (say) 20-year life: the years 5–20 are then just a repetitive extension of the expectations of the 4th year. Much of this short-cut policy stems from a lack of experience and/or lack of confidence in practical long-term planning – *L.E.R.*

Exhibit 108

Evaluation of investments by average annual income per £
invested

Details	Project A	Project B	Project C
Total cash flows	£6,000	£9,000	£12,000
Average per year	£2,000	£3,000	£4,000
Investment cost	£5,000	£7,500	£10,000
Desirability index	0.4	0.4	0.4

Average annual income as a percentage of the book value of investment

There are numerous variants of this measure of return: the average annual income may be calculated before or after depreciation, before or after tax, for example. Such inconsistencies reflect the lack of uniformity of many expressions used in accounting, for the 'book rates of return' are based upon accounting concepts and accounting statements. For the purposes of this publication, however, it is intended to use the term 'income' to indicate profit after depreciation charges have been levied. Now after the average annual income has been determined, the resultant sum is then expressed as a percentage of the capital investment cost as shown in Exhibit 109.

A further variant of this rate of return is introduced by presenting the average annual income as a percentage of the *average* book value of the capital asset. Average book value (on straight-line depreciation) means one half of the original cost. The result upon the rate of return index is simply to double the percentages shown in Exhibit 109. Thus again it must be emphasised that consistency of treatment of the data in calculating the rate of return is of prime importance. Book rates of return are widely used in

Exhibit 109

Evaluation of investments by average annual income expressed as a percentage of
investment book value

Project	Average income	Depre- ciation*	Net income	Invest- ment cost	Percentage return index
A	£2,000	£1,667	£333	£5,000	6.7
B	£3,000	£2,500	£500	£7,500	6.7
C	£4,000	£3,333	£667	£10,000	6.7

*Straight-line depreciation

view of their simplicity. The major criticism to be directed against their operation is once more the lack of consideration given to the timing of the proceeds of innovation.

Discounted cash flow method (DCF)

Several methods of capital expenditure evaluation have now been presented. Each one has the fundamental drawback of its complete lack of consideration for the timing of cash returns. Furthermore in the hypothetical projects given in the above tables, none of the criteria so far examined has been able to present a positive tool of choice to the investor. In every instance the previously studied measures of return give identical assessments to the several projects. What is required therefore is some positive indicator of desirability, some rating index which can be regarded as a reliable guide for the analysis of investment worth. In this context investment worth will be taken to apply to proposals where profitability can be measured and is furthermore the desirable objective.

(Some investment proposals may be undertaken in order to improve welfare and medical facilities for the company's employees. Assessing the profitability of this type of capital expenditure is practically impossible. Again, all proposed capital investment must be considered in the light of the company's business objectives. It may be that the policy maker's plans are being directed to the achievement of a certain growth in sales, or growth in the asset value of the company. In such circumstances there could be occasions where *profitable* investment opportunities would not satisfy the objectives set out in the corporate long-term plan: these proposals, though profitable, might well be rejected where the firm's directing managers considered the long-term strategy to be of greater importance than short-term profitability.)

Time-adjusted rates of return give emphasis to the incidence of cash returns in each year of a proposed investment's expected economic life. The emphasis is given by applying, to the forecast returns, an interest discounting factor which has the effect of levying a rate of interest *charge* on each year's budgeted cash receipts. This charge reduces, i.e. discounts, the cash flows of the future years to an amount which represents their worth at the present time. The investor is then able to compare the cost today of the proposed capital expenditure, with the evaluation – also in present day terms – of the related future cash receipts. Like is being compared with like and the assessment becomes more meaningful.*

There are three forms of time-adjusted return, which are finding increasing acceptance for the evaluation of industrial capital expenditure.

*The different worths attributed here to £1 today and £1 at a specified future time is a function of the rate of interest. This function, which is fully explained in Appendix C, has *nothing* to do with prices rising in the future because of a monetary inflation.

The three DCF return indexes are:

1 The yield method.
2 The net present value method.
3 The annual value method.

Before studying the impacts of these time-adjusted rates of return upon the assessment of the projects shown in Exhibits 106–109, it is advisable that the simple mathematics of discounting and compounding are understood. For this purpose the reader is referred to Appendix C, 'Discounting Techniques Explained'.

The yield method
The object of the yield method of investment appraisal is to ascertain the rate of interest which, when applied to the future cash flows, will reduce, i.e. discount, their monetary size until, in total, they are equal to the initial cost of the investment. Frequently referred to as the internal rate of return or the marginal efficiency of capital, yield presents a percentage rating which can be used as a tool of choice by the investment analyst; it answers the question – 'What rate of interest could the company pay to finance the project yet still enable the investment to break even?'

The following calculations demonstrate applications of the DCF yield technique. Exhibit 110 deals with the cash flows of project A.

The present value (PV) of the cash flows is obtained by multiplying each year's cash flow sum by its appropriate discount factor. At a rate of 10 per cent the aggregate PV of the future cash flows is £5,047. Clearly the discount, i.e. interest, rate is not big enough to bring the future flows' PV to equality with the initial outlay cost of the project. At the higher rate of 15 per cent, the total PV of the future flows is £4,666. Here the higher rate is too

Exhibit 110
DCF yield evaluation of Project A

Year	Cash flows	10% Discount factor*	PV of cash flows (2) × (3)	15% Discount factor*	PV of cash flows (2) × (5)
(1)	(2)	(3)	(4)	(5)	(6)
	£		£		£
1	2,000	0.909	1,818	0.870	1,740
2	3,000	0.826	2,478	0.756	2,268
3	1,000	0.751	751	0.658	658
Total	6,000		5,047		4,666

*See interest tables in Appendix D for factors used

269

great for the project to bear (the total PV of the future cash flows is LESS than the initial outlay costs of the project). Therefore the correct yield percentage for project A must lie between 10 and 15 per cent. Linear interpolation will show the correct yield to be 10.6 per cent: the relevant calculations are given below:

		£
(1) Present value of future cash flows at 10%		5,047
at 15%		4,666
Difference		£381
(2) Present value of future cash flows at 10%		5,047
Initial outlay costs		5,000
Difference		£47

The next stage involves dividing the difference at (2) above by the difference at (1) above. When the resulting fraction is multiplied by the interest gap of 5 per cent (15−10 per cent) we arrive at the additional percentage sum to be added to 10 per cent, to raise that percentage figure to the correct yield:

$$\frac{47}{381} \times \frac{5}{100} = 0.0061 = 0.61\%$$

$$= 0.61\% + 10\% = 10.61\% \text{ yield}$$

If the reader utilises similar arithmetical processes for B and C he will find that their DCF yield ratings are 12.3 and 11.9 per cent, respectively. The first of the discounting criteria thus says that – from the standpoint of profitability –project B is better than C which is better than A.

The net present value method
This method shows the monetary difference between the original cost, and the total future cash flows when they are *discounted at a specific percentage rate*. On the other hand yield seeks the rate of interest which will discount the future cash flows until they equal capital costs; it does not therefore specify the rate for discounting. Once the yield rate is found it can be used as an indicator of investment worth. The decision-maker would be prepared to accept proposals where yield is above a certain minimum rate which he considers may have to be paid in order to raise finance for the

270

project. Now net present value (NPV) specifies in advance a minimum percentage interest factor at which the future cash flows must be discounted. Then the difference between the capital cost and the total discounted sum of the future cash flows is termed the net present value. If this sum is positive the investment is *prima facie* acceptable; if the net present value calculated in this way is negative, the investment should be rejected. The present value of project A is given in Exhibit 110 as £5,047, using an interest factor of 10 per cent. Subtracting the capital cost £5,000, the *net* present value of the investment is £47, at a 10 per cent cost of financing.

Comparisons of yield and net present value
In the same way we can ascertain that the net present values of projects B and C are £236.5 and £260, respectively. Now the above two time-adjusted rates of return give ratings which have brought to account the time distributions of the future cash flows of each project. But the two methods of appraisal do not appear to agree on the order of preference – the ranking – to be accorded to the several investment opportunities. This is not an unusual result in the comparisons of yield and NPV for a group of investment projects. Before passing final judgement on the evaluations, however, we should consider the widely varying capital costs of the three projects. Clearly a more expensive project, or one having a longer life, *ought* to generate a higher NPV. In our three examples the expected future life of each project is the same as the other two. Therefore if the NPVs are expressed as a percentage of the related capital cost, we shall obtain a more realistic indication of each project's powers to create additional wealth. Project A's profitability index is calculated as follows:

$$\text{Project A} \quad \frac{47 \times 100}{5,000} = 0.94\%$$

The percentage ratings of B and C are 3.15 and 2.6 per cent respectively, and the order of preference is the same as that recommended by the yield method. Where projects have varying lives, then the NPV should be expressed per year of project life as shown below for project A:

$$\frac{47/3}{5,000} \times 100 = \frac{15.6}{5,000} \times 100$$
$$= 0.312\%$$

Thus the annual rate at which the project generates corporate wealth (the

NPV) is, in simple average terms, 0.31 per cent. Project B has an annual rate of 1.05 per cent and C has a rate of 0.87 per cent. Again the order of preference for project choice is the same as that indicated by the yield percentages.

Both yield and net present value are sound measures to employ when seeking a 'yes' or 'no' answer to the question of whether to invest or not. But where the problem arises of which (of several) investments to undertake, the profitability ranking order may well be a decisive factor in the decision. The ranking of projects in order of their desirability is wanted especially in those instances where a company has a limited supply of funds but a goodly supply of investment needs and ideas. Now discounted rates of return just compare input (cost of all capital resource use caused by the investment) with output (cash earnings). It is essential, *after this comparison has been made*, that the calculated return index should be related to the cost of capital financing. Net present value does this automatically where the discount rate chosen is in fact the investor's cost of capital. It has been noted (see above) that where the net present value is positive, i.e. gives a gain in excess of the financing cost, the project may be accepted (subject to any other limitations imposed by corporate objectives).

On the other hand the yield percentage arises as a result of averaging the returns implicit in the cash flows of each of a series of years. The percentage index has then to be compared with the cost of financing and if the yield is *above* the cost of financing, the project may be accepted. So, whilst the yield method demonstrates a percentage *rate of growth*, net present value reveals an absolute *quantity* of growth in money terms. This latter measure indicates the extent of the growth in wealth which would accrue to the firm if the related investment is undertaken. Furthermore where the firm has several investment opportunities open to its choosing, the sum of the NPVs of the investments selected will indicate the probable total increase in corporate wealth resulting from that selection. This assumes that the capital expenditure proposals have equal risks, or that each NPV has been determined after an analysis of the inherent risks and uncertainties. No such conclusion could be drawn from an aggregation of yield percentages, each of which would simply reveal the rate of interest at which the relevant investment could be financed without incurring a loss or making a gain.* Yield is the break-even cost of capital rate for the investment.

Finally to complete a brief comparison of these two methods of appraisal, it must be pointed out that assessment of yield index can produce somewhat disturbing results. Certain combinations of cash flows will give forth no yield result at all. Another series will present *two* measures of return. Whilst these results stem from the mathematical relationships involved in the

*The situation is best expressed by imagining that the investment is financed by a loan *from the company* to the investing department. The earnings from the project must then repay principal and interest to the company before being able to contribute to corporate profits.

calculations, they do not give comfort in the practical situation where it is necessary to make a choice between various available projects. Several writers point out* how the problem, presented by two rates, may be overcome: they also assert that the conditions which give rise to uncommon results (two rates of return for one project) are themselves uncommon. The reader is encouraged to study the methods suggested for rationalising the apparent paradox of double rates of return. However the fact remains that such results can happen: the measures to be taken to solve the problem present further complications to the unsophisticated user of indexes of investment worth. For these and other reasons the writer's preference rests on the use of net present value for evaluation of investment worth. This statement should not be regarded as a recommendation to be applied on all occasions, however, and it will be necessary to return to this problem in a later chapter. For the moment it must be re-emphasised that corporate long-term planning and/or short-term liquidity will certainly affect some capital spending decisions. It could be that two or more indexes of worth should be used to obtain a *comprehensive* view of any single investment. Here the decision-maker might use a liquidity index (payback), a growth index (net present value) and a long-term earnings rate (yield).

Discounted payback
Before studying the third DCF criterion – the annual value method – we will return to the payback index to see how the application of discounting techniques will result in more meaningful payback indexes for ranking investment projects. Make no mistake, PB still has its disadvantages in that the PB appraisal method does not consider the whole of the forecast life of an investment proposal. However the method has some uses – as a measure of the risk period, and as a primary screening device at the first stage of a comprehensive evaluation programme.

In Exhibit 106 (page 263) three projects were given identical PB measures of worth. These results were obtained despite the markedly uneven patterns of cash inflows expected from the proposed investments. Now in order to arrive at a discounted PB we have to determine the discount rate to be used in the calculations. If we assume that the company has to bear a net 7 per cent interest charge in order to obtain the capital money to finance the projects A, B and C, we can use this percentage rate as the discount rate in the refined PB index.

Now the simple payback version shown in Exhibit 106 used the absolute values of the yearly cash inflows, in calculating the PB index for each project. In this more realistic appraisal we shall use the *discounted* values for the future cash flows, in order to calculate the payback period. The

*MERRETT, A.J., and SYKES, A., *The Finance and Analysis of Capital Projects*, Longmans (1963).

Exhibit 111
Discounted payback – Project A

Year	Net cash flows £	7% Discount factor	PV of net cash flows £
1	2,000	0.935	1,870
2	3,000	0.873	2,619
3	1,000	0.816	816
TOTAL	£6,000		£5,305

paybacks given in Exhibit 106 were 2 years for each project, but when each year's cash flows are reduced in numerical size (through the discounting process), then clearly the project payback periods must be longer. Exhibit 111 shows that the summation of discounted cash flows for years 1 and 2, gives a figure of £4,489. In order to recoup the whole of the initial outlay cost therefore, the project needs £511 from the year 3 amount of £816. On the assumption that each year's cash flows are evenly distributed throughout the year, a discounted payback of £5,000 will be achieved when 0.63 of the third has elapsed, i.e. 511/816 = 0.63. Thus the discounted payback of A is 2.63 years and those of B and C are 2.52 and 2.55 years, respectively.

All that we have done in our revised PB index is to take account of the cost of the money involved in the initial investment outlay. Therefore we do *not* specify the new PB as a rate of return measure. This function is reserved for criteria such as DCF yield or NPV. A payback rating should not be used to rank projects in an order preference where profitability is the principal aim. PB is a liquidity measure. As such the discounted version will give a more practical view of the payback period.

Annual value method
Whilst the writer's clear preference for net present value as a criterion of investment worth has been stated, the picture of indexes of worth would not be complete without a study of the annual value (AV) method of appraisal. Nearly all the discussions surrounding the appraisal of capital expenditures refer to the assessment of proposals as projects. The constituents of the proposals are frequently overlooked so it must be pointed out that most investment opportunities involve the purchase and use of assets. Many proposals consist of a mixture of different types of assets such as land,

buildings, machinery equipment and vehicles. Now whilst the project may have an extensive life, the assets themselves will have economic operational lives different from the proposal life. Machinery, plant and vehicles would need to be replaced during the life of the proposed investment project. Therefore the annual value calculations are based upon the initial outlay costs, or replacement costs, of the separate assets which form part of the whole project. This evaluative principle is regarded as a major improvement in investment analysis. However other discounting criteria produce project ratings which have brought to account the various cost and benefit impacts of the several assets involved. So we are not dealing with a new concept at all. It is just that the annual value method presents data in a different way. AV shows both the initial outlay costs and the related net cash flows as uniform annual sums. If the annual value of the expected earnings is greater than the project's annual cost, the investment would therefore be worth considering, as shown below:

Constituents of Annual Value

---

1 The annualised value of the expected earnings, i.e. an averaged per annum value of the NCFs forecast for project life

less

2 The annualised total cost of the project, i.e. the annual capital charge necessary to finance the project

equals

3 The annual value of the proposed investment, i.e. the value of the investment to the firm, expressed as an annuity

---

Now in order to ascertain annualised or annuity values of item 2, AV uses the accountant's sinking fund. The sinking fund is a concept which shows how much would have to be set aside each year, at a specified rate of interest, in order to accumulate sufficient funds

1　For the replacement of a fixed asset at a specified future date.
　or
2　For the discharge of a debt, e.g. a debenture, at a specified future date.

No new complicated arithmetical calculations are necessary: sinking fund tables are available in just the same way as the discount tables given in Appendix D. All we need to know in determining the annuity sum is the ultimate size of the sinking fund, the period during which it will operate and the rate at which the interest contributions to the fund are expected to grow. The following example will demonstrate the method's application.

275

Example

A project costing £15,000 has the following cash flows over its expected life of 5 years:

Year	1	2	3	4	5
£	3,000	2,000	5,000	6,000	7,000

The cost of capital to the company is 10 per cent per annum.

The first stage in the analysis must be to express the initial outlay costs as an annualised cost or annual capital charge. Here AV charges interest on the total capital outlay plus the annual cost of amortisation, i.e. renewal or depreciation charge, in respect of the project assets.

The total of £3,957 given in Exhibit 112 quantifies the annuity which an investor would receive from investing £15,000 for five years at 10 per cent per annum. At the end of the five years the whole of the initial fund of £15,000 and its interest receipts would be extinguished. It is calculated in the following way:

Annual Capital Charge = Initial outlay cost × Sinking fund factor

Exhibit 112
Calculation of the annual capital charge: I

Investment Cost £15,000

	£
Depreciation or Amortisation £15,000 at £0.1638 per £	2,457
Interest £15,000 at 10 per cent per annum	1,500
ANNUAL CAPITAL CHARGE (ACC)	£3,957

The sinking fund factor can be found by taking the reciprocal of the 10 per cent discount factor (the rate used will vary according to the cost of capital of the firm involved) for a series of years ending at year 5:

$$\frac{1}{3.7908} = 0.2638$$

Therefore ACC = £15,000 × 0.2638

= £3,957

Clearly in allocating the whole of the annual capital charge between the two constituents of the annualised cost, 10 per cent must be regarded as the interest charge, as this is the firm's cost of capital. Therefore the proportion of the sinking fund relating to depreciation of the project asset will be

$$£15,000 \times (0.2638 - 0.1) = £15,000 \times 0.1638$$

$$= £2,457$$

Annualising cash flows

Now in the context of investment appraisal the £3,957 is termed the annual capital charge, a description which relates to the spreading of the initial cost plus interest charges, over the economic life of the project. (Similarly to straight-line depreciation, the annual capital charge is a notional sum: it does not represent a specific capital payment.) Here the AV project appraisal process next requires that the annual capital charge be compared with the project's cash flows. But in most practical business circumstances the year by year variations in cash flows would make such a comparison meaningless. Therefore the future cash flows have to be annualised also and we return to the NCF's of the above example to show the nature of the problem (see Exhibit 113).

Exhibit 113
Project net cash flows

Year	Net cash flows, £	10% Discount factor	PV of cash flows, £
1	3,000	0.9091	2,727.3
2	2,000	0.8264	1,652.8
3	5,000	0.7513	3,756.5
4	6,000	0.6830	4,098.0
5	7,000	0.6209	4,346.3
TOTALS	£23,000	3.7907	£16,580.9

We can represent the annualised value of the above cash flows as a simple arithmetical average, thus

$$£ \frac{23,000}{5} = £4,600$$

or, more satisfactorily, as a weighted, i.e. discounted, average

$$£ \frac{16,580.9}{3.7907} = £4,374$$

and immediately we face a major problem which is involved in applying the principles of AV to investment choice where competing projects have differing patterns of cash inflows. Depending upon our version of the annualised cash flow sum, its comparison with the annual capital charge given in Exhibit 112 will determine the AV of the project (see Exhibit 114).

Exhibit 114
Project annual value

Details	Simple average £	Weighted average £
Annualised cash flows	4,600	4,374
Annual capital charge	3,957	3,957
ANNUAL VALUE	£643	£417

Investment 'chains'

Where the decision-maker is faced with having to choose from a list of investment proposals, each of which has a different expected economic life, the problem is compounded. In these circumstances it is suggested that effective comparisons can be made only if the projects are regarded as potential investments into perpetuity – the same investment is repeated, at each life end, for ever. For AV purposes this means that the cash flows must be annualised on a perpetuity basis. AV achieves this aim by assuming that the last year's cash flows are repeated onwards into perpetuity. This is a most unsatisfactory process for the perpetuity annual value of the cash flows would be greatly influenced by their *trend* as forecast for the investment actually proposed.

The cash flows expected in the fifth year of our project example are £7,000 and the trend portrays a rising one. Projecting this sum into perpetuity results in £7,000 × 6.8301* = £47,810.7 and the discounted average of the project's cash inflows would be

$$£\ \frac{60,045}{9.999} = {}^{!}£6,005$$

Clearly the discounted annual average, and thus the annual value, would be markedly different if the trend of cash flows had been reversed, with the fifth year accruing £3,000 only!

*Ascertained from the PV of a £ per year in perpetuity, e.g. the reciprocal of 10 per cent, less the present value of a pound a year for 4 years (= 10 − 3.1699 = 6.8301).

Annual capital charge from mix of assets

A better view of the annual capital charge will be achieved if we assume that our £15,000 project consists of the following assets:

1 A machine with a 20-year life, costing £10,000.
2 Equipment with a 5-year life, costing £5,000.

If we use the initial outlay cost of these assets in our calculations the annual capital charge will be as shown in Exhibit 115.

Exhibit 115
Calculation of the annual capital charge: II

	£
Investment Cost £15,000	
Depreciation or amortisation	
Machine: £10,000 at £0.0175* per £	175
Equipment: £5,000 at £0.1638 per £	819
Interest	
£15,000 at 10 per cent per annum	1,500
ANNUAL CAPITAL CHARGE	£2,494

*The sinking fund calculation for the machine is:

Reciprocal of PV of £ p.a. for 20 years at 10 per cent	= 0.1175
Less the interest factor at 10 per cent	0.1000
Sinking fund factor	0.0175

In the stated project the expected life of the investment is five years so no asset replacement in this period is expected. Nevertheless we ought to take the *net* cost of the machine in the 5-year life of the investment, not its full cost. Furthermore where the project life embraces a period during which assets would be replaced, it is suggested that the depreciation sums should be based upon the replacement cost. The proponents of AV put this forward as a major analytical benefit of the AV method. However if there are several replacements of a particular asset within a project life, they do not state which of the several replacement costs should be used. NPV can deal with a string of asset replacements, in its cash flow analyses, and can therefore present a wholly better appraisal index.

Self-examination questions

1 Explain the meaning and relevance for investment appraisal of the following terms:
   (*a*)   incremental costs
   (*b*)   incremental incomes
   (*c*)   net present value
   (*d*)   yield
   (*e*)   payback and discounted payback.

2 Which investment appraisal criteria are most likely to appeal to corporate investors in
   (*a*)   a recession
   (*b*)   a period of trade expansion
   (*c*)   evaluating non-cash flow projects?

3 What would be the Equal Annual Charge (Annual Capital Charge) of a project costing £10,000, with a life expectancy of 10 years, if the cost of capital was 20 per cent?

4 Compare and contrast the implications of a specified yield percentage with a net present value sum. Does NPV have any advantages over DCF yield?

5 In what way does the 'return' in return on capital employed differ from the 'return' (NCF) used in a time adjusted yield calculation?

6 Does the annualising of project cash flows offer a viable means of comparing those cash flows with an Annual Capital Charge based upon the project's initial outlay costs?

Recommended reading

ROCKLEY, L. E., *Capital Investment Decisions*, Business Books (1968).

FIRTH, M., *Investment Analysis*, Harper and Row (1975), see chapter 10.

YEATS, A., et al., *Financial Tables*, Stanley Thornes (1978).

WATTS, B. K. R., *Business and Financial Management*, Macdonald and Evans (1978), see chapter 12.

HINGLEY, W., and OSBORN, F., *Financial Management*, W. H. Allen (1978), see chapter 3.

14 The cost of capital

Introduction

The examination of time-adjusted rates of return and net present values in the previous chapter has been presented as a means of indicating those investments which could be accepted where acceptance implied their being judged from the point of view of profitability. Profitability was measured by a yield of a certain percentage – a rate of return above the minimum requirement laid down by the company's planners. Similarly a positive net present value, when calculated by using a minimum rate of discount, revealed a desirable project whereas a negative net present value showed a project which should be rejected. However, it must be pointed out that to judge proposed capital investments *solely* upon their profitability *rate* is to take a narrow view of corporate development. All investment proposals must be considered in the light of long-term strategic plans for the firm's progress, its future markets and future products. This topic will be discussed in later chapters. It is mentioned here to ensure that the reader does not attribute to the index of choice more than its own intrinsic value. A rate of return is a part only of the whole concept of capital expenditure planning.

The supply of capital

Thus we come to the determination of a minimum cut-off rate for DCF yield or a minimum discounting percentage to be used in NPV, AV and discounted PB calculations. It is here that we are concerned with what is called the cost of capital. Now a company has many sources of finance; it can, for example:

1 Borrow from the bank.
2 Issue debentures.
3 Increase trade creditors (delay payments).

4   Sell assets.
5   Issue more Ordinary shares. And/or
6   Use funds generated by profitable operations.

Each of these sources of money can have a different cost. That cost may also change with time, according to the stability or instability of the economy or of trade. Some of the above types of finance have a well defined cost. A loan or overdraft from the bank will carry an interest charge which is fixed having regard, amongst other things, to the current level of the Minimum Lending Rate. Again the level of debenture interest will be affected by the current market rate for long-term loans whilst funds obtained from profitable operations have a lower cost than that of a new issue of shares. These comments indicate that there could be a wildly fluctuating cost of capital over a period of years. On the other hand the cost could well vary even within a short period of *one* year, where it was considered that different investments were being financed by specific allocations of these different types of capital. Nevertheless it is reasonable to suggest that the whole of the corporate financial base should be deemed to be available for each branch of the corporate activities. Thus with certain exceptions the definition of the cost of capital must rest upon some average rate which takes into account the differing costs of the major groups of capital finance.

Before examining the concept of an average cost of capital, two items need to be settled. They are:

1   What is the 'cost' of Ordinary shares?
2   What mix of the total capital supply ought to be used in the calculation?

The cost of Ordinary shares is the reward which must be provided to the Ordinary shareholder to induce him to buy those shares. It has been shown* that over the period 1919 to 1966 shareholders would have received a discounted rate of return post-tax of about 6 per cent from a continuous annual investment during this period.

If the shareholder had invested a lump sum then his discounted rate of return would have been about 8 per cent. Furthermore, throughout the period 1919 to 1966 the Ordinary shareholder's real return, for 75 per cent of the 10 year cycles, was 7 per cent per annum both for the continuous investment and the lump sum investment. The question which begs an answer is whether this kind of performance can be expected to continue. Opinion used to favour the continuance of an 8 per cent *real return post-tax* to shareholders for the forthcoming 10 to 20 years.

However public policies in regard to taxation, dividend restriction and price controls will vary with different governments, and thus may well affect

*MERRETT, A. J., and SYKES, A., 'Return on equities and fixed interest securities, 1919–1963', *District Bank Review* (December 1963). See also *Capital Budgeting and Company Finance* by the same authors, published by Longmans, (1966).

the overall return from long term investment. Moreover the rates of inflation experienced during a project's life can reduce a forecast positive return to a negative real return. Clearly, the problem of forecasting the investor's return is a difficult one, but equally clearly it is the *long-term* expectations of shareholder returns which must be the deciding factor. During the coming years, financial managers will need to watch the general movements of share prices and dividends in order to test the maintenance of shareholder expectations of reward from investment in business activities. Here we have to remember that the Ordinary shareholder's reward is made up of two elements, namely the dividend yield plus a capital growth in terms of an increasing share price. It is this combined return requirement which must be met by the user of subscribed share capital (the company). The better the investing public is served in this way, the easier it will be to raise further capital for future corporate developments. A capital asset investment cut-off rate therefore needs to be set at that level which will ensure a corporate earning power which is capable of sustaining the Ordinary shareholders' expectation of a long-term real return of around 6 to 8 per cent after tax. That is the problem which bedevils the low investment policies of UK industry: until it is recognised that business investment in fixed assets must be given the opportunity of a satisfactory return for risk-taking, the corporate investment profiles will remain low.

Two relatively simple methods of establishing a corporate cost of capital have been put forward by various writers. Both methods demonstrate an immediate concern with current post-tax profits and their expected growth in the future. The first example is expressed by

Dividend yield + Rate of dividend growth in future

Now in the context of a corporate dividend policy, the rate of growth of dividends must depend on the rate of growth of post-tax profits. Therefore we are recognising the relevance, for the cost of capital, of a firm's own profit expectations. We can relate a rate of profit growth to a rate of dividend growth, and conversely an *expected* rate of dividend growth to a *required* rate of profit growth. The *Financial Times* daily index reports the dividend yields of industrial groups and we can use this in an example:

Cost of capital = FT index dividend yield + Expected rate of growth in dividends

= 6.5% + 10%

= 16.5% cost of capital post-tax

but we have to remember that the shareholder is interested in the *long-term* yield to his investment.

The second of the two methods consists merely of taking the earnings yield of the firm's shares as its cost of capital. It is important to recognise that both systems are greatly influenced by the market price for the relevant shares. Where dividends and earnings per share are relatively static, it could be that the share price would fall relative to the market as a whole. In this event the cost of capital, as defined above, would rise, thus reflecting the investing public's opinion of a higher risk attending the investment in such shares.

Financing structures

But Ordinary shares do not constitute the whole of a firm's capital supply. Neither do they form the largest element in the total capital structure of companies. Retained earnings, long- and short-term debts such as debentures, bank loans and overdrafts, also play a large part in financing business development. Each of these will have a different cost and it is the proportions of these different costs, as parts of the whole capital supply, which need to be considered. A company's long-term capital structure will change from year to year if only from the growth in retained earnings resulting from each succeeding year's profitable operations.

Furthermore it will be necessary for the company to take up additional permanent capital or long-term loans from time to time because its business growth demands further injections of liquid funds in excess of the cash generated by trading operations. Such expansions of capital finance are rarely effected by the issue of several kinds of share or debt certificates at the same time. A company's financial structure will change by periodic issues of different kinds of long-term capital. Thus the corporate capital structure is not made up of precisely the same proportions of each type of finance in each year. The long-term trend may well present an average picture. Whilst this average picture will vary from trade to trade because of the ability of some businesses to raise a greater proportion of loan money,* the concept of a normal capital structure for an individual company is not unreasonable. The question that arises therefore is whether the cost of capital should be calculated having regard to the *long-term* intentions of the firm's planners for corporate financing.

Before this question is answered the impact of the various forms of capital upon the whole corporate capital cost must be considered. So long as

---

*'Firms with relatively low risk can afford to secure much, if not most, of their total capital requirements from creditors .... Firms with higher relative variance in expected earnings must have larger equity contributions. Thus business firms as a group average about 65 per cent equity ....' ARCHER, S. H., and D'AMBROSIO, C. A., *Business Finance: Theory and Management*, p521, Collier-MacMillan (1966).

The reader should also consider the availability of capital assets for mortgaging as security for debt issues. See BIERMAN, H., and SMIDT, S., *The Capital Budgeting Decision*, pp165–8, Collier-MacMillan (1966).

dividends are paid to the shareholder net of tax, then undistributed profits (retained earnings) will constitute a cheaper form of equity money than new issues of shares. This arises because an investor who invests in a new share issue does so out of income which has suffered a tax charge of so much in the £. Retained earnings do not have to bear this further imposition. For example if an investor wishes to buy £1,000 of shares in a company which is going to use the money for capital expansion, the cost of these shares to the Ordinary share investor would be £1,000 of his income *after tax*. If, however, the ordinary shareholder provides this finance by going without dividends, or by receiving lower dividends, the capital expansion will be financed from retained earnings. In this case the cost to the shareholder will be the £1,000 left with the company LESS the tax he would have suffered on the £1,000 if it had been distributed as dividend. With a standard tax rate of 30p in the £, the shareholder would have been surrendering a net receipt of £700, i.e. £1,000 less 30p in the £, in order to enable the company to invest £1,000 in corporate expansions.

On the other hand if retained earnings are not used for the proposed capital development, then the shareholder would have to receive £1,428.57 in order to invest, after 30 per cent tax deduction, £1,000 in the company's shares. For this reason retained earnings are able to generate the required 8 per cent return for the company's Ordinary shareholders, even though the return demanded from the employment of retained earnings is set lower than that required from the employment of new issue money. Nevertheless it is suggested that it is the duty of company managements to secure as high a return from retained earnings as from subscribed ordinaries. In this case the company is considered to be investing on behalf of the shareholder who could have invested his £700 with some other high yielding project. However the gap between the potential returns to £1,000 in the hands of the company and £700 in the hands of the shareholder is large: a 20 per cent return achieved by the company's £1,000 would need the shareholder to achieve 29 per cent on his £700 in order to break-even.

In the cost of a capital mix, we must also consider the use of fixed interest loan capital. Now the cost of borrowing money has risen considerably in recent years due both to inflation and to a greater preference by investment managers for fixed interest stocks rather than low yielding UK industrial equities.* Even so we have to consider the costs of capital over the medium to long term and it may be considered that the gross interest costs of loan

*' ... since 1959 fears of inflation and expectations of continued full employment have led to the *reverse yield gap* ... dividend yields on equities have been lower than the yields of fixed interest securities ... for most investors the opportunity cost of an investment in an equity portfolio is the return that could have been earned by investing the same sum at fixed interest .... In the long run investors will look for higher average returns at constant prices and after tax, on equities than on relatively riskless fixed interest securities.' CARR, J. I., *Investment Economics*, pp47–8, Routledge and Kegan Paul (1969).

financing over such periods will be about 10 per cent. But interest on debt is a cost which is charged in the profit and loss account before profit is determined. So while dividends are paid out of *taxed* profits, loan interest is a cost allowed *before the tax on those profits is assessed*. The net cost of a 10 per cent loan interest charged to a company is therefore 10 per cent, less the tax rate levied on company profits. With a 52 per cent Corporation tax this gives a net-of-tax cost, for such an interest charge, of 4.8 per cent. Each of the above features impact upon the return a company must seek from its investments. Therefore these factors must be taken into account when considering what is termed 'the weighted average cost of capital'. This concept will now be examined by the calculation of a weighted average cost of capital for a hypothetical company.

Weighted (average) cost of capital

For the purpose of a cost of capital assessment, it is necessary to postulate a long-term capital structure, so that the cost of each type of capital can be given its due influence in calculating the cost of the whole. The assumed capital structure for use in the following examples will be

Ordinary shares, 30 per cent.
Reserves, 50 per cent.
Debentures, 20 per cent.

Ordinary shares

Several factors affect the rate to be earned on this type of capital. Firstly the costs of issue of the shares for a good 'blue chip' share will be around 3 per cent of the issue price; in other cases the issue costs will be much higher. Therefore the share proceeds actually received and employed by the company must gain a return capable of satisfying the *whole* subscription, not just the 97 per cent which is received by the firm after deduction of issue costs. Furthermore, because dividends payable to shareholders are subjected to a further tax deduction, companies must justify new share issues by earning a return thereon higher than that demanded of retained earnings. This higher rate required of Ordinary shares brings the Ordinary share capital cost into line with the cost to be attributed to retained earnings. In other words the minimum rate required, around 8 per cent, needs to be increased for Ordinary share capital by the net of tax percentage which is applied to the income from which the shareholder finances his subscriptions to new share issues. Thus the cost of Ordinary share capital finance is derived from the following.

1   The basic minimum requirement, which is taken to be 8 per cent in real terms.
2   Because of issue costs, the capital actually subscribed will be greater than that received by the firm: assuming the issue costs to be 3 per cent, then the equity must earn $8 \times 1.03 = 8.24$ per cent in order to cover an 8 per cent return on the gross capital subscribed.
3   The influence of tax on the shareholder's income results in a company having to justify its equity issues by earnings in excess of the above 8.24 per cent: the increased level of earnings is determined by dividing 8.24 per cent by 0.7 – the net of tax rate for shareholder income (with the standard rate of income tax at 30 per cent): this raises the required rate to an 11.77 per cent real return.
4   Finally with a continuous inflation of about 15 per cent per annum, the shareholder's *real* return can be preserved only if the 11.77 per cent is increased by the expected future inflation rate: thus if the expected inflation rate is 15 per cent per annum, the final *money* cost of Ordinary share capital will be $(111.77 \times 1.15) - 100 = 28.54$ per cent. This 28.54 per cent is the post-tax money return which Ordinary share capital needs to earn in order to give the shareholder a real return after tax of 8 per cent.

Retained earnings

1   Again the basic minimum requirements for all forms of equity is taken to be 8 per cent in real terms.
2   As inflation will affect the return on retained earnings in the same way as that for Ordinary shares, the expected post-tax money rate of return requirement will be $(108 \times 1.15) - 100 = 24.2$ per cent.

Long-term debt

Here we shall specify that the expected interest rate for long-term lenders will be about 10 per cent per annum, and in consequence the cost of loan capital will be based upon that percentage. The reader is reminded that the loan capital interest rate will reflect the security and standing of the company which is borrowing, so this basic rate could fluctuate widely. In this instance the basic 10 per cent is the *money* cost of loan capital, and the following calculations will determine the real cost of debt financing.

1   As with equity issues the cost of issuing debentures is being taken to be about 3 per cent of the issue price (though it could be much higher). Therefore the influence of issue costs upon the return required will be $10 \times 1.03 = 10.3$ per cent.

2 Now debenture interest is an expense which is allowed in assessing the amount of the firm's tax liability: with Corporation tax at 52 per cent the firm will bear 48 per cent only of the gross money cost, and the net cost will be $10.3 \times 0.48 = 4.94$ per cent. This rate is still a *money* cost of loan capital.

3 The impact of inflation must be considered in the same way as for equity capital. To convert this money cost of loan interest to a *real* cost (post-tax) for the company, our rate of 4.94 per cent is divided by the 15 per cent inflation rate thus $(104.94 \div 1.15) - 100 = -8.75$ per cent. A negative real cost of 8.75 per cent is revealed, due to the high level of inflation!

The weighted average cost of capital

The incorporation of the above factor costs into the total costs of the whole capital supply is demonstrated below:

Type of capital	Real cost	Money cost	Weighting	Weighted real cost	Weighted money cost
	%	%		%	%
Ordinary shares	11.77	28.54	0.3	3.53	8.56
Retained earnings	8.00	24.20	0.5	4.00	12.10
Loan capital	−8.75	4.94	0.2	−1.75	0.99
WEIGHTED AVERAGE COST OF CAPITAL SUPPLY				5.78	21.65

The calculations given above show the assessment of the cost of capital to the second decimal place. In practical business circumstances no company would specify its cost of capital cut-off rate in these terms. The resultant figure would be rounded off to the nearest whole sum. Again we have to consider changing economic conditions, because with an inflation rate of 18 per cent and a standard rate of tax of 33 per cent, the above weighted money cost of capital would be 23.16 per cent: with an inflation rate of only 6 per cent the weighted money cost of capital would be 13.31 per cent. Clearly the encouragement for business managers to invest in capital assets will be more greatly stimulated with the lower cut-off rate requirement. Either the inflation rate must be reduced or the prices of industrial products must rise to enable the higher cut-off rates to be achieved from outputs of operational activities.

Cost of capital applications

The relevance of the post-tax weighted average money costs and real costs of capital concerns the method of forecasting, thus:

1   The money cost of capital should be used where forecasts are compiled in money terms.
2   The real cost of capital should be used where forecasts are compiled having regard to the influences of inflation on the various factor cost and income groups which are the determinants of a project's expected future performance.

We have questioned earlier in this chapter whether the cost of capital should be calculated on the basis of a planned long-term capital structure, or whether the cost of capital should be determined in a way which reflects every change in the proportions of the whole capital supply. It is to be expected that a company would have a planned pattern of growth, and that it would always be enlarging its total of long term finance within the planned growth pattern. If this is so then the weighted costs of capital should be based upon that planned capital structure even though there will be periodic divergencies from the precise pattern as the firm develops from one level of capital size to the next higher level. This is a view which is expressed frequently. However the writer favours a marginal approach to the weighted average cost of capital, and this is dealt with below.

Investment is concerned with change, and when we appraise investment proposals we are measuring the consequences of changes at the margin of business activity. For this reason we ought also to consider a marginal cost of capital. Now it is not suggested that each package in a series of capital cash inflows should identify the cost of capital for the projects it finances. Rather does it imply that we should take a moving marginal weighted average cost of capital. Such a moving average would reflect the time pattern necessary to effect changes in the corporate image and its operational outputs. Thus it would be based upon the actual changes in a capital structure during a five-year period (for example) and we would be constantly looking forward over a series of five-year periods. In this way the effectiveness of the firm's management, the profitability of its trading operations are being readily reflected in its cost of capital. The firm's ability to secure additional finance has a regular impact upon that cost of capital. The firm's plans for development, expansion and modernisation are being evaluated against a more relevant 'current marginal' cost of obtaining the required financial support.

However, practice has its own divergencies. The writer has discussed with many financial managers the problems of capital supply and the measurement of corporate efficiency. Several of the best growth companies in the UK take the view that the cost of capital must be based upon the cost of equity shares only: any method of financing which ensures a lower cost of capital just increases the profitability of operations. Thus whilst the cost of Ordinary share capital determined as above is used as the firm's cost of capital, any project-financing that utilises loan capital or retained earnings still has to meet the minimum earning rate required by equity shares. A further restriction on the use of the weighted cost of capital refers to the situation where a project being appraised is so large as to need a special supply of finance to support it. In such cases, and particularly where the project is of such a size as to bring about a considerable change in the firm's total asset structure, then the cost of capital should be the cost of that finance specially raised to meet the cost of establishing the project.

Other reservations concerning the use of the weighted cost must now be referred to. It is suggested that such weighted costs should be reserved for *relatively* risk-free investments. The basic 8 per cent which started the whole calculation is based upon *average* returns to the ordinary shareholder over a period of 47 years and it must therefore reflect an *average* experience of risk. Consequently, where a project is thought to have inherent risks greater than the average it is suggested that a premium should be added to the weighted cost of capital requirement to cover that risk. Here the capital planner departs from the facts of

1   A historical rate of return received by Ordinary shareholders.
2   The current level of taxation on incomes.
3   The recent historical experience of the annual rates of inflation.

which have been used in the assessment of the weighted cost of capital. Upon a reasonable basis of fact is superimposed an element of judgement. In many cases the experienced businessman's judgement will be the most valuable factor in investment appraisal. However, the application of practices for the analysis of risk and uncertainty will show more clearly (see Chapter 16) the potential risk element in that a *probability* of loss or gain can be quantified. Here at least the decision-maker can see the measured extent of the risks involved and can compare them with the expected most likely returns for the project. In this way the presence of risk can be brought into the decision and can affect a choice between alternative investments. Again there are circumstances where the aim of best available profitability from alternative business opportunities may be set aside where it is considered that other objectives are temporarily paramount. These other objectives may include the desire for a specific rate of growth* or a large market share or may refer to the provision of welfare amenities for company employees, etc. On the other hand a higher return than the weighted cost of capital may be necessary when the company does not intend to raise capital (or cannot)

*The form of growth is not specified here but may include growth of asset size, sales, share price or earnings per share, etc.

to satisfy the demands of all available investment opportunities. These circumstances will be found where the proprietors or directors do not wish to go to the market for money because they fear that they may suffer some loss of control of their business – an experience of numerous private limited companies.

(The writer has encountered several private limited companies which were operating quite efficiently. The demand for the products, both for the home market and abroad, was strong. It appeared that output could be increased, with profit, if the necessary finance for expansion had been forthcoming. The directors could not subscribe the necessary finance themselves because '... the high level of taxation did not leave enough money for the individual ...' to enable them to invest the *total* quantity of finance required. At the same time they did not intend going to the equity issues market because they could see that such action would weaken *their* control of *their 'own'* company.)

Finally the power of all companies to make profit from capital investment must rest with its managerial ability to *manage* their projects *profitably*. Any shortage of the right management calibre will limit the company's ability to run its affairs at the most efficient level: such a limitation will therefore restrict the company's power to expand through accepting all the investment opportunities which come its way. It should undertake only those projects which it can effectively and efficiently manage, no matter what returns are forecast.

Objects of cost-of-capital determination

Any discussion of the cost of capital would be inadequate without some reference to the object of the calculations. Business activity must be directed to profitability, for profitability is necessary for corporate continuance and for all the other non-profitable activities to be sustained. Whilst operational incomes and costs can be identified, within the limits of the power to forecast events, it must be remembered that a normal profitability statement does not include the costs of dividends or of loan interest. Therefore the rate of profit generation which is forecasted for a proposal needs to be sufficient to pay the costs of financing at least. It is for this reason that a cost-of-capital yardstick is assessed to show how a proposal's expected rate of return matches with the cost of getting the money to finance that proposal. The financial manager should be concerned with assessing the right cost of capital and choosing the right criteria of investment evaluation. His advice on these topics needs to be well informed advice in order that the directing managers can choose that investment pattern which will enable the company to achieve the objectives of its long-term plans. It is in this context that the cost of capital is so

Exhibit 116

Profile of net present values: I

Rates	5% £	10% £	15% £	20% £	25% £
Discounted NCFs	2,723	2,487	2,283	2,107	1,952
Investment cost	2,200	2,200	2,200	2,200	2,200
Net present values	523	287	83	−93	−248

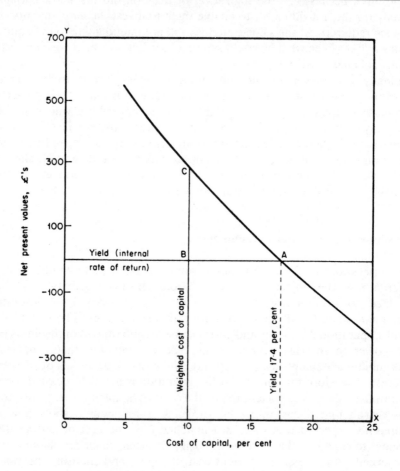

important: it is for this reason that its impact on investment worth must be studied.

Exhibit 116 shows a profile of net present values of the net cash flows of a project. The net present values are calculated at varying rates of discount from 5 to 25 per cent.

At the point where the profile crosses (A) the line of investment cost, the yield is given by the corresponding discount rate on the horizontal axis OX. If at this stage the cost of capital is assumed to be 10 per cent, then the NPV of the proposal is measured by the line BC. The financial value of the NPV, shown on the OY axis, represents the growth in wealth which would accrue to the firm as a result of implementing the investment.

Exhibit 117
Project returns with varying costs of capital: I

Project	Details	Cost of capital				
		5% £	10% £	15% £	20% £	25% £
A	Discounted NCFs	15,443	12,289	10,038	8,385	7,141
	Investment cost	10,000	10,000	10,000	10,000	10,000
	Net present values	5,443	2,289	38	−1,615	−2,859
B	Discounted NCFs	23,165	18,434	15,056	12,578	10,712
	Investment cost	13,000	13,000	13,000	13,000	13,000
	Net present values	10,165	5,434	2,056	−422	−2,288
C	Discounted NCFs	30,887	24,578	20,075	16,770	14,282
	Investment cost	16,000	16,000	16,000	16,000	16,000
	Net present values	14,887	8,578	4,075	770	−1,718

Exhibit 117 gives details of the discounted net cash flows, initial investment costs and net present values of three separate investment proposals. These data of project returns have again been discounted at varying rates from 5 to 25 per cent. The resultant profiles of net present worths are then displayed on the graph in Exhibit 118.

Here the reader can see the discounted cash flow yield and the net present value for each project (if the cost of capital remains at 10 per cent). Clearly project C has a higher value, for both yield and NPV, than B: furthermore B has higher values than A. Whichever cost of capital is chosen or calculated for the company, the above order of preference will be maintained. The only feature to vary will be the net present values, because these emerge from the application of different discounting, i.e. cost of capital, rates.

Two further examples are examined in Exhibit 119, where future cash flows of two potential investments are discounted at rates varying from 5 to

Exhibit 118

Profiles of net present values: II

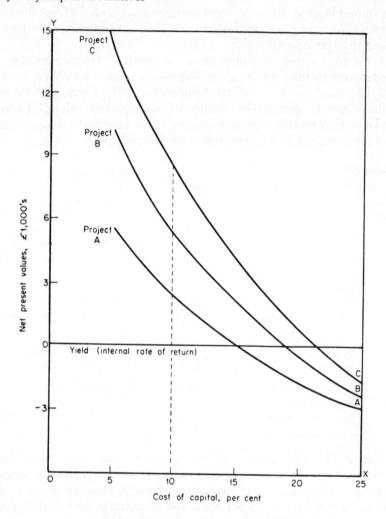

30 per cent. Again the sequence of net present values is represented in profile form on a graph in Exhibit 120. The importance of correct determination of the cost of financing is emphasised here when yields and NPVs are calculated. The yields of A and B are shown to be 28.1 and 23.4 per cent respectively. By this criterion of measurement, A is shown to be superior to B when the constraints of corporate policy are removed from a comparative evaluation.

In these circumstances project A would be chosen rather than project B. However, if the cost of capital is assessed at 10 per cent, then from the graph

Exhibit 119

Project returns with varying costs of capital: II

Project	Details	Cost of capital					
		5% £	10% £	15% £	20% £	25% £	30% £
A	Discounted NCFs	2,749	2,538	2,360	2,205	2,072	1,954
	Investment cost	2,000	2,000	2,000	2,000	2,000	2,000
	Net present values	749	538	360	205	72	−46
B	Discounted NCFs	3,379	2,888	2,496	2,177	1,917	1,699
	Investment cost	2,000	2,000	2,000	2,000	2,000	2,000
	Net present values	1,379	888	496	177	−83	−301

and from the data in Exhibit 119 it can be seen that the NPV of A is £538 whilst that of B is £888. On *this* basis project B will generate a greater growth in wealth for the company than A: B ought therefore to be chosen rather than A, when the cost of capital is 10 per cent.

In fact, for any cost of capital up to 19 per cent, project B is superior to A: beyond that discounting rate the reverse position arises. The changing fortunes of these two investment proposals arise from the nature of their cash flows, which are given in Exhibit 121. These time periods of cash flows show that it takes four years before A and B are roughly equal in total cash receipts; for years 1, 2 and 3 project A earns higher aggregate cash returns than B. Such a pattern of returns will always be influenced to a lesser extent by the higher discount rates than by lower rates. Thus at rates in excess of 19 per cent, proposal A is more acceptable than B.

Cut-off rates

The lesson shown in Exhibits 119 and 120 concerns not the importance of the cost of capital only, but also the criterion of choice. It is pointed out that both criteria (yield and NPV) give the same answer to a question of whether or not to invest. The answer would be 'yes' in both cases assuming that the cost of capital was set at any rate of discount up to 23 per cent. From the point of ranking the investments in order of preference, however, NPV has the advantage: the growth *sum* is revealed and the *rate* of growth can be determined. The appreciation of NPV's value stems from a clear knowledge and understanding of the cost of capital. It is this concept which has forced the issue of choosing between yield and NPV.

Exhibit 120
Profiles of net present values: III

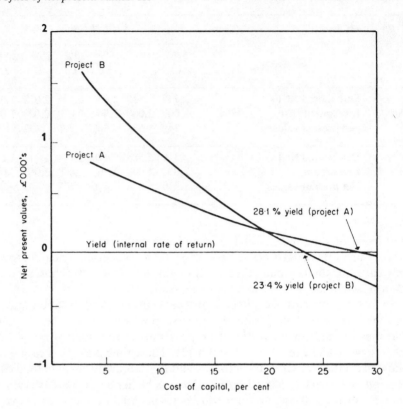

Exhibit 121
Project net cash flows

Project	Investment cost	Net cash flows in year				
	Year 0 £	1 £	2 £	3 £	4 £	5 £
A	2,000	2,000	250	250	250	250
B	2,000	400	600	800	1,000	1,200

Perhaps the main use of the cost-of-capital rate for each firm relates to the policy of identifying acceptable investment projects. It is suggested that the cost of finance must represent the minimum level of return for a project, if it is to receive the 'go ahead' from the firm's directing managers. Whilst the minimum return may be set in this way, it does not necessarily mean that enough projects will be sought and approved in each year, until the marginal project just covers its cost of financing as promulgated in the cut-off rate. This is because the net cash flows of investment proposals are the final outcomes of numerous estimates of incomes and costs. Many of these estimates will be based on very sound premises: others may well be pure aspirations. The point is that the forecasted rate of return will rarely be achieved so precisely. Thus to safeguard against losses which could arise from imperfect forecasts, investment approval procedures frequently propound a cut-off rate higher than the arithmetically determined cost of finance.* The point at which the company's policy makers fix the cut-off rate will depend upon the cost of finance and upon other matters of policy also. For example, the available time of top management is limited: if managerial time is dispersed over too many projects, the efficiency of control and direction will eventually decline. Therefore the company's directing managers recognise the need to use top management's time to the best advantage. This best advantage will not be secured if too much time and thought is concerned with an overlarge investment programme.

(This is especially true if that programme is made overlarge by accepting projects of low return, even if these low returns are still just above the cost of capital. If managerial control declines, so eventually will the total return on capital employed. A decline in the total return may eventually result in a reduction of the dividend paid to shareholders or at least it will affect the growth of the total shareholders' interest. Results such as these would cause the market price of the company's shares to fall and up will go the cost of capital.)

A high cut-off rate may also be adopted because of limited liquid resources but at the same time it may discourage profitable proposals which do not attain the required exalted return. The higher is set the ante for investment proposals to overcome, the greater will be the danger that proposals of real urgency relating to the improvement of existing operations may be postponed. For management to be constantly delaying capital expenditures until the *high* return is obtained might result in investments being postponed until present equipment is so inefficient that the profitability of any investment must rise considerably. To reach this stage, however, the years of operating inefficient assets will have caused reduced profits and increasingly uncompetitive outputs.

On the other hand, a low cut-off rate needs to be examined within the context of opportunity cost – can the company use some of its cash resources on more profitable ventures elsewhere on the industrial scene? While a low cut-off rate for proposed investments should not cause the company to

*ROCKLEY, L. E., *Capital Investment Decisions*, pp56–7, Business Books (1968).

suffer from a stifling of new ideas or proposals for capital spending, it becomes much more important that capital expenditure proposals should be subjected to precise appraisal of expected benefits. The margin of error is reduced when the cut-off rate is reduced. The determination and use of an investment proposal cut-off rate needs continual re-assessment. It should be used mainly as a moderator between investment opportunities coming forward, the availability of funds to meet those opportunities, and the quantity and quality of management capable of directing the projects during and after installation. It is here that data on the cost of capital is so pertinent to policy making.

Self-examination questions

1 A high debt/equity ratio frequently results in the market prices of a company's Ordinary shares standing at levels lower than the related industry averages. As a result would you expect the company's cost of capital to be decreased or increased?

2 The Ordinary shares of the XYZ Company are quoted on the Stock Exchange at £4 each whilst the current dividend payments amount to 20p per share. With an expected dividend growth of 8 per cent per annum, estimate the cost of the company's Ordinary shares.

3 If a third of the XYZ Company's long-term capital finance is comprised of 12 per cent debentures (the remaining two thirds being Ordinaries), and if the corporation tax rate is 50 per cent, what would the company's weighted average cost of capital be?

4 Explain the relationship between a higher market price for a company's Ordinary shares and a consequently lower corporate cost of capital.

5 Why should the concept of a single cost of capital be an untenable proposition for a large multi-product company to hold? In what circumstances would you vary the cut-off rate for investment appraisal purposes?

6 What are the arguments for using a marginal cost of capital rather than a weighted average cost of a standard capital mix for project evaluations? How would you define marginal in this context?

Recommended reading

BROWN, H. P., 'The present theory of investment appraisal: a critical analysis', *Bulletin, Oxford University Institute of Economics and Statistics*, 31(2), (1969).

298

SOLOMON, E., (Editor), *The Management of Corporate Capital*, Collier-MacMillan (1964), see part III.

BROMWICH, M., *The Economics of Capital Budgeting*, Penguin Books (1976), see chapters 6 to 10.

BULL, R. J., *Accounting in Business*, Butterworth (1976), see chapter 15.

15 Analysis of project returns

Introduction

The application of discounting techniques to the appraisal of capital expenditure proposals will now be displayed in a series of examples. The first few cases studied show net present values of the proposals using 10 per cent as the firm's cost of capital: yield ratings are also shown and the reader should remember that a project can be regarded as acceptable provided that:

1 The net cash flows give a positive net present value when they are discounted at the given cost of capital.
   and/or
2 The yield rating is in excess of the cost of capital percentage.

Again the importance of corporate long-term objectives must be stressed. All investments, whatever their NPV or yield, need to be directed towards fulfilling the company's strategic plans. The appraisal indexes, which are used to indicate the worthwhileness of a proposal, do not of themselves select those proposals which are to be implemented. The criteria of investment appraisal are only aids for the decision-maker when he faces problems of choice between, and preferential ordering of, a selection of available investment opportunities.

Investment profiles

Three investment projects, A, B and C, are detailed in Exhibits 122, 123 and 124 respectively. By using the discounting tables at pages 362–70 the reader will be able to verify the calculations of yield and NPV for each of the three proposals. Their net cash flows have been discounted at the percentage rate shown at the head of the 'Interest factor' column.

Exhibit 122

Project A: investment cost £15,000

Year of life	NCFs	Interest factor 10%	Present value of NCFs	Interest factor 15%	Present value of NCFs	Interest factor 20%	Present value of NCFs
	£		£		£		£
1	2,000	0.9091	1,818.2	0.8696	1,739.2	0.8333	1,666.6
2	3,000	0.8264	2,479.2	0.7561	2,268.3	0.6944	2,083.2
3	4,000	0.7513	3,005.2	0.6575	2,630.0	0.5787	2,314.8
4	5,000	0.6830	3,415.0	0.5718	2,859.0	0.4823	2,411.5
5	6,000	0.6209	3,725.4	0.4972	2,983.2	0.4019	2,411.4
6	7,000	0.5645	3,951.5	0.4323	3,026.1	0.3349	2,344.3
TOTAL	£27,000		£18,394.5		£15,505.8		£13,231.8

Net present value at 10% cost of capital = £3,394.5

$$\text{Yield by interpolation} = 15 + \left(\frac{505.8}{2,274} \times \frac{5}{100}\right) = 16.1\%$$

Exhibit 123

Project B: investment cost £15,000

Year of life	NCFs	Interest factor 10%	Present value of NCFs	Interest factor 20%	Present value of NCFs	Interest factor 30%	Present value of NCFs
	£		£		£		£
1	7,000	0.9091	6,363.7	0.8333	5,833.1	0.7692	5,384.4
2	6,000	0.8264	4,958.4	0.6944	4,166.4	0.5917	3,550.2
3	5,000	0.7513	3,756.5	0.5787	2,893.5	0.4552	2,276.0
4	4,000	0.6830	2,732.0	0.4823	1,929.2	0.3501	1,400.4
5	3,000	0.6209	1,862.7	0.4019	1,205.7	0.2693	807.9
6	2,000	0.5645	1,129.0	0.3349	669.8	0.2072	414.4
TOTAL	£27,000		£20,802.3		£16,697.7		£13,833.3

Net present value at 10% cost of capital = £5,802.3

$$\text{Yield by interpolation} = 20 + \left(\frac{1,697.7}{2,864.4} \times \frac{10}{100}\right) = 25.9\%$$

Exhibit 124

Project C: investment cost £15,000

Year	NCFs per year	Interest factor 10%	Present value of NCFs	Interest factor 15%	Present value of NCFs	Interest factor 20%	Present value of NCFs
	£		£		£		£
6	4,500	4.3553	19,598.8	3.7845	18,030.2	3.3255	14,964.7

Net present value at 10% cost of capital = £4,598.8

$$\text{Yield by interpolation} = 15 + \left(\frac{3,030.2}{3,065.5} \times \frac{5}{100} \right) = 19.9\%$$

Now for determination of a yield rating, the object of discounting is to find that percentage discount which will reduce the future net cash flows until they equal the capital cost of the investment (see Appendix C). For project A, it is evident that a 15 per cent rate of discount is not a high enough *rate of charge*, for the present value of the future cash flows is greater than the initial investment outlay.* Therefore a higher rate must be chosen and at 20 per cent the resultant present value total is lower than the cost of the investment, showing that 20 per cent is too high a rate of charge. In these circumstances DCF yield must fall between the two rates tested and interpolation reveals the result to be 16.1 per cent. In each of the Exhibits, the future cash flows have been discounted at a 10 per cent rate (the cost of capital) in order to ascertain the NPV for each proposal.

Project C earns net cash returns of £4,500 in each year of its life. With uniform cash flows, such as those found in C, it is not necessary to calculate *separately* the present value of *each year's* flows in order to determine the total present value of the whole cash flows of the project. A single interest factor, which represents the present worth of £1 per year for each of the six years, is used in this case. Reference to the interest tables on page 367 shows that the factor for a six-year life at 10 per cent discount is 4.3553. Now this single interest factor equals the sum of the individual factors for each of the years during which the proposal is expected to generate net cash flows of £4,500. Thus for investments producing equal annual cash flows, the calculations are greatly reduced. Furthermore, location of the yield percentage is easier. A DCF yield rating results from a comparison of an investment's initial cost with its net cash flow returns. It is determined by finding out the value for *r* in the following equation:

---

*Another way of explaining this point would be to say that the returns to the investment can support a higher interest charge in order to finance the project.

$$C = \frac{A_1}{(1 + r)} + \frac{A_2}{(1 + r)^2} + \frac{A_3}{(1 + r)^3} + \dots + \frac{A_n}{(1 + r)^n}$$

where C is the investment cost, A the net cash flows in each year up to n years, r the rate of discount and n the number of years.

If the net cash flows are the same amount in every year of the proposal's operating life, the equation can be written as

$$\frac{C}{A} = \frac{1}{(1 + r)} + \frac{1}{(1 + r)^2} + \frac{1}{(1 + r)^3} + \dots + \frac{1}{(1 + r)^n}$$

Now the answer to the right-hand side of the equation produces that interest factor which is equal to the sum derived from dividing the investment's initial cost by its uniform annual net cash flow amount. Applying the method to project C above we have

$$\frac{15,000}{4,500} = 3.3333$$

This solution represents the factor of interest for a six-year life, where a project's future net cash flows are equated with its original cost of installation. By examining Table B of Appendix D and looking along the line of interest factors for a six-year life, the reader will see that the amount 3.3333 falls between interest rates of 18 and 20 per cent. It follows therefore that the yield will fall between 18 and 20 per cent: in fact the calculations at the foot of Exhibit 124 show the yield to be 19.9 per cent.

The work involved in finding out the percentage yield can be simplified in another way. Exhibit 125 is a form that can be used by clerical staff to ascertain a yield rating.

Discount factors for percentages from 4 to 30 are printed on the form: in the second column after the heading 'actual' should be entered:

1 The capital cost in year 0.
2 The estimated future net cash flows in years 1 to 6.

Interest factors shown under the various percentages must be multiplied by the forecast cash flows. Thereby present values of the project's net cash flows in each year of its forecast life are produced. It is then a simple matter to ascertain the NPVs of the investment at given costs of capital. The squared section of the form is provided for drawing a profile line of the NPVs which were produced by the calculations in the top half of the document. A vertical scale must be devised for the NPV data of the investment proposal which is being studied. When the profile is drawn on the graph, the point at which it intersects the horizontal line of a nil NPV can be read on the horizontal scale as the DCF yield. Exhibit 126 shows a form completed in respect of project A.

A study of project worth can be greatly aided by the profile method. Exhibit 127 displays net present value profiles for each of the projects A, B

Exhibit 125

Project appraisal by DCF yield

PROJECT ....

Year	Actual	Net cash flow, £									
		4%		10%		15%		20%		30%	
		Factor	Present value	Factor	Present value	Factor	Present value	Factor	Present value	Factor	Present value
0		1.00		1.00		1.00		1.00		1.00	
1		0.962		0.909		0.870		0.833		0.769	
2		0.925		0.826		0.756		0.694		0.592	
3		0.889		0.751		0.658		0.579		0.455	
4		0.855		0.683		0.572		0.482		0.350	
5		0.822		0.621		0.497		0.402		0.269	
6		0.790		0.565		0.432		0.335		0.207	
NPV											

PRESENT VALUE PROFILE

Net present values, £

Discount, %

and C which have been discussed in this chapter. Each profile is based on the data in the table at the head of the exhibit: the table shows the NPV of each investment at the *end of each year* of its expected economic life. Clearly the figures given for year 6 must equal the NPV for each investment, and the reader can verify this by referring to the exhibits on pages 301–2. The table of data also records the expected DCF yield for each project. The important

304

Exhibit 126

Project appraisal by DCF yield

PROJECT ....

Year	Actual	4%		10%		15%		20%		30%	
		Factor	Present value	Factor	Present value	Factor	Present value	Factor	Present value	Factor	Present value
0	(15,000)	1.00		1.00	(15,000)	1.00	(15,000)	1.00	(15,000)	1.00	
1	2,000	0.962		0.909	1,818	0.870	1,740	0.833	1,666	0.769	
2	3,000	0.925		0.826	2,478	0.756	2,268	0.694	2,082	0.592	
3	4,000	0.889		0.751	3,004	0.658	2,632	0.579	2,316	0.455	
4	5,000	0.855		0.683	3,415	0.572	2,860	0.482	2,410	0.350	
5	6,000	0.822		0.621	3,726	0.497	2,982	0.402	2,412	0.269	
6	7,000	0.790		0.565	3,955	0.432	3,024	0.335	2,345	0.207	
NPV					£3,396		£506		(£1,769)		

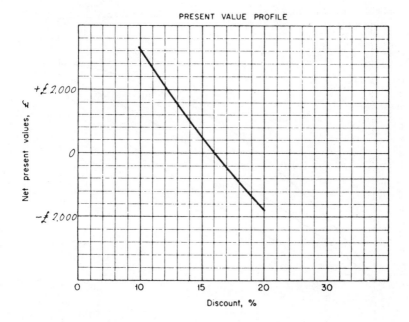

PRESENT VALUE PROFILE

Net present values, £ — +£2,000, 0, −£2,000

Discount, % — 0, 10, 15, 20, 30

element revealed by *these* NPV profiles concerns the point of intersection of the zero line by the profile line. When related to the horizontal scale, the point of intersection shows the discounted payback period in years for each project. Conclusions which can be drawn from the exhibit include:

1 Project B has a risk period of approximately 3 years: its net present value up to that point is a negative quantity.

Exhibit 127

Projects A, B and C yearly NPV profiles

Years	A	B	C
	£	£	£
1	(13,182)	(8,636)	(10,909)
2	(10,703)	(3,678)	(7,190)
3	(7,698)	78	(3,809)
4	(4,283)	2,810	(736)
5	(558)	4,673	2,058
6	3,395	5,802	4,598
YIELDS	16.1%	25.9%	19.9%

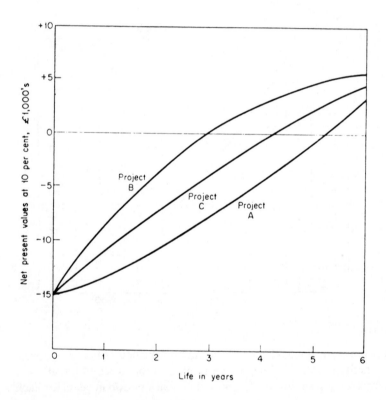

2   Project C has a risk period of approximately 4.3 years.
3   Project A has a risk period of approximately 5.2 years.
4   At the time when project B passes from being a wholly risk project into the profit-making stage, project A still has over £7,600 of unrecovered capital expenditure at risk.

Influence of taxation and other allowances

Projects A, B and C were easy proposals to assess, and ranking them in an order of desirability presents few problems – if they are to be graded according to their respective profitabilities. The evaluation of an investment's net cash flows is not always so straightforward, however. Net cash flows refer to the cash flow *changes* resulting from implementing a proposal and it is essential that the *cash flow changes remaining with the company* are used in the investment appraisal. Therefore it is the *after-tax* gains of an investment which are vital to correct evaluation. This means that where grants are received towards the cost of a project, the amount of the grant and the timing of its receipt should be brought into the appraisal. Similarly annual capital allowances (now called writing-down allowances) which are given in consequence of certain capital expenditures and which operate to reduce the amount of tax on company profits, must be included in the assessment of an investment's expected rate of return.

Thus in the next series of investment examples, the influence of grants and writing-down allowances will be studied. The reader must recognise that taxation rates, allowances and grants change frequently. The important point is that the influence, on investment worth, of net cash flows after tax is appreciated. When these after tax, after grant influences on net cash flows are fully understood and when the methods by which these allowances are brought to the investment appraisal are followed, then future variations in investment incentives, i.e. tax allowances, can be brought to the account also.

Project D

Government and Parliament have made available certain grants and taxation allowances aimed at stimulating industrial and commercial capital investment. Full information about these investment incentives can be obtained from the Department of Trade and Industry at their London Headquarters or at any of the Regional offices of the DTI. Our next project evaluation exercise is designed to show how the incentives can operate to turn an unacceptable project into one which promises a worthwhile return on the initial outlay cost.

307

The Alpha Manufacturing Company Limited has decided to make a new product which is expected to have a marketable life of six years. The life of this product should be adequate, for it will enable the development of longer term plans in this particular field. Other products should be fully tested in time for their release to the public in six years' time. Machinery and equipment for production are expected to cost £30,000, whilst the net cash flows arising from the project should be £7,000 in each of the six years of the expected life of the investment. An investment grant of 20 per cent will be received in consequence of the expenditure on machinery and equipment. This machinery should have a disposal value of £3,000 at the end of its life and will attract 100 per cent first year taxation allowances on the expenditure incurred. Corporation tax is levied at 52 per cent. The company assess its cost of capital at 15 per cent and the board would like to know if the project is worth adopting on the basis of its forecast profitability.

In order to emphasise the importance of grants, tax allowances and the *post-tax* cash flows in the process of appraising a proposal's profitability rating, it is proposed in the first instance to evaluate the project *without* considering these incentives. (The reader should appreciate that this first evaluation is an incorrect method of appraising the proposal, because it ignores the actual whole effects on the firm's cash flows.)

Evaluation 1

	£
Capital cost of investment proposal	£30,000
Net cash flows: present values at 15% discount rate:	
Years 1–6: £7,000 × 3.7845	26,492
Year 7*: £3,000 × 0.3759	1,128
Total present value of future NCFs at 15%	£27,620
Net cash flows: present values at 10% discount rate:	
Years 1–6: £7,000 × 4.3553	30,487
Year 7: £3,000 × 0.5132	1,540
Total present value of future NCFs at 10%	£32,027

Therefore, by interpolation the yield is found to be

$$10\% \times \left(\frac{2,027}{4,407} \times \frac{5}{100} \right) = 12.2\%$$

*We make the practical assumption that the machinery was sold in the year after that in which the project was terminated.

308

Thus we have a negative NPV, at the 15 per cent cost of capital, of £2,380 and a yield which is less than that cost of capital. By both criteria the proposal should be rejected – on grounds of insufficient profitability. Each of the above interest factors can be verified in the interest tables on pages 362–70.

Evaluation 2

Here we shall bring to account the 20 per cent development grant, and in doing this we assume that the grant was received 12 months after the machinery was paid for. Thus the grant is shown amongst the project's cash flows. It does not have to be done in this way however: the discounted value of the grant could have been deducted from the capital cost of the investment proposal. Again the reader is reminded that the appraisal exemplified is still not a wholly correct assessment of the project's worth.

		£
Capital cost of the investment proposal		£30,000

Net cash flows: present values at 15% discount rate:

Year 1:	(Grant) £6,000 × 0.8696	5,218
Years 1–6:	£7,000 × 3.7845	26,492
Year 7:	£3,000 × 0.3759	1,128
Total present value of future NCFs at 15%		£32,838

Net cash flows: present values at 20% discount rate:

Year 1:	(Grant) £6,000 × 0.8333	5,000
Years 1–6:	£7,000 × 3.3255	23,279
Year 7:	£3,000 × 0.2791	837
Total present value of future NCFs at 20%		£29,116

By interpolation the yield is found to be

$$15\% + \left(\frac{2,838}{3,722} \times \frac{5}{100}\right) = 18.8\%$$

The mere fact of including the receipt of a grant has increased the yield calculation by 54 per cent, to a rate which shows a return in excess of the cost of capital. At the same time the NPV is a positive £2,838, and therefore both criteria would indicate Project D to be an acceptable venture. Yet we still have not produced an authentic evaluation of our proposed investment. Such a realistic appraisal can only result from an examination of the *post-tax* future cash flows because our object is to appraise the worth of the incremental benefits of the investment to the company, i.e. the cash flows which will remain with the company. This will be accomplished when we evaluate the after-tax cash flows which the proposal is expected to earn for the corporate treasury.

Evaluation 3 – post-tax returns

The procedure for allowing the net capital costs of capital expenditure against the income of a business activity, is achieved by taxation allowances. These writing-down allowances, as they have been termed, constitute permissible charges against the taxable profits of a venture: they act to reduce the taxation bill. Now the project data (page 308) specified that the machinery and equipment '...will attract 100 per cent first year taxation allowances...'. This means that in the tax year following that in which the capital expenditure was incurred, the whole of the £30,000 can be set against the total corporate taxable profits. Therefore in year 1 of our appraisal the tax *saved* by this capital allowance will be

Allowed capital expenditure × Corporation tax rate

= £30,000 × 52%

= £15,600

The fact that we expect the scrap value of the machinery to be £3,000 in year 7 will be brought to account in year 8. If the £3,000 is actually received for the retired plant, and in the evaluation we shall assume this to be so, it would mean that the writing-down taxation allowance received in year 1 was too great. The £3,000 scrap value clearly acts to reduce the gross capital cost of the machinery, to a NET £27,000. Thus year 8 must bear a balancing taxation charge of £3,000. Here the after tax effect will be to reduce the corporate cash flows by a sum equal to

£3,000 × 52% = £1,560

in year 8, if we assume the tax rate to remain at 52 per cent for the forthcoming 8 years. Exhibit 128 now presents Project D's post-tax NCFs for its expected life.

Completion of the project appraisal is now accomplished by using the post-tax cash flows to find out the correct yield and NPV. Exhibit 129 demonstrates the calculations.

Therefore with an initial outlay cost of £30,000, the yield is found by interpolation to be

$$15\% + \left(\frac{3,914}{4,201} \times \frac{10}{100}\right) = 24.3\%$$

and the NPV at a cost of capital of 15 per cent is a healty £3,914, i.e. 13 per cent of the gross capital cost. Exhibits 128 and 129 highlight the very real benefits which the current investment incentives do bring to appropriate capital expenditure projects.

Whereas the project seemed to be an unprofitable venture (see Evaluation 1), the realistic post-tax cash flows together with the development grant give a completely different picture. In fact the post-tax cash flows

310

Exhibit 128

Project D: Post-tax net cash flows
(Corporation tax 52 per cent)

Year	Grant	NCFs	Corporation tax on previous year's NCFs	Tax saved by writing-down allowances	Post-tax NCFs Cols (2) + (3) + (5) − (4)
(1)	(2)	(3)	(4)	(5)	(6)
	£	£	£	£	£
1	6,000	7,000	—	15,600	28,600
2		7,000	(3,640)	—	3,360
3		7,000	(3,640)	—	3,360
4		7,000	(3,640)	—	3,360
5		7,000	(3,640)	—	3,360
6		7,000	(3,640)	—	3,360
7		3,000	(3,640)	—	(640)
8				(1,560)	(1,560)
Total	£6,000	£45,000	£21,840	£14,040	£43,200

Exhibit 129

Project D: Evaluation of post-tax cash flows

Year	Post-tax NCFs	Interest factor, 15%	PV of net cash flows	Interest factor, 25%	PV of net cash flows
(1)	(2)	(3)	(4)	(5)	(6)
	£		£		£
1	28,600	0.8696	24,871	0.8000	22,880
2	3,360				
3	3,360				
4	3,360	2.9149	9,794	2.1514	7,229
5	3,360				
6	3,360				
7	(640)	0.3759	(241)	0.2097	(134)
8	(1,560)	0.3269	(510)	0.1678	(262)
TOTAL	£43,200		£33,914		£29,713

311

show that 76 per cent of the initial outlay cost is recovered in the first year of the project's life at a 25 per cent interest charge, and 82 per cent is recovered in the first year of life at the firm's own cost of capital (15 per cent)! But the important point to remember, in connection with project D, is that regional investment grants and taxation incentives are not available at uniform rates over the whole of the UK. These incentives have a locational incentive for corporate investment. They can turn an apparently unprofitable investment in the London area to a profitable investment in, say, Middlesborough. The business manager must consult the DTI booklets on investment incentives.

Project E

When we first direct our attention to the appraisal of investment proposals we tend to forget that variations in the level or mix of trading operations will most likely lead to variations in the sum of corporate working capital. Such a variation can arise from the need for additional cash for wages, from increased stocks necessary to support the higher levels of production and from the increased debtors arising out of the increased sales. Now any increase in working capital has the same effect, on the firm's cash flows, as expenditure on plant and machinery; a long-term investment of company funds is involved. If this extra investment is ignored, it may lead to the acceptance of proposals which are, in reality, unprofitable. Therefore we must increase the initial outlay cost of such a project by the amount of additional working capital required. When the project comes to the end of its economic life, the working capital will be released to other corporate activities. When that release takes place, the relevant amount must be treated as an additional cash flow. The following example will show how these working capital aspects of investment projects are brought to account.

The Gamma Machine Company Limited is considering extending its range of products by producing a line of high quality tools for the export market. The cost of new plant and machinery would be £75,000 but this expenditure would rank for a regional development grant of 22 per cent which would be received about a year after the initial expenditure. In addition the capital expenditure would rank for 100 per cent first year taxation allowances. It is anticipated, furthermore, that extra working capital of £5,000 a year will be necessary to finance additional stocks of materials, and some increase in the amount of debtors. The increase in working capital would be needed from the first year of operations.

The incremental incomes (net cash flows) stemming from the project are anticipated to be £15,000 per annum for 10 years: the extra working capital should be released from the project by the end of year 11. Finally, no scrap value is expected to accrue from the sale of plant and machinery when it is retired from use.

With Corporation tax at 52 per cent, and a corporate cost of capital of 20 per cent, should the investment be undertaken?

Evaluation

A new factor for investment appraisal arises in this proposal – the requirement of an additional amount of working capital. Therefore the first stage of the evaluation shows how the working capital investment is brought into the assessment of project total cost. At the same time an alternative method of dealing with the regional development grant is shown. Here this discounted value of the grant is used to reduce the initial outlay cost of the project, rather than to increase its subsequent net cash flows. Either method is quite acceptable because the results revealed by the calculations will be the same by either method.

	£
Capital cost of investment proposal	£75,000
Add: Working capital increase, from	
year 1: £5,000 × 0.8333	4,167
	79,167
Less: Regional development grant of	
22% of expenditure on plant and	
machinery, received in year 1:	
£16,500 × 0.8333	13,749
PV cost of investment proposal	£65,418

The post-tax and the writing-down allowance impacts on the project's net cash flows are presented in Exhibit 130. The reader should also note that the release of working capital, after the project has ended, is shown as a cash inflow in year 11.

Again our completion of the project appraisal is now accomplished by using the post-tax cash flows to find out the correct yield and NPV. Exhibit 131 demonstrates the calculations.

The yield is found by interpolation to be

$$20\% + \left(\frac{3,389}{5,900} \times \frac{5}{100}\right) = 22.8\%$$

and the NPV at the corporate cost of capital is £3,389, i.e. 5.2 per cent of the adjusted capital cost.

Project F

The investment decision becomes more interesting where there are NO cash

Exhibit 130

Project E: Post-tax net cash flows
(Corporation tax 52 per cent)

Year	NCFs	Corp. tax on previous year's NCFs	Tax saved by writing-down allowances	Post-tax NCFs (2) + (4) − (3)
(1)	(2)	(3)	(4)	(5)
	£	£	£	£
1	15,000	—	39,000	54,000
2	15,000	(7,800)	—	7,200
3	15,000	(7,800)	—	7,200
4	15,000	(7,800)	—	7,200
5	15,000	(7,800)	—	7,200
6	15,000	(7,800)	—	7,200
7	15,000	(7,800)	—	7,200
8	15,000	(7,800)	—	7,200
9	15,000	(7,800)	—	7,200
10	15,000	(7,800)	—	7,200
11	5,000	(7,800)	—	(2,800)
TOTAL	£155,000	£(78,000)	£39,000	£116,000

inflows directly attributable to the project being appraised. Now the nil cash flow situation is not unusual. It will arise in circumstances such as

1 The choice of a computer installation.
2 The exchange of a company car for a new model.
3 The replacement of a heating pump.

and, in the public service, by

4 The construction of roads or reservoirs.

With investments such as these, calculation of the Annual Capital Charge (see the Annual Value criterion on page 319) will enable us to annualise the total costs involved in the project. In this way a weighted annual cost, or an annuity cost, of the proposed investment is derived. Whilst the annualised cost will not represent any sum of cash cost outflows, and cannot be traced to the cash account or the profit and loss account, it does reveal how the total cost is to be shared equally by each year in the project's economic life. The equivalent annual charge – the annuity cost – uses the sinking fund principle and therefore brings to the appraisal the application of discounting techniques. The following example demonst-

314

Exhibit 131

Project E: Evaluation of post-tax cash flows

Year	Post-tax NCFs	Interest factor 20%	PV of net cash flows	Interest factor 25%	PV of net cash flows
(1)	(2)	(3)	(4)	(5)	(6)
	£		£		£
1	54,000	0.8333	44,998	0.8000	43,200
2	7,200				
3	7,200				
4	7,200				
5	7,200				
6	7,200	3.3592	24,186	2.7705	19,948
7	7,200				
8	7,200				
9	7,200				
10	7,200				
11	(2,800)	0.1346	(377)	0.0859	(241)
TOTAL	£116,000		£68,807		£62,907

rates the method as it could be applied to the exchange of a company car for a new model.

The transport manager of the Beta Company Limited has obtained the following data about one of the fleet of cars used by company directors:

		£
Annual maintenance costs:	year 1	500
	year 2	1,000
	year 3	1,500
	year 4	2,000
	year 5	2,500
	year 6	3,000
	year 7	3,500

A new model would cost £5,000 and the trade-in values for a similar type of car would be as given below

	£
Trade-in value at end of year 1	3,000
at end of year 2	2,000
at end of year 3	1,000

at end of year 4	500
at end of year 5	100

With the company's cost of capital of 20 per cent, the transport manager has to decide the most economic time, from a total cost standpoint, to recommend for replacement of the vehicle and others of a similar type.

Evaluation 1

An inadequate valuation would have regard to the absolute totals of cost and express their annual equivalent by means of a simple arithmetical average. Exhibit 132 shows the results of this method.

Exhibit 132

Project F: Average net costs per annum

Years of life	Initial outlay costs	Total main tenance costs to end of life	Resale value at end of life	Net total cost over life	Average net cost per annum
(1)	(2)	(3)	(4)	(5)	(6)
	£	£	£	£	£
1	5,000	500	3,000	2,500	2,500
2	5,000	1,500	2,000	4,500	2,250
3	5,000	3,000	1,000	7,000	2,334
4	5,000	5,000	500	9,500	2,375
5	5,000	7,500	100	12,400	2,480
6	5,000	10,500	—	15,500	2,583
7	5,000	14,000	—	19,000	2,714
TOTAL	£35,000	£42,000	£6,600	£70,400	£17,236

Clearly the simple average cost per annum indicates that a vehicle life of two years is the most economic policy to adopt. Annual average costs rise when we keep the vehicle for three years: therefore trade-in the vehicle at the end of its second year.

Evaluation 2

In this evaluation we shall use the Annual Capital Charge method of appraisal. The object of the exercise is to identify that vehicle-life which results in the lowest annual cost, where this is defined by the lowest equivalent annual charge for a specified vehicle-life. Exhibit 133 below

Exhibit 133
Project F: Present values of total net costs (capital cost £5,000)

Years of vehicle life	Maintenance costs in each year	Interest factor at 20%	PV of annual maintenance costs	Total PV of maintenance costs to end of vehicle life	Estimated vehicle trade-in value	Interest factor at 20%	PV of trade-in value	PV of total net cost
(1)	(2)	(3)	(4)	(5)	(6)	(7)	(8)	(9)
	£		£	£	£		£	£
1	500	0.8333	417	417	3,000	0.8333	2,500	2,917
2	1,000	0.6944	694	1,111	2,000	0.6944	1,389	4,722
3	1,500	0.5787	868	1,979	1,000	0.5787	579	6,400
4	2,000	0.4823	965	2,944	500	0.4823	241	7,703
5	2,500	0.4019	1,005	3,949	100	0.4019	40	8,909
6	3,000	0.3349	1,005	4,954	—	—	—	9,954
7	3,500	0.2791	977	5,931	—	—	—	10,931

317

summarises the costs incurred by deciding to retain the vehicle for any series of years up to a maximum of seven years.

Column 2 states the maintenance, etc., costs incurred in each separate year that the vehicle is retained in the company's service – up to the maximum proposed of seven years. The PV of each of these separate annual sums is shown in column 4 having been discounted at a 20 per cent cost of capital. Column 5 aggregates the present values of each year's annual maintenance costs. Thus we have the present values of the total maintenance costs for any series of years up to seven. The trade-in values, discounted by the 20 per cent factor given in column 7, are shown in present value terms in column 8.

Bringing the £5,000 initial outlay cost to add to the data in column 5, less the PV of the trade-in value, we now arrive at the present value of the total net cost in column 9. The next stage in the appraisal process demands that the totals given in column 9 of the above exhibit are annualised. That is, we must convert for each of the life-series, the total costs into equivalent annual charges – the annual capital charge as we have previously termed it. To do this we need the sinking fund factor for each of the several life cycles, using 20 per cent as our cost of capital. The reciprocal of the relevant discounting factor provides the answer, as is explained below.

$$\text{Single year life} = \text{Reciprocal of 1st year factor}$$

$$= 1/0.8333$$

$$= 1.20$$

$$\text{Two-year life} = \text{Reciprocal of aggregate of 1st and 2nd year factors}$$

$$= 1/1.5278$$

$$= 0.655$$

These calculations should be continued for each of the vehicle life-series up to the maximum of seven. The results which demonstrate the equal annual charges for keeping the vehicle for one, two, three or up to seven years are given in Exhibit 134.

This exhibit shows that the lowest annualised cost is achieved when the vehicle is kept for four or five years. Therefore we would recommend that the trade-in should take place at the end of year 4 or 5 (the difference between the annualised costs of these two years is of no consequence, and perhaps the decision would then hinge on availability of actual cash to finance the change!). It is pointed out however that the example has been kept as simple as possible in order to demonstrate the annual capital charge concept. Clearly we must bring into a full evaluation,

1   The taxation consequences of the running costs.

Exhibit 134

Project F: annual capital charges

Years of vehicle life	Present value of total net cost over life, £	Sinking fund interest factor: 20 per cent	Equivalent annual capital charge, £
(1)	(2)	(3)	(4)
1	2,917	1.20	3,500
2	4,722	0.655	3,093
3	6,400	0.475	3,040
4	7,703	0.386	2,973
5	8,909	0.334	2,975
6	9,954	0.301	2,996
7	10,931	0.277	3,028

2   Any available writing-down allowances in respect of the car.

Our final note refers to the total cost figures in column 2. These sums represent, for the relevant vehicle life, the capital sums which would have to be invested at 20 per cent compound interest, in order to receive an annuity of the value given in column 4.

Project G

Our next example of capital expenditure appraisal will review the cost impacts of alternative ways of financing the acquisition of a specific asset which is required for certain manufacturing operations. In this instance we shall not bring the expected operating net cash flows into our calculations. This is because such operational cash flows will be identical for all methods of financing the asset acquisition. Clearly the appraisal must be directed towards ascertaining the lowest discounted cost of having the asset available for use.

The Delta Company Limited has decided to acquire a machine tool for a new manufacturing process. The process final product has an assured market and the forecast incomes are substantial. However there are three methods of financing the asset acquisition which are available to the company, and the managing director seeks advice about which method to select. The machinery costs £10,000 but no regional development grant is applicable though 100 per cent first year taxation allowance is available for the full amount of the capital expenditure. The plant has a five-year life, and the corporation tax rate is 50 per cent. The various financing strategies are detailed below.

Purchase of asset
Acquisition cost £10,000; installed in year 0; 100 per cent taxation allowance receivable in year 1; no scrap value on retirement of the asset.

Lease of asset
Details of plant cost and life, etc., are as given above. The lease terms require payments of £2,500 per annum for five years; each payment to be made at the beginning of each year.

Hire-purchase of asset
Details of plant cost and life etc. are as given above. The hire-purchase contract requires a deposit of £2,500 in year 0. Annual payments of £1,500 are to be made at the end of each year; interest on the balance of £7,500 is also to be charged at a rate of 10 per cent.

The first stage must be to establish the cost cash flows of the three financing strategies. Exhibit 135 presents the yearly cost impacts of purchasing, leasing or buying by hire purchase the assets involved. In each instance the net effect of inflows and outflows is shown at the 'net cost' line. If we were to consider the net totals derived from the undiscounted cost flows, then the cheapest financing strategy is clearly the outright purchase method. The most costly method is shown – in this way – to be the hire-purchase strategy.

However when the yearly patterns of cost flows are discounted at the corporate cost of capital, a different picture emerges. Exhibit 136 demonstrates the effect of discounting the yearly flows and immediately the importance of the cost of capital rating becomes apparent: the order of preference of financing strategy changes within the range of 5 to 20 per cent discounting rates. It is pointed out that these conclusions, regarding choice of the method of financing, reflect the costs of the three methods. It should be recognised that other policy factors may have an impact on the choice of financing the asset acquisition. Even at a cost of capital of 5 per cent, it may be considered advisable to lease or buy by hire-purchase in order to conserve corporate cash resources. In any case a decision based upon data given in Exhibit 135 alone, could be completely erroneous.

Self-examination questions

1 Refer to Exhibits 133 and 134: recalculate the present values of the investments net cost, and the equivalent annual charges for years 1 to 7, after assuming a cost of capital of (a) 15 per cent and (b) 25 per cent.

Exhibit 135
Project G: Yearly cash flows — financing costs

Details	Years 0 £	1 £	2 £	3 £	4 £	5 £	6 £	TOTALS £
1 PURCHASE								
Initial outlay cost	(10,000)	—	—	—	—	—	—	(10,000)
100% tax allowance on capital cost	—	5,000	—	—	—	—	—	5,000
Net cost	(10,000)	5,000	—	—	—	—	—	£(5,000)
2 LEASE								
Annual payments	(2,500)	(2,500)	(2,500)	(2,500)	(2,500)	—	—	(12,500)
Tax relief on payments — in succeeding year	—	1,250	1,250	1,250	1,250	1,250	—	6,250
Net cost	(2,500)	(1,250)	(1,250)	(1,250)	(1,250)	1,250	—	£(6,250)
3 HIRE PURCHASE								
Deposit	(2,500)							(2,500)
Annual instalments		(1,500)	(1,500)	(1,500)	(1,500)	(1,500)	—	(7,500)
10% Interest on balance of £7,500		(750)	(750)	(750)	(750)	(750)		(3,750)
Tax relief in interest payment			375	375	375	375	375	1,875
100% Tax allowance on capital cost		5,000						5,000
Net cost	(2,500)	2,750	(1,875)	(1,875)	(1,875)	(1,875)	375	£(6,875)

Exhibit 136
Project G: Discounted yearly cash flows

Year	Cost of capital 5% Int. factor	Purch. £	Lease £	HP £	Cost of capital 10% Int. factor	Purch. £	Lease £	HP £	Cost of capital 15% Int. factor	Purch. £	Lease £	HP £	Cost of capital 20% Int. factor	Purch. £	Lease £	HP £
0	1.00	(10,000)	(2,500)	(2,500)	1.00	(10,000)	(2,500)	(2,500)	1.00	(10,000)	(2,500)	(2,500)	1.00	(10,000)	(2,500)	(2,500)
1	0.95	4,750	(2,500)	2,613	0.91	4,550	(2,500)	2,503	0.87	4,350	(2,500)	2,392	0.83	4,150	(2,500)	2,283
2	0.91	—	{(4,425)	—	0.83	—	{(3,963)	—	0.76	—	{(3,575)	—	0.69	—	{(3,225)	—
3	0.86	—		{(6,319)	0.75	—		{(5,400)	0.66	—		{(4,669)	0.58	—		{(4,031)
4	0.82	—			0.68	—			0.57	—			0.48	—		
5	0.78	—	975		0.62	—	775		0.50	—	625		0.40	—	500	
6	0.75	—	—	281	0.56	—	—	210	0.43	—	—	161	0.33	—	—	124
PV total cost		(5,250)	(5,950)	(5,925)		(5,450)	(5,688)	(5,187)		(5,650)	(5,450)	(4,616)		(5,850)	(5,225)	(4,124)
Ranking		1	3	2		2	3	1		3	2	1		3	2	1

2 To what extent do cash flow methods of investment evaluation (DCF) displace the value of judgement in appraising the worths of alternative projects?

3 What do you understand by a project's risk period?

4 Calculate the minimum sum which you could afford to pay now for an investment promising net cash flows of £1,000 in year one, £2,500 in years two and three and £3,000 in year four. You wish to achieve a break-even situation with a cost of borrowing the necessary capital being set at 12 per cent. If the lender demanded a variable interest rate with the interest cost being 15 per cent in year four, how would your present capital funds requirement be affected?

5 Compare the effectiveness of DCF yield, Net Present Value and Payback as techniques for appraising the wealth creating powers of proposed investments.

Recommended reading

ROCKLEY, L. E., *Finance for the Purchasing Executive*, Business Books (1978), see chapters 10 and 11.

ED29, Accounting for leases and hire purchase contracts, Institute of Chartered Accountants in England and Wales, October 1981, see also the related Guidance Notes.

BROMWICH, M., *The Economics of Capital Budgeting*, Penguin Books (1976), see chapters 4 to 8.

VLIELAND–BODDY, C., and M., 'The Tax Advantages of Equipment Leasing' *Accountancy*, February 1980, pp. 82–4.

16 Risk and uncertainty

Introduction

Capital investment decisions have been portrayed, up to this stage, as though they were based invariably upon accurate statements of future costs and incomes. From these figures a forecasted rate of return for a particular proposal has then emerged. In examples demonstrated in the previous chapters, investment lives varied from 5 to 10 years, whilst industrial forecasters can instance investments where much longer lives are being forecast. Few investment projects are limited to the precise lives quoted in their original forecast information, because any capital expenditure decision is always subject to unknown developments in the future. Such developments may affect an investment's initial cost, its running costs, the size of the market and thus the ultimate sales volume, price at which the output can be sold and the life of the project itself. No single table of DCF calculations can bring together all of the imponderables which may affect a project's outcome, yet business decisions are being based upon the type of single estimated rate of return which has been demonstrated in the earlier chapters.

The place of judgement

This is not to say that the evaluation criteria used in Chapter 15 are badly conceived. They make the best use of the information upon which they are based. They represent a conventional approach to investment appraisal – assessing future outcomes as a result of 'best guesses' of the timing of future events, of the level of future costs and incomes. With such best guess forecasted single rates of return, a business manager can then apply his own judgement of the proposed expenditure's chances of survival or of profit. In other words, hunch still plays a vital part in investment choice. Nevertheless it is true to say that investment decision-making has experienced considerable improvements, in the method and technique of proposal evaluation, during the last ten years. Not the least of these improvements concerns the use of time-adjusted rates of return which take into account the time value of money. However these changes in method are not enough, by themselves, for ensuring the best decisional aids in the investment analysis of the future. Even if it is accepted that the experienced manager's judgement (of a future cash flow's potential) can be a viable criterion in selecting between alternative investment choices, it is still not enough to enable him to assess an average value of his hunch appraisal. This can be achieved only with considerable experience of specific investment types. A sufficient historical experience of certain capital expenditure proposals may well form a judgement base for appraising similar projects in the future. Where a company undertakes frequent small investment projects, it is likely that the ultimate variations between forecasted and actual returns will average out over the whole range of such projects. In these instances the single best-guess indicator of project desirability may well be sufficient.

On the other hand, where a capital expenditure project is expected to have considerable impact on a firm's existing capital and asset structure, the same conclusions about the sufficiency of the single best-guess criterion cannot be supported. It is very probable that a poor actual performance of the large project would have a significant influence upon the firm's total rate of return. In consequence the company's dividend potential and market rating (P/E ratio) could be adversely affected, and therefore its power to raise further long-term capital for expansion severely restricted. With the relatively large capital expenditure proposal, more information on possible future outcomes for a project's returns is essential for better corporate long-term planning. Exhibits 137, 138 and 139 below show the

Exhibit 137
Forecast data of investment proposal

Sales price of product	£10 each
Sales volume	36,000 units per annum
Running costs	£250,000 per annum
Economic life	12 years
Investment cost	£75,000
Net cash flows per annum	£360,000 − £250,000
	= £110,000
Present value of net cash flows at 15 per cent cost of capital	£110,000 × 5.4206
	= £596,266
Net present value	£596,266 − £75,000
	= £521,266

Exhibit 138

Likely ranges of future outcomes for proposal data

Sale price of product	£9 to £12 each
Sales volume	32,000–40,000 units p.a.
Running costs	£240,000–£270,000 p.a.
Economic life	10 to 20 years
Investment cost	£70,000–£100,000

Exhibit 139

Best and worst outcomes from forecast data

	Best result	Worst result
Sales price of product	£12	£9
Sales volume	40,000 units	32,000 units
Running costs	£240,000	£270,000
Economic life	20 years	10 years
Investment cost	£70,000	£100,000
Sales income	£480,000	£288,000
Running costs	£240,000	£270,000
Net cash flows per annum	£240,000	£18,000
PV of net cash flows at		
15 per cent	£1,502,160	£90,342
Net present value	£1,432,160	−£9,658

problems a decision-maker might have to face when he has to apply his judgement to appraising the worth of a particular investment proposal.

The results in Exhibit 137 were obtained by the single best-guess approach and look attractive, they represent a growth in wealth which should accrue to the company *after charging a 15 per cent cost of capital rate of interest*. However a closer examination of the proposal's prospects reveals quite a range of potential outcomes for the various factors affecting the proposal's whole performance. The additional information is given in Exhibit 138.

In order to assess the limits of the risks attaching to the investment proposal, a decision-maker may now calculate a most optimistic and a most pessimistic rate of return. These returns are based upon the likely extremes of the values shown for the various factors affecting the proposal. Exhibit 139 shows how this concept is applied. These two extremes of *possible* net present values of the proposal should be compared with the single best-guess result of £521,226. It then becomes very obvious that such widely varying estimates of future returns present the decision-maker with totally

326

inadequate information for reliable investment forecasting. The question which must be answered is – 'How can the basic data be improved to make the ultimate evaluation of a project more meaningful?'

Improving decisional data

A first priority should be the improvement of forecasts. In so far as errors and uncertainties can be removed by, for example, an extension of market research or extrapolation of cost trends from internal cost data, this should be done. However, just as the cost of costing has always been a major point of concern for management accountants, so should the costs of forecasting be weighed against the additional benefit which it produces. Where a considerable expenditure is necessary to achieve a minimal increase in forecasting accuracy, it may well prove to be not worth the expense.

Again most managers can cite instances of the optimistic and the pessimistic estimator. The writer has met instances where decision-makers have known of a certain manager's propensity for over-confidence. Where these circumstances have produced estimates which were, say, 10 to 15 per cent in excess of the actual outcomes for 90 per cent of the time, then clearly a specific adjustment of such future forecasts ought to be made. A more frequently used method for countering hidden risks and uncertainties arises where the decision-maker demands a higher return for a proposal which *he considers* is risky. Where it seems that sizeable uncertainties could be hidden in the many variable factors which determine a project's profitability, then the raising of the cut-off rate for proposal acceptance may provide some 'cover' for taking on the uncertainty. It is suggested however that the method is somewhat weak because the decision-maker can never know the size of the final risk he is accepting, neither can he know the true extent of the risks he is avoiding. Furthermore, the practice of an unreasoned raising of the cut-off rate can restrict the flow of profitable opportunities which are necessary for the continued existence and growth of the company.

A further and more acceptable first approach to the quantification of uncertainties, which may lie in business investment, concerns selectivity. By this procedure the project appraiser selects a value from the normal single best-guess estimates in a proposal evaluation. This particular factor's value is then varied by a specific percentage or quantity: the project's expected rate of return is then recalculated, incorporating the one (arbitrary) variation in the forecast data, in order to find out what effect such a variation would have on the ultimate expected rate of return for the proposal. When this process has been repeated several times, giving a number of percentage variations in the average expected return, then the extent of importance of each factor's forecast in the eventual outcome will be revealed. Here the reader should remember that if the likelihood of the forecasts in Exhibit 137

327

being achieved is only a 70 per cent chance for each factor, then the likelihood of all of them attaining the forecasted values *at the same time* is only 17 per cent.

Examining the results of a selectivity study will indicate those estimates which are critical to the proposal's outcome. Consequently the areas where further research is necessary into the accuracy of forecasted data can be emphasised. Extra attention to these areas vital to proposal productivity may well enable the forecasts to be improved. At least the figures should be blessed with sounder bases from which to draw conclusions. The investment's forecasts and its ultimate evaluation will be giving better information to the decision-maker, consistent with forecasting cost and available business knowledge. Exhibit 140 demonstrates the value of a selective analysis of the importance of cost and income in a proposal's estimated returns.*

The horizontal line grades percentage changes for the variable factors in a particular investment. Assuming a 5 per cent increase in plant cost, the broken lines on the chart show that a 2 per cent reduction in the rate of return could be expected. Similarly a 5 per cent decrease in building costs should give a 1.7 per cent increase in the expected return from the proposal. Such visual expressions of capital expenditure profitabilities have considerable presentation value for the busy decision-makers: their appreciation of the risks involved is easily heightened. It must be emphasised however that the above exhibit does not present a general picture for all investment projects. It is applicable to the circumstances of that project only which is represented in the exhibit.

A further example of project sensitivity to variations in forecast data is given in Exhibits 141 to 143. Here again the forecasted information is shown to have a (limited) range of possible outcomes.

It is here that present value profiles can be used once more to show the relative worths of the various groups of factor values affecting the investment's forecasted returns. Exhibit 142 demonstrates the sensitivity of the project's returns to variations in (a) net cash flows and (b) investment life. The point at which the profile line crosses the line of investment initial outlay indicates discounted payback periods for the project, where there are variations in the forecast net cash flows. The graph shows that a doubling of net cash flows from £75 to £150 per annum will reduce the discounted payback by *more* than 50 per cent. The conclusions to be drawn from such a presentation can be impressive where more variables are introduced into the calculations. Next, Exhibit 143 shows the same information being used to produce DCF yields for the several combinations of factors which can influence the project's returns. In this case the possible economic life has been extended to 20 years.

*See MCFALL, I., and DENHOLM, J., 'The complete investment picture', *Management Today*, p 74 (February 1967).

Exhibit 140

Project return sensitivity to cost/income variations

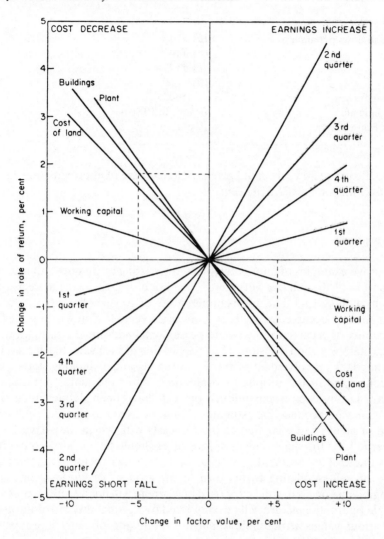

This arbitrary extension of project life gives a clear indication that, after a certain period, length of economic life is of minor importance to the forecasted return. In particular, if the capital expenditure proposal should prove to have a longer profitable life than the 10 years quoted in the original forecast, then, with net cash flows of £150 per annum, little improvement in the rate of return can be expected *from such an extension of life*. However with net cash flows of £75 per annum, a lengthening of the proposal's

329

Exhibit 141
Forecast data of investment proposal

Net cash flows per annum	(*a*) £75
	(*b*) £100
	(*c*) £125
	(*d*) £150
Investment cost	£300
Economic life	From 2 to 10 years
Cost of capital	10 per cent

economic life to 20 years could give a yield increase of approximately 7 per cent *over the forecast 21.5 per cent.*

Risk profiles

The above examples of improvements in forecasting techniques still lack an evaluation of the relative variations' likelihood of arrival. If the decision-maker could be told that, for example, a life of 10 years has a 60 per cent probability of occurrence whereas a life of 20 years has only a 20 per cent probability of occurrence, he would possess vital additional information to aid his making a good decision. The presentation of such valuable decisional data needs the involvement of those forecasting and estimating staffs who are concerned in the proposal's evaluation. After the major influencing factors, in any capital expenditure project, have been defined then the managers who produce the estimates should be asked to give the probable range of values to be applied to the forecasts with which they have been concerned. At the same time each forecaster should be encouraged to give his estimate of the probability of achievement for each sector of the forecast range of values relating to his own factor groups. By these means the intangibles associated with a proposed investment will not be represented by a single figure: the picture will be completed by a probability distribution of the various values attributable to each of the major influencing groups of costs and incomes found in any proposed capital investment.

The next stage in the process of reaching an assessment of the proposed investment would be to find out the rates of return, for the project, which would result from random combinations of the probability values for each of the major influencing factor groups. Common sense will have to lay down some restriction on the 'random' combinations. There would have to be a realistic limit to the share of the market attainable by the investment plus existing resources. The end result will be an assessment of the return to an investment which gives not only the spread of various likely returns, but also

Exhibit 142

Sensitivity analysis – influence on proposal's present value.
Cost of capital – 10 per cent

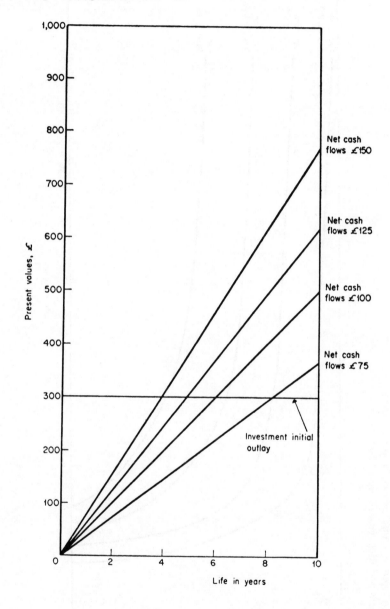

Exhibit 143
Sensitivity analysis — influence on proposal's yield
Investment cost £300, cost of capital 10 per cent

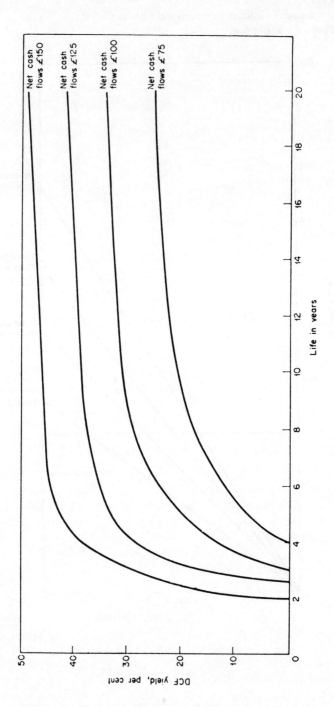

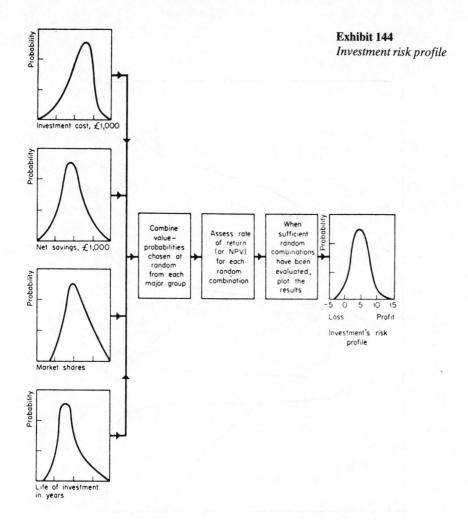

Exhibit 144
Investment risk profile

Probability

Investment cost, £1,000

Probability

Net savings, £1,000

Probability

Market shares

Probability

Life of investment
in years

| Combine value— probabilities chosen at random from each major group |

| Assess rate of return (or NPV) for each random combination |

| When sufficient random combinations have been evaluated, plot the results |

Probability

-5 0 5 10 15

Loss   Profit

Investment's risk
profile

a *weighting to the likelihood* of the actual return falling at any point within the potential whole range. Exhibit 144 shows the sequence of events in evaluating the risks and uncertainties implicit in planning the installation of long-term capital assets. The final chart of investment risk profile measures, on the vertical axis, the probabilities that the investment will achieve the returns graduated on the horizontal axis.

The final risk profile, which incorporates the range of all the variable factors for the project, shows not only the average or expected rate of return but also the probability of their being achieved. The likelihood that other rates of return, expressed by any point on the profile, will be achieved is similarly expressed in probability ratings. Thus the decision-maker knows the probability of loss or of large gain and he is the better equipped to place his own subjective value on the worthwhileness of the

333

334

Exhibit 145
Risk profiles of alternative investments

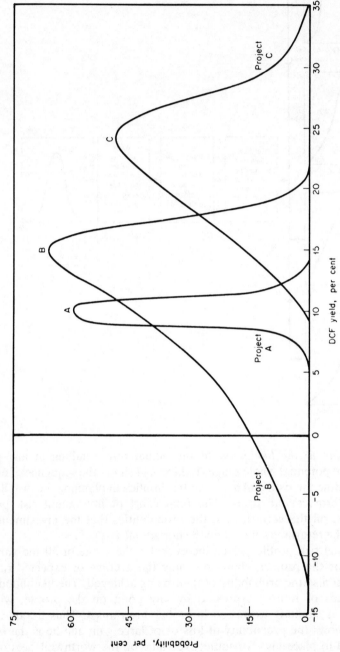

Project A

Project B

Project C

B

A

C

Probability, per cent

DCF yield, per cent

gamble. The usefulness of such risk profiles is shown to advantage by Exhibit 145.

Here three alternative proposals are presented for the choice of the decision-maker. He can have project A with its assured 10 per cent return but with no prospect of high returns, or of loss. Proposal B offers a higher average return of 15 per cent; it also rates a higher probability for the 15 per cent. Unfortunately project B has a 15 per cent probability of loss. Finally proposal C's expected return, 24 per cent, is given the lowest probability rating of the three proposals. On the other hand it offers no prospect of loss and a 10 per cent probability of a high return of 30 per cent. The reader is invited to place himself in the position of the decision-maker, who is about to spend say £500,000 on *one* of the three proposals. Which investment project should be chosen for implementing?

Self-examination questions

1 How would you attempt to improve the reliability of data used in the forecasts of project cost/incomes, so as to reduce the element of uncertainty about its forecast rate of return?

2 What do you understand by (*a*) selectivity, (*b*) sensitivity and (*c*) probability?

3 The inherent risks of a project are perhaps a matter for entrepreneurial judgement. How would you bring risk *measurement* into the value assessments of three competing investment proposals?

4 What do you understand by the 'risk profile' of a project? Does it enable better appreciation of project possible outcomes than the solely numerical rate of return etc. criteria?

Recommended reading

TOWNSEND, E. C., *Investment and Uncertainty*, Oliver and Boyd (1969).

SIZER, J., *An Insight Into Management Accounting*, Penguin Books (1978), see chapter 6.

BROMWICH, M., *The Economics of Capital Budgeting*, Penguin Books (1976), see chapters 12 and 13.

CARSBERG, B., *Economics of Business Decisions*, Penguin Books (1976), see chapters 13, 14 and 15.

Appendices

A 1981 Companies Act: account formats

Balance sheet formats

Format 1

A *Called up share capital not paid (1)*

B *Fixed assets*

   I Intangible assets
- 1 Development costs
- 2 Concessions, patents, licences, trade marks and similar rights and assets (2)
- 3 Goodwill (3)
- 4 Payments on account

   II Tangible assets
- 1 Land and buildings
- 2 Plant and machinery
- 3 Fixtures, fittings, tools and equipment
- 4 Payments on account and assets in course of construction

   III Investments
- 1 Shares in group companies
- 2 Loans to group companies
- 3 Shares in related companies
- 4 Loans to related companies
- 5 Other investments other than loans
- 6 Other loans
- 7 Own shares (4)

C *Current assets*

   I Stocks
- 1 Raw materials and consumables
- 2 Work in progress
- 3 Finished goods and goods for resale
- 4 Payments on account

II Debtors (5)
    1 Trade debtors
    2 Amounts owed by group companies
    3 Amounts owed by related companies
    4 Other debtors
    5 Called up share capital not paid (1)
    6 Prepayments and accrued income (6)
III Investments
    1 Shares in group companies
    2 Own shares (4)
    3 Other investments
IV Cash at bank and in hand

D *Prepayments and accrued income (6)*

E *Creditors: amounts falling due within one year*
    1 Debenture loans (7)
    2 Bank loans and overdrafts
    3 Payments received on account (8)
    4 Trade creditors
    5 Bills of exchange payable
    6 Amounts owed to group companies
    7 Amounts owed to related companies
    8 Other creditors including taxation and social security (9)
    9 Accruals and deferred income (10)

F *Net current assets (liabilities) (11)*

G *Total assets less current liabilities*

H *Creditors: amounts falling due after more than one year*
    1 Debenture loans (7)
    2 Bank loans and overdrafts
    3 Payments received on account (8)
    4 Trade creditors
    5 Bills of exchange payable
    6 Amounts owed to group companies
    7 Amounts owed to related companies
    8 Other creditors including taxation and social security (9)
    9 Accruals and deferred income (10)

I *Provisions for liabilities and charges*
    1 Pensions and similar obligations
    2 Taxation, including deferred taxation
    3 Other provisions

J *Accruals and deferred income (10)*

K *Capital and reserves*
  I Called up share capital (12)
  II Share premium account
  III Revaluation reserve

IV Other reserves
    1 Capital redemption reserve
    2 Reserve for own shares
    3 Reserves provided for by the articles of association
    4 Other reserves
V Profit and loss account

Format 2

ASSETS

A *Called up share capital not paid (1)*

B *Fixed assets*
  I Intangible assets
    1 Development costs
    2 Concessions, patents, licences, trade marks and similar rights and assets (2)
    3 Goodwill (3)
    4 Payments on account
  II Tangible assets
    1 Land and buildings
    2 Plant and machinery
    3 Fixtures, fittings, tools and equipment
    4 Payments on account and assets in course of construction
  III Investments
    1 Shares in group companies
    2 Loans to group companies
    3 Shares in related companies
    4 Loans to related companies
    5 Other investments other than loans
    6 Other loans
    7 Own shares (4)

C *Current assets*
  I Stocks
    1 Raw materials and consumables
    2 Work in progress
    3 Finished goods and goods for resale
    4 Payments on account
  II Debtors (5)
    1 Trade debtors
    2 Amounts owed by group companies
    3 Amounts owed by related companies
    4 Other debtors
    5 Called up share capital not paid (1)
    6 Prepayments and accrued income (6)

III Investments
    1 Shares in group companies
    2 Own shares (4)
    3 Other investments
IV Cash at bank and in hand

D *Prepayments and accrued income (6)*

A Capital and reserves
  I Called up share capital (12)
  II Share premium account
  III Revaluation reserve
  IV Other reserves
    1 Capital redemption reserve
    2 Reserve for own shares
    3 Reserves provided for by the articles of association
    4 Other reserves
  V Profit and loss account

B Provisions for liabilities and charges
    1 Pensions and similar obligations
    2 Taxation including deferred taxation
    3 Other provisions

C Creditors (13);
    1 Debenture loans (7)
    2 Bank loans and overdrafts
    3 Payments received on account (8)
    4 Trade creditors
    5 Bills of exchange payable
    6 Amounts owed to group companies
    7 Amounts owed to related companies
    8 Other creditors including taxation and social security (9)
    9 Accruals and deferred income (10)
D Accruals and deferred income (10)

Notes on the balance sheet formats

(1) *Called up share capital not paid*
(Formats 1 and 2, items A and C.II.5)
This item may be shown in either of the two positions given in Formats 1 and 2.

(2) *Concessions, patents, licences, trade marks and similar rights and assets*
(Formats 1 and 2, item B.I.2)

Amounts in respect of assets shall only be included in a company's balance sheet under this item if either:

(*a*) the assets were acquired for valuable consideration and are not required to be shown under goodwill

(*b*) or the assets in question were created by the company itself.

(3) *Goodwill*

(Formats 1 and 2, item B.I.3)

Amounts representing goodwill shall only be included to the extent that the goodwill was acquired for valuable consideration.

(4) *Own shares*

(Formats 1 and 2, items B.III.7 and C.III.2)

The nominal value of the shares held shall be shown separately.

(5) *Debtors*

(Formats 1 and 2, items C.II.1 to 6)

The amount falling due after more than one year shall be shown separately for each item included under debtors.

(6) *Prepayments and accrued income*

(Formats 1 and 2, items C.II.6 and D)

This item may be shown in either of the two positions given in Formats 1 and 2.

(7) *Debenture loans*

(Format 1, items E.1 and H.1 and Format 2, item C.1)

The amount of any convertible loans shall be shown separately.

(8) *Payments received on account*

(Format 1, items E.3 and H.3 and Format 2, item C.3)

Payments received on account of orders shall be shown for each of these items in so far as they are not shown as deductions from stocks.

(9) *Other creditors including taxation and social security*

(Format 1, items E.8 and H.8 and Format 2, item C.8)

The amount for creditors in respect of taxation and social security shall be shown separately from the amount for other creditors.

(10) *Accruals and deferred income*

(Format 1, items E.9, H.9 and J and Format 2, items C.9 and D)

The two positions given for this item in Format 1 at E.9 and H.9 are an alternative to the position at J, but if the item is not shown in a position corresponding to that at J it may be shown in either or both of the other two positions, as the case may require.

The two positions given for this item in Format 2 are alternatives.

(11) *Net current assets (liabilities)*

(Format 1, item F)

In determining the amount to be shown for this item any amounts shown under 'prepayments and accrued income' shall be taken into account wherever shown.

(12) *Called up share capital*

(Format 1, item K.I and Format 2, item A.I)

The amount of allotted share capital and the amount of called up share capital which has been paid up shall be shown separately.

(13) *Creditors*
      (Format 2, items C.1 to 9)
      Amounts falling due within one year and after one year shall be shown
      separately for each of these items and their aggregate shall be shown
      separately for all of these items.

Profit and loss account formats

Format 1

1   Turnover
2   Cost of sales (14)
3   Gross profit or loss
4   Distribution costs (14)
5   Administrative expenses (14)
6   Other operating income
7   Income from shares in group companies
8   Income from shares in related companies
9   Income from other fixed asset investments (15)
10 Other interest receivable and similar income (15)
11 Amounts written off investments
12 Interest payable and similar charges (16)
13 Tax on profit or loss on ordinary activities
14 Profit or loss on ordinary activities after taxation
15 Extraordinary income
16 Extraordinary charges
17 Extraordinary profit or loss
18 Tax on extraordinary profit or loss
19 Other taxes not shown under the above items
20 Profit or loss for the financial year

Format 2

1   Turnover
2   Change in stocks of finished goods and work in progress
3   Own work capitalised
4   Other operating income
5   (*a*) Raw materials and consumables
    (*b*) Other external charges
6   Staff costs:
    (*a*) wages and salaries
    (*b*) social security costs
    (*c*) other pension costs
7   (*a*) Depreciation and other amounts written off tangible and intangible fixed
           assets

       (*b*)   Exceptional amounts written off current assets
  8   Other operating charges
  9   Income from shares in group companies
10   Income from shares in related companies
11   Income from other fixed asset investments (15)
12   Other interest receivable and similar income (15)
13   Amounts written off investments
14   Interest payable and similar charges (16)
15   Tax on profit or loss on ordinary activities
16   Profit or loss on ordinary activities after taxation
17   Extraordinary income
18   Extraordinary charges
19   Extraordinary profit or loss
20   Tax on extraordinary profit or loss
21   Other taxes not shown under the above items
22   Profit or loss for the financial year

Format 3

A   Charges
    1   Cost of sales (14)
    2   Distribution costs (14)
    3   Administrative expenses (14)
    4   Amounts written off investments
    5   Interest payable and similar charges (16)
    6   Tax on profit or loss on ordinary activities
    7   Profit or loss on ordinary activities after taxation
    8   Extraordinary charges
    9   Tax on extraordinary profit or loss
   10   Other taxes not shown under the above items
   11   Profit or loss for the financial year
B   Income
    1   Turnover
    2   Other operating income
    3   Income from shares in group companies
    4   Income from shares in related companies
    5   Income from other fixed asset investments (15)
    6   Other interest receivable and similar income (15)
    7   Profit or loss on ordinary activities after taxation
    8   Extraordinary income
    9   Profit or loss for the financial year

Format 4

A   Charges
    1   Reduction in stocks of finished goods and in work in progress

2 (*a*) Raw materials and consumables
   (*b*) Other external charges
3 Staff costs:
   (*a*) wages and salaries
   (*b*) social security costs
   (*c*) other pension costs
4 (*a*) Depreciation and other amounts written off tangible and intangible
          fixed assets
   (*b*) Exceptional amounts written off current assets
5 Other operating charges
6 Amounts written off investments
7 Interest payable and similar charges (16)
8 Tax on profit or loss on ordinary activities
9 Profit or loss on ordinary activities after taxation
10 Extraordinary charges
11 Tax on extraordinary profit or loss
12 Other taxes not shown under the above items
13 Profit or loss for the financial year
B Income
   1 Turnover
   2 Increase in stocks of finished goods and in work in progress
   3 Own work capitalised
   4 Other operating income
   5 Income from shares in group companies
   6 Income from shares in related companies
   7 Income from other fixed asset investments (15)
   8 Other interest receivable and similar income (15)
   9 Profit or loss on ordinary activities after taxation
   10 Extraordinary income
   11 Profit or loss for the financial year

Notes on the profit and loss account formats

(14) *Cost of sales: distribution costs: administrative expenses*
      (Format 1, items 2, 4 and 5 and Format 3, items A.1, 2 and 3)
      These items shall be stated after taking into account any necessary provisions
      for depreciation or diminution in value of assets.
(15) *Income from other fixed asset investments: other interest receivable and similar
      income*
      (Format 1, items 9 and 10; Format 2, items 11 and 12; Format 3, items B.5
      and 6; Format 4, items B.7 and 8)
      Income and interest derived from group companies shall be shown separately
      from income and interest derived from other sources.
(16) *Interest payable and similar charges*
      (Format 1, item 12; Format 2, item 14; Format 3, item A.5; Format 4, item
      A.7)
      The amount payable to group companies shall be shown separately.

(17)   *Formats 1 and 3*

The amount of any provisions for depreciation and diminution in value of tangible and intangible fixed assets falling to be shown under items 7(a) and A.4(a) respectively in Formats 2 and 4 shall be disclosed in a note to the accounts in any case where the profit and loss account is prepared by reference to Format 1 or Format 3.

B Glossary of common accounting and financial terms

Absorption costing A method of costing where all costs are identified with – absorbed by – units of output and stock: thus all costs of a particular period are allocated between that period's output and the stocks in hand at the end of the period.

Amortisation A reduction in a debt or fund by periodic payments, covering interest and part of the principal; also a charge against earnings to write off the cost of an intangible asset over a period of years.

Articles of Association The regulations governing the internal affairs of the company: the Articles specify (*inter alia*) the rights, duties and powers of the members of the company together with the powers of the directors: the Articles are filed with the Registrar of Companies.

Asset turnover The ratio of sales to assets employed which is expressed as sales per £ of assets employed. An increase in the ratio implies a more efficient use of corporate assets.

Assets Everything a business owns or is due to it: *current assets*, such as cash, short-term deposits, debtors, stocks of raw materials, work-in-progress and finished goods; *fixed assets*, such as buildings and machinery; and *intangible assets*, such as patents and goodwill.

Authorised shares The total amount of capital which a company is authorised to issue: the total amount is recorded in the Memorandum of Association which is filed with the Registrar of Companies. Also referred to as *Registered Capital*.

Balance sheet A statement showing the nature and amount of a company's assets, liabilities and capital on a given date. In money terms, the balance sheet shows what the company owned, what it owed, and the ownership interest in the company of its shareholders. A *consolidated balance sheet* is one showing the financial condition of a holding or parent company and its subsidiaries. A *narrative balance sheet* is one that is written in vertical – rather than two-sided – form.

Basic accounts Those prepared substantially in accordance with established conventions on the basis of historical cost, including those in which some or all of the fixed assets have been revalued and/or some or all current assets are shown at estimated realisable value.

Bond or debenture A written promise to pay the holder a sum of money at a certain date (more than one year after issue) at a stated annual rate of interest. Debentures are frequently secured on the assets of the company. Where not so secured they are termed 'naked' debentures.

Book value The book value of an Ordinary share is determined from a company's records, by adding all assets (generally excluding such intangibles as goodwill), then deducting all debts and other liabilities, plus the liquidation price of any preference shares. The sum arrived at is divided by the *number* of Ordinary shares outstanding and the result is the book value per share. Book value of the assets of a company or a security may have little or no significant relationship to market value. The book value of an Ordinary share is also termed the 'net asset value' of the share.

Break-even point The level of output or value of sales where total costs equal total revenue.

Budget A financial or quantitative statement of a firm's desired or intended activity for a stated (future) operating period. Normally prepared and approved prior to commencement of the related period, it reflects the policies to be pursued during the specified period for the purpose of attaining the desired objectives or targets.

Budget variance The difference between actual costs incurred in an operation, and the costs which were expected when the plan was made. It may be favourable, i.e. less than the planned expenditure, or unfavourable.

Called-up capital Denotes that portion of the total sums due on the issued capital, which has been 'called-up' by the company from the shareholders.

Capacity costs Those costs necessary in order to provide the operational assets and corporate organisation to be ready to manufacture and sell the related goods – up to a planned maximum volume of output. (See *Fixed costs*.)

Capital budgeting Long-term planning for future capital expenditures: involves forecasting of initial outlays, their financing and the expected future cash flow effects.

Capitalisation Total amount of the various securities issued by a company. Capitalisation may include loan stock, preference and Ordinary shares. They are usually shown in the books of the issuing company at their nominal or face value.

Cash budget A schedule of expected cash receipts and payments over a limited future period.

Cash flow Reported net income of a company plus non-cash charges such as depreciation and charges to reserves (which are bookkeeping deductions and not paid out in cash). Other terms such as gross cash flow and net cash flow are derived from the pre- and post-tax net incomes plus non-cash charges.

Collateral Securities or other property pledged by a borrower to secure repayment of a loan.

Conservatism The practice of a prudent accountant in not anticipating gains as yet unrealised, but providing for all losses which have arisen or are likely to arise.

Consistency An accounting convention: where there are alternative, acceptable, methods of calculating or treating specific terms in the accounts and balance sheets, the method actually chosen and operated should be used consistently: if this is not done comparisons between different accounts and balance sheets would be impaired.

Continuous budget A method of budgeting which continually covers a specific future period: it adds a future month or quarter at the end of the planning period as the month or quarter just completed is deleted from the start of the planning period.

Contribution The amount by which sales price exceeds the variable, i.e. direct, expenses.

Controllable cost A cost that may be directly regulated or influenced by action at a given level of managerial authority.

Conversion The process of translating figures from historical pounds to pounds of current purchasing power.

Conversion cost The total amount of direct labour and factory overhead expenses which are incurred when raw material is transformed into a finished product.

Convertible A debenture that may be exchanged by the owner for Ordinary shares or another security of the same company, in accordance with the terms of the issue.

Cost allocation The assignment or allotment of proportions of the total overhead costs of an organisation to one or more cost centres or segments of a firm by reference to the benefits received by, or responsibilities of, those various cost centres, etc.

Cost apportionment The assignment or sharing out of allocated costs to cost services or cost units.

Cost centre The unit of activity or responsibility for which relevant costs are aggregated, and used for cost control.

Costing The methods and means by which costs of processes and products, for example, are ascertained.

Cost of sales The cost of stock sold, i.e. the total purchase cost of goods sold (retail or wholesale trades) or the total manufacturing cost (manufacturing business): also termed *Cost of goods sold*.

Current assets Those assets of a company that are reasonably expected to be realised in cash, or sold, or consumed during the normal operating cycle of the business. These include cash, debtors, short-term investments and all forms of stock. Frequently called *circulating assets* because they are (or should be) constantly on the move, being converted, in the production and marketing process, from raw material stock to cash (received from sales).

Current liabilities Money owed and payable by a company, usually within the normal operating cycle of the business. Items due and payable within one year may also be classified as current liabilities.

Current ratio   An index of liquidity or creditworthiness; derived from dividing the book value of total current assets by the book value of the total current liabilities.

Debentures   A written acknowledgement of a debt owing by a company. Normally the document is under seal, the debt carries a fixed rate of annual interest and it is repayable within a fixed term of years. The debt may be secured on certain of the company's assets, or it may be unsecured.

Depreciation   Charges against earnings to write off the cost, less salvage (resale) value, of a fixed asset over its estimated useful life. It is a bookkeeping entry and does not represent any cash outlay, nor are any funds earmarked for the purpose.

Direct costing   The form of output costing that charges manufacturing and other overhead costs to the revenue account of the period during which the costs were incurred. Direct costs include those costs which tend to vary directly in proportion with variations in output. (Compare with *Absorption costing*.)

Direct labour cost   Expenditure on labour that is directly attributable to a product: it is clearly identified with the product in course of manufacture.

Direct material   Expenditure on raw material which is incorporated in the finished product: it forms part of that product.

Dividend   The payment recommended by the board of directors to be distributed to shareholders. On preference shares, it is generally a fixed percentage of the share's nominal value. On Ordinary shares, the dividend varies with the fortunes of the company and the amount of cash on hand, and may be omitted at the discretion of the directors if business is poor or if they determine to withhold earnings to invest in plant and equipment, research and development, and so on. Sometimes a company will pay a dividend out of past earnings even if it is not currently operating at a profit. The proposed rate of dividend on Ordinary shares must be approved by the members in general meeting, before it is paid.

Earnings per share (EPS)   Profits after tax available for the ordinary shareholders, divided by the *number* of Ordinary shares in issue, fully paid.

Equity (or owner's equity)   The sum invested in a business either by way of the initial purchase of shares or injection of capital, plus the earnings retained in the business: also called net assets or net worth. Equity value reflects the excess of the value of total assets over total liabilities.

Extraordinary gain (or loss)   The difference between amounts actually realised from disposal transactions which do not form part of a company's trading activities, and the value to the company of the items involved at the time of disposal.

Factory cost   The cost of manufacture of the product or service: it includes prime cost (*q.v.*) plus factory overheads but excludes selling, distribution and administrative expenditures.

Factory overhead   All factory costs other than direct labour, direct materials and direct expenses. (See also *Direct costing*.)

Fictitious assets   Expenditures not charged to the profit and loss account of the year in which they were incurred: the relevant amounts are shown in balance sheets until written off to profit and loss appropriation accounts in future years, i.e. the sums involved are spread over those future years to achieve more realistic matching of income with expenditure.

Fixed assets   The capital expenditure of a business in respect of its permanent or semi-permanent physical structure: these possessions are not held for resale but will be retained for the purpose of earning income throughout future years.

Fixed charges   A class of business expense which cannot be identified with a specific output, except by some kind of subjective allocation. These expenses do not generally vary in money size as production varies and most fixed expenses will continue even if production were discontinued.

Fixed costs   A cost which, for a particular capacity structure, does not change in total during a given period. Fixed costs per unit tend to decrease as the volume of output increases – within the maximum output available from the specific capacity structure. (See *Capacity costs* and *Fixed charges*.)

Flexible budget   A budget that is prepared for a range of possible activity levels, rather than for a single level of activity: it is usually related to overhead costs only but variable materials and labour costs may also be included.

Garnishee order   Order by a court to a creditor restraining a debtor disposing of property until a sum of money to clear debts has been handed to the creditor.

Gearing   The ratio between (*a*) the issued preference shares and debentures and (*b*) the issued Ordinary shares: the various shares and debentures are expressed in nominal value terms.

Historical costing   The ascertainment of the cost of some activity by reference to costs which have already been incurred.

Holding gain (or loss)   The difference between the value to a business of an asset and the (depreciated) initial acquisition cost incurred by the company in purchasing that asset.

Ideal output   The maximum number of items that could be produced in a given period with a given physical capacity, no allowance being made for any form of production stoppage.

Ideal standard   The standard of cost and efficiency performance that can be attained under the most favourable conditions possible: no allowance is given for stoppages.

Incremental costs   The difference between the total costs of two alternative courses of action.

Indirect labour cost   Any expenditure on labour that is not directly attributable to a product being manufactured.

Intangible assets   Those assets that cannot be seen or touched, although they may have some value: patents, trademarks and goodwill are typical examples.

Internal check   The self-regulatory methods and procedures in an organisation

352

which operate continuously in checking the day-to-day transactions of the firm as part of the routine system.

Internal control   The complete system of controls whether financial or otherwise which are designed to promote efficiency, ensure adherence to corporate plans and policies, verify the accuracy of corporate data and to safeguard the continuing retention of corporate assets.

Investments   When appearing on a balance sheet, this term represents the investment in another company. The value shown is usually the original cost of the investment. The Companies Acts require balance sheet entries to show investments in two main groups – listed investments and unlisted investments.

Issued shares   That portion of the authorised share capital (*q.v.*) which has been issued to shareholders. Shares may be issued for cash or for other consideration.

Job costing   A method of apportioning manufacturing costs to specific single orders or batches of identical products.

Labour efficiency variance   The difference between the actual hours expended and the standard hours specified, multiplied by standard rate specified for the work.

Labour rate variance   See *Rate variance*.

Liabilities   All the claims against a company. Liabilities include accounts and wages and salaries payable, dividends declared payable, accrued taxes payable and fixed or long-term liabilities, such as mortgage bonds, debentures and bank loans.

Liquid assets   Cash, short-term investments, securities and debtors which can be turned into cash relatively quickly.

Liquidity ratio   A more stringent index of liquidity or creditworthiness than the current ratio (*q.v.*). It is derived from dividing the book values of (*a*) total current assets minus all stocks by (*b*) the book values of total current liabilities: also termed the *Quick ratio*.

Management by exception   The practice of directing the attention of management staffs to significant deviations of actual from expected results.

Management by objectives   Setting out the functions and responsibilities of executive management at all levels, with the aim of ensuring economic achievement of tasks and maximisation of corporate profits.

Manufacturing overhead   See *Factory overhead*.

Marginal costing   See *Direct costing*.

Material price variance   See *Price variance*.

Material usage variance   See *Quantity variance*.

Memorandum of Association   The document setting out the powers of the company in its dealings with the outside world: the Memorandum is filed with the Registrar of Companies.

Minority interests   In consolidated balance sheets, this term describes the liability of the group towards the minority shareholders, being that part of the total assets and earnings due to them. This arises where, for example, the accounts of a less than 100 per cent owned subsidiary are consolidated and shown in the group accounts; 100 per cent of the subsidiary assets are consolidated in the group accounts; the fraction of assets belonging to the minority shareholders in the subsidiary are shown as a liability of the group.

Monetary items Assets, liabilities or capital, the amounts of which are fixed by contract or statute in terms of the numbers of pounds regardless of changes in the purchasing power of the pound.

Mortgage debenture A bond secured by a mortgage on a property. The value of the property may or may not equal the value of the bonds issued against it.

Net present value A method of calculating and evaluating a project's expected returns: future cash flows are discounted at a predetermined rate (cost of capital) and their summation is then matched against the initial capital expenditure.

Net worth Total assets less amounts due to creditors. It includes both issued shares and reserves: also called *Total shareholders' interest*.

Non-absorption costing The practice of charging all variable costs to the related operations or products or processes, whilst charging indirect costs, i.e. overhead costs, to the income of the period in which they arise.

Non-monetary items All items that are not monetary items, with the exception of total equity interest, i.e. share capital, reserves and retained profits. The total equity interest is neither a monetary nor a non-monetary item.

Normal standard The standard cost and efficiency performance which is regarded as attainable over a future operating period.

Operating gain (or loss) The difference between the value of a business's output – its sales of goods and services – and the replacement costs of the goods and services consumed in achieving that output.

Opportunity cost The benefits and gains foregone when the next most profitable, alternative use for one's efforts is not undertaken; in other words, the potential gains lost from not engaging activity B – the next best alternative – must be considered as part of the costs of engaging activity A.

Ordinary shares The ownership interest in a limited company. If the company has also issued preference shares, both Ordinary and preferred have ownership rights. However, the preferred normally has prior claim on dividends and, in the event of liquidation, on assets as well. Claims of both Ordinary and preference shareholders are junior to claims of debenture holders and other creditors of the company. Ordinary shareholders assume the greater risk, but generally exercise the greater control and may gain the greater reward in the form of dividends and capital appreciation.

Overhead costs The total of indirect materials, wages, salaries and expense costs of the organisation (see *Depreciation* as an example).

Paid-up shares Denotes that the sum due on the issued capital has been paid to the company (after issue expenses, where appropriate).

Payback   The time taken to repay to the corporate treasury the initial cash outlays involved in a capital investment.

Period cost   A cost which belongs to, and aggregates as a result of, a particular period of time, and which tends to be unaffected by fluctuations in levels of activity.

Preference share   A class of share with a claim on the company's earnings, at a specified rate, before payment may be made to the Ordinary shareholders. Also usually entitled to priority over Ordinary shareholders if the company goes into liquidation. *Cumulative preference shares* have a provision that if one or more dividends are omitted, the omitted dividends must be paid before dividends may be paid on the company's Ordinary shares.

Price-earnings ratio   A ratio derived from dividing the market price of an Ordinary share by the earnings per share (*q.v.*). It is used as a basis for comparing market prices of Ordinary shares.

Price variance   The difference between actual price and standard price per item, multiplied by the number of items purchased.

Prime cost   The total of the direct material costs, direct wages and direct expenses.

Process costing   A cost centre which consists of a continuous sequence of operations which are necessary to produce the goods at the end of the operational series – it is normally used in high-volume situations, where total costs are divided by equivalent units of production output.

Profit and loss statement or **income statement**   A statement summarising the income and expenditure of a company to show net profit or loss for the period involved.

Quantity variance   The difference between the actual quantity used and the standard quantity specified – for the output actually produced – multiplied by the standard price per item.

Quick ratio   See *Liquidity ratio*.

Reserve gearing   See *Gearing*. Where the company has substantial reserves recorded in the Total Shareholders' Interest, then the issued preference shares and debentures are expressed in relationship with the issued Ordinary shares *plus* the reserves.

Reserves   Reserves represent funds which have been appropriated from after-tax profits, and used for the purpose of increasing capital, investing in fixed assets. Generally, reserves show the growth in corporate wealth and represent a strengthening of the company's financial position.

Semi-variable cost   A cost which is partly fixed and partly variable (*q.v.*). Telephone and power costs are common examples.

Service departments   Those departments whose sole function is to assist production departments to complete their tasks, by providing specialised assistance in certain aspects of the firm's overall activities, e.g. canteens, maintenance, power supply.

Share dividend   A dividend paid in shares rather than cash. The dividend is usually additional shares of the issuing company.

Sinking fund   Money regularly set aside by a company to redeem its loan stock or preference shares from time to time. A sinking fund may also be used to make provisions for fixed asset replacement.

Standard cost   A predetermined cost based upon an expected attainable level of operations.

Standard hours   The time allowed for the completion of a predetermined amount of work.

Stock appreciation   The increase in the money costs of a given volume of stockholding.

Stock profits   A term describing the consequences of rising replacement costs of stocks, where the company (or trader) is able to increase the selling price of its products immediately the higher replacement costs are experienced: stock 'profit' is thus gained on stocks purchased before increased prices are introduced.

Sunk cost   A cost which has already been incurred and which is irrevelant to any current or future decision-making process (compared with *Fixed costs* and *Overhead costs*).

Surplus   The excess of assets over liabilities and issued shares. When accumulated from profits, it is called retained earnings and may be shown – in part – as a general reserve. If from other sources, it is called capital surplus. The sale of shares at prices above the nominal value results in a premium equal to the excess of sale price over nominal value. This premium is shown in the balance sheet as a 'share premium account' – a form of capital surplus.

Tangible assets   Those assets of a company which can be seen and touched: physical assets such as plant, machinery, vehicles and stocks rather than ownerships resulting from legal or economic rights.

Tax avoidance   A use of taxation provisions and legislation to produce a result more favourable to the taxpayer than was intended by the legislative authority.

Tax evasion   Concealment of appropriate data with a view to defrauding the taxation authorities.

Time cost   A cost which exists and aggregates as a result of the passage of time and which tends to be unaffected by fluctuations in levels of activity. (See *Fixed costs*.)

Total materials cost variance   The difference between the actual cost of materials used and the standard cost of the standard quantity specified for the actual output.

Total wage cost variance   The difference between the actual wages paid and the standard cost specified for the actual output.

Turnover of capital employed   The ratio of sales to capital employed which is expressed as sales per £ of capital employed. The greater the ratio, a more efficient use of the capital employed is implied. (See *Asset turnover*).

Uncontrollable cost   A cost that is not regulated or influenced by any action at a given level of managerial authority.

Uniform costing The application by different business firms of the same costing methods and practices.

Updating The process of translating figures of an earlier accounting period from pounds of current purchasing power at one date to pounds of current purchasing power at another, later date.

Usage variance The difference between the actual quantity of material used and the predetermined standard quantity, multiplied by the number of goods produced.

Variable cost A cost that tends to vary in the same proportion as variations of output (see *Direct costing*). Variable costs per unit tend to be fixed or uniform.

Working capital The difference between current assets and current liabilities.

Works cost See *Factory cost*.

Yield Also known as a return. The dividends or interest paid by a company expressed as a percentage of the current market price of the shares or debentures involved.

C Discounting techniques explained

Introduction

1   The object of these examples is to enable the reader to become accustomed to the use of interest tables for determining the *present* value of a sum of money which is *receivable in the future*. Conversely the growth, through the passage of time, of a present sum of money which is invested at a specified rate of interest, will also be demonstrated.

2   A sum of £500 is invested for six years at a 10 per cent per annum interest rate.

	£
Amount of initial investment	500
First year's interest (£500 × 0.1)	50
On hand at end of first year	550
Second year's interest (£550 × 0.1)	55
On hand at end of second year	605
Third year's interest (£605 × 0.1)	60.5
On hand at end of third year	665.5
Fourth year's interest (£665.5 × 0.1)	66.5
On hand at end of fourth year	732
Fifth year's interest (£732 × 0.1)	73.2
On hand at end of fifth year	805.2
Sixth year's interest (£805.2 × 0.1)	80.5
On hand at end of sixth year	£885.7

The above sequence of computations presents three facts to the analyst. These are:

(*a*)   Assuming an interest rate of 10 per cent, £500 today is comparable with the right to receive £885.7 in six years' time.

358

(b)   Conversely, and making the same assumption concerning interest, the receipt of a sum of £885.7 in six years' time has a present value of £500 today, and

(c)   a sum of £500 invested today to produce £885.7 in six years' time has a yield of 10 per cent.

Discounting and compounding

3   Turning to the present value interest tables on page 363 it will be seen that today's value of a £ receivable in six years' time, at a discount rate of 10 per cent, is £0.5645. Therefore to find the present value of £885.7 which is receivable at the end of six years, using the same discounting rate, it is necessary to work the following simple multiplication sum:

£885.7 × 0.5645 = £500

In this calculation, the resultant £500 is given after allowing for the very slight approximations which led to the original calculation of the £885.7. Now in this instance £500 is the present value referred to in para. 2(b) above: it is the future sum of £885.7 which has been discounted over six years to the present time. It should be noted that *the capital sums are therefore equal after allowing for a financing cost of 10 per cent per annum*.

4   Compounding is the reverse of discounting. It means the aggregation of the original capital invested, plus interest upon interest and upon that invested sum, throughout the life of the investment. Looking back at the example in (2) above, in order to ascertain the amount to which £500 will increase in six years' time at a rate of 10 per cent, the reader may use either compound interest tables, or take the reciprocal of the factor shown in (3). The arithmetical calculation is

£500 × 1/0.5645, i.e. times the reciprocal

= £500 × 1.7714, i.e. times the compound interest factor*

= £885.7

5   The interest factors for discounting and compounding, etc., can be obtained by referring to various publications devoted to presenting this information.* Interest tables such as these will be used in normal circumstances to save laborious calculations. However, the reader ought to understand how they have been derived. Now the discounting factors are arrived at by starting with the value of £1 today; all that one has to remember is that today's pound (year 0) is next years' pound (year 1) plus 10 per cent, assuming this to be the discounting rate, and the arithmetical display is

Year 1   1 × 100/110 = 0.90909

Year 2   0.90909 × 100/110 = 0.82644

Year 3   0.82644 × 100/110 = 0.75131

*LAWSON, G.H., and WINDLE, D.W., *Tables for DCF Annuity, Sinking Fund Compound Interest and Annual Capital Charge Calculations*, Oliver and Boyd (1965).

For years 4, 5 and 6, the interest factors will be found to be 0.68301, 0.62092 and 0.56447, respectively. In this way we are able to obtain the discounting factors, at a 10 per cent interest rate, for a series of years one to six. To simplify the calculations which will follow in para. 6, the interest factors have been restricted to three decimal places.

Capital and interest recovery – present value

6   Assume an investment which can show cash flows of £100 in each of the next six years, and assume also that the capital to carry out this investment can be borrowed at 10 per cent. The above interest factors will show *the present value* of those *future* cash flows, thus:

Year 1   100 × 0.909 =   £90.9
Year 2   100 × 0.826 =   £82.6
Year 3   100 × 0.751 =   £75.1
Year 4   100 × 0.683 =   £68.3
Year 5   100 × 0.621 =   £62.1
Year 6   100 × 0.565 =   £56.5

Present value of
   cash flows   £435.5

From this statement it can be said that if the investment costs £435.5 today and this capital sum can be obtained at 10 per cent annum interest, then the future cash flows will just break even with investment cost. It should be noted that the future cash flows:

(*a*)   Repay the original capital cost.
(*b*)   Pay a capital financing charge of 10 per cent.

Capital and interest recovery – net present value

7   If the capital cost of the above investment were LESS than £435.5 then the difference between that lower cost and the £435.5 [shown in (6) as the present value of the future series] would represent the increase in wealth or the profitability stemming from the project. The difference is referred to as the *net present value* of the investment and again it should be very carefully noted that this increase in wealth would have been obtained:

(*a*)   After repaying the original capital cost.
(*b*)   After paying a capital financing charge of 10 per cent.

Uniform cash flows and the annuity

8   The interest factors in para. 6 can be used in different ways. The reader will observe that these present value factors total to a sum of 4.355. This use of present value techniques appertains to an annuity which is concerned with equal payments over equal periods of time. Thus the factor of 4.355 informs us that, in order to obtain an income of £1 per year for the next six years at an interest rate of 10 per cent, it is necessary to invest £4.355 today. Similarly, and by the same conditions, in order to receive £100 in each of the next *three years* it is necessary to invest £248.6 today (the factors for the first three years total to 2.486). Put in another way, the receipt of £100 in each of the next three years, allowing for a financing charge of 10 per cent, will cost £248.6 today.

DCF yield or investment rate of return

9   The above examples of compounding and discounting enable a flat rate of return to be obtained by showing

(a)   A present value or
(b)   A terminal value of a series of cashflows.

The yield or investment rate of return (see page 269) is the rate of interest which discounts the future incomes produced by an investment, to the point where investment cost and the present value of future incomes are equal. In simpler vein, this is the same as saying that the yield rate is the rate of interest which could be paid on a bank overdraft, necessary to finance the investment, without the investor showing a profit or a loss. In this case the annual cash flows are then treated as repayments of principal and interest as Exhibit 146 shows.

Exhibit 146
Investment costing £435.5 returns £100 p.a. in each of six years
(Interest rate 10 per cent)

Year	Initial advance o/s at beginning of each year	Interest due for year	Principal + interest due at end of year	Cash flows used to repay Interest	Principal	O/s at end of year
	£	£	£	£	£	£
1	435.5	43.6	479.1	43.6	56.4	379.1
2	379.1	37.9	417.0	37.9	62.1	317.0
3	317.0	31.7	348.7	31.7	68.3	248.7
4	248.7	24.9	273.6	24.9	75.1	173.6
5	173.6	17.4	191.0	17.4	82.6	91.0
6	91.0	9.0	100.0	9.0	91.0	Nil
				164.5	435.5	
				£600		

D Tables A and B

TABLE A
Present value of £1 (what £1 due in the future is worth today)

$(1 + r)^{-n}$

Year	1%	2%	3%	4%	5%	6%	7%
1	0·9901	0·9804	0·9709	0·9615	0·9524	0·9434	0·9346
2	0·9803	0·9612	0·9426	0·9246	0·9070	0·8900	0·8734
3	0·9706	0·9423	0·9151	0·8890	0·8638	0·8396	0·8163
4	0·9610	0·9238	0·8885	0·8548	0·8227	0·7921	0·7629
5	0·9515	0·9057	0·8626	0·8219	0·7835	0·7473	0·7130
6	0·9420	0·8880	0·8375	0·7903	0·7462	0·7050	0·6663
7	0·9327	0·8706	0·8131	0·7599	0·7107	0·6651	0·6227
8	0·9235	0·8535	0·7894	0·7307	0·6768	0·6274	0·5820
9	0·9143	0·8368	0·7664	0·7026	0·6446	0·5919	0·5439
10	0·9053	0·8203	0·7441	0·6756	0·6139	0·5584	0·5083
11	0·8963	0·8043	0·7224	0·6496	0·5847	0·5268	0·4751
12	0·8874	0·7885	0·7014	0·6246	0·5568	0·4970	0·4440
13	0·8787	0·7730	0·6810	0·6006	0·5303	0·4688	0·4150
14	0·8700	0·7579	0·6611	0·5775	0·5051	0·4423	0·3878
15	0·8613	0·7430	0·6419	0·5553	0·4810	0·4173	0·3624
16	0·8528	0·7284	0·6232	0·5339	0·4581	0·3936	0·3387
17	0·8444	0·7142	0·6050	0·5134	0·4363	0·3714	0·3166
18	0·8360	0·7002	0·5874	0·4936	0·4155	0·3503	0·2959
19	0·8277	0·6864	0·5703	0·4746	0·3957	0·3305	0·2765
20	0·8195	0·6730	0·5537	0·4564	0·3769	0·3118	0·2584
21	0·8114	0·6598	0·5375	0·4388	0·3589	0·2942	0·2415
22	0·8034	0·6468	0·5219	0·4220	0·3419	0·2775	0·2257
23	0·7954	0·6342	0·5067	0·4057	0·3256	0·2618	0·2109
24	0·7876	0·6217	0·4919	0·3901	0·3101	0·2470	0·1971
25	0·7798	0·6095	0·4776	0·3751	0·2953	0·2330	0·1842
26	0·7721	0·5976	0·4637	0·3607	0·2812	0·2198	0·1722
27	0·7644	0·5859	0·4502	0·3468	0·2678	0·2074	0·1609
28	0·7568	0·5744	0·4371	0·3335	0·2551	0·1956	0·1504
29	0·7493	0·5631	0·4243	0·3207	0·2429	0·1846	0·1406
30	0·7419	0·5521	0·4120	0·3083	0·2314	0·1741	0·1314
40	0·6717	0·4529	0·3066	0·2083	0·1420	0·0972	0·0668
50	0·6080	0·3715	0·2281	0·1407	0·0872	0·0543	0·0339

$(1 + r)^{-n}$

Year	8%	9%	10%	12%	14%	15%	16%
1	0·9259	0·9174	0·9091	0·8929	0·8772	0·8696	0·8621
2	0·8573	0·8417	0·8264	0·7972	0·7695	0·7561	0·7432
3	0·7938	0·7722	0·7513	0·7118	0·6750	0·6575	0·6407
4	0·7350	0·7084	0·6830	0·6355	0·5921	0·5718	0·5523
5	0·6806	0·6499	0·6209	0·5674	0·5194	0·4972	0·4761
6	0·6302	0·5963	0·5645	0·5066	0·4556	0·4323	0·4104
7	0·5835	0·5470	0·5132	0·4523	0·3996	0·3759	0·3538
8	0·5403	0·5019	0·4665	0·4039	0·3506	0·3269	0·3050
9	0·5002	0·4604	0·4241	0·3606	0·3075	0·2843	0·2630
10	0·4632	0·4224	0·3855	0·3220	0·2697	0·2472	0·2267
11	0·4289	0·3875	0·3505	0·2875	0·2366	0·2149	0·1954
12	0·3971	0·3555	0·3186	0·2567	0·2076	0·1869	0·1685
13	0·3677	0·3262	0·2897	0·2292	0·1821	0·1625	0·1452
14	0·3405	0·2992	0·2633	0·2046	0·1597	0·1413	0·1252
15	0·3152	0·2745	0·2394	0·1827	0·1401	0·1229	0·1079
16	0·2919	0·2519	0·2176	0·1631	0·1229	0·1069	0·0930
17	0·2703	0·2311	0·1978	0·1456	0·1078	0·0929	0·0802
18	0·2502	0·2120	0·1799	0·1300	0·0946	0·0808	0·0691
19	0·2317	0·1945	0·1635	0·1161	0·0829	0·0703	0·0596
20	0·2145	0·1784	0·1486	0·1037	0·0728	0·0611	0·0514
21	0·1987	0·1637	0·1351	0·0926	0·0638	0·0531	0·0443
22	0·1839	0·1502	0·1228	0·0826	0·0560	0·0462	0·0382
23	0·1703	0·1378	0·1117	0·0738	0·0491	0·0402	0·0329
24	0·1577	0·1264	0·1015	0·0659	0·0431	0·0349	0·0284
25	0·1460	0·1160	0·0923	0·0588	0·0378	0·0304	0·0245
26	0·1352	0·1064	0·0839	0·0525	0·0331	0·0264	0·0211
27	0·1252	0·0976	0·0763	0·0469	0·0291	0·0230	0·0182
28	0·1159	0·0895	0·0693	0·0419	0·0255	0·0200	0·0157
29	0·1073	0·0822	0·0630	0·0374	0·0224	0·0174	0·0135
30	0·0944	0·0754	0·0573	0·0334	0·0196	0·0151	0·0116
40	0·0460	0·0318	0·0221	0·0107	0·0053	0·0037	0·0026
50	0·0213	0·0134	0·0085	0·0035	0·0014	0·0009	0·0006

$(1 + r)^{-n}$

Year	18%	20%	22%	24%	25%	26%	28%
1	0·8475	0·8333	0·8197	0·8065	0·8000	0·7937	0·7813
2	0·7182	0·6944	0·6719	0·6504	0·6400	0·6299	0·6104
3	0·6086	0·5787	0·5507	0·5245	0·5120	0·4999	0·4768
4	0·5158	0·4823	0·4514	0·4230	0·4096	0·3968	0·3725
5	0·4371	0·4019	0·3700	0·3411	0·3277	0·3149	0·2910
6	0·3704	0·3349	0·3033	0·2751	0·2621	0·2499	0·2274
7	0·3139	0·2791	0·2486	0·2218	0·2097	0·1983	0·1776
8	0·2660	0·2326	0·2038	0·1789	0·1678	0·1574	0·1388
9	0·2255	0·1938	0·1670	0·1443	0·1342	0·1249	0·1084
10	0·1911	0·1615	0·1369	0·1164	0·1074	0·0992	0·0847
11	0·1619	0·1346	0·1122	0·0938	0·0859	0·0787	0·0662
12	0·1372	0·1122	0·0920	0·0757	0·0687	0·0625	0·0517
13	0·1163	0·0935	0·0754	0·0610	0·0550	0·0496	0·0404
14	0·0985	0·0779	0·0618	0·0492	0·0440	0·0393	0·0316
15	0·0835	0·0649	0·0507	0·0397	0·0352	0·0312	0·0247
16	0·0708	0·0541	0·0415	0·0320	0·0281	0·0248	0·0193
17	0·0600	0·0451	0·0340	0·0258	0·0225	0·0197	0·0150
18	0·0508	0·0376	0·0279	0·0208	0·0180	0·0156	0·0118
19	0·0431	0·0313	0·0229	0·0168	0·0144	0·0124	0·0092
20	0·0365	0·0261	0·0187	0·0135	0·0115	0·0098	0·0072
21	0·0309	0·0217	0·0154	0·0109	0·0092	0·0078	0·0056
22	0·0262	0·0181	0·0126	0·0088	0·0074	0·0062	0·0044
23	0·0222	0·0151	0·0103	0·0071	0·0059	0·0049	0·0034
24	0·0188	0·0126	0·0084	0·0057	0·0047	0·0039	0·0027
25	0·0160	0·0105	0·0069	0·0046	0·0038	0·0031	0·0021
26	0·0135	0·0087	0·0057	0·0037	0·0030	0·0025	0·0016
27	0·0115	0·0073	0·0047	0·0030	0·0024	0·0019	0·0013
28	0·0097	0·0061	0·0038	0·0024	0·0019	0·0015	0·0010
29	0·0082	0·0051	0·0031	0·0020	0·0015	0·0012	0·0008
30	0·0070	0·0042	0·0026	0·0016	0·0012	0·0010	0·0006
40	0·0013	0·0007	0·0004	0·0002	0·0001		
50	0·0003	0·0001					

$(1 + r)^{-n}$

Year	30%	35%	40%	45%	50%
1	0·7692	0·7407	0·7143	0·6897	0·6667
2	0·5917	0·5487	0·5102	0·4756	0·4444
3	0·4552	0·4064	0·3644	0·3280	0·2963
4	0·3501	0·3011	0·2603	0·2262	0·1975
5	0·2693	0·2230	0·1859	0·1560	0·1317
6	0·2072	0·1652	0·1328	0·1076	0·0878
7	0·1594	0·1224	0·0949	0·0742	0·0585
8	0·1226	0·0906	0·0678	0·0512	0·0390
9	0·0943	0·0671	0·0484	0·0353	0·0260
10	0·0725	0·0497	0·0346	0·0243	0·0173
11	0·0558	0·0368	0·0247	0·0168	0·0116
12	0·0429	0·0273	0·0176	0·0116	0·0077
13	0·0330	0·0202	0·0126	0·0080	0·0051
14	0·0254	0·0150	0·0090	0·0055	0·0034
15	0·0195	0·0111	0·0064	0·0038	0·0023
16	0·0150	0·0082	0·0046	0·0026	0·0015
17	0·0116	0·0061	0·0033	0·0018	0·0010
18	0·0089	0·0045	0·0023	0·0012	0·0007
19	0·0068	0·0033	0·0017	0·0009	0·0005
20	0·0053	0·0025	0·0012	0·0006	0·0003
21	0·0040	0·0018	0·0009	0·0004	0·0002
22	0·0031	0·0014	0·0006	0·0003	0·0001
23	0·0024	0·0010	0·0004	0·0002	
24	0·0018	0·0007	0·0003	0·0001	
25	0·0014	0·0006	0·0002		
26	0·0011	0·0004	0·0002		
27	0·0008	0·0003	0·0001		
28	0·0006	0·0002			
29	0·0005	0·0002			
30	0·0004	0·0001			
40					
50					

Table B

Present value of £1 per year (what £1 receivable annually is worth today)

$$\frac{1 - (1 + r)^{-n}}{r}$$

Year	1%	2%	3%	4%	5%
1	0·9901	0·9804	0·9709	0·9615	0·9524
2	1·9704	1·9416	1·9135	1·8861	1·8594
3	2·9410	2·8839	2·8286	2·7751	2·7232
4	3·9020	3·8077	3·7171	3·6299	3·5460
5	4·8534	4·7135	4·5797	4·4518	4·3295
6	5·7955	5·6014	5·4172	5·2421	5·0757
7	6·7282	6·4720	6·2303	6·0021	5·7864
8	7·6517	7·3255	7·0197	6·7327	6·4632
9	8·5660	8·1622	7·7861	7·4353	7·1078
10	9·4713	8·9826	8·5302	8·1109	7·7217
11	10·3676	9·7869	9·2526	8·7605	8·3064
12	11·2551	10·5753	9·9540	9·3851	8·8633
13	12·1337	11·3484	10·6350	9·9856	9·3936
14	13·0037	12·1062	11·2961	10·5631	9·8986
15	13·8651	12·8493	11·9379	11·1184	10·3797
16	14·7179	13·5777	12·5611	11·6523	10·8378
17	15·5623	14·2919	13·1661	12·1657	11·2741
18	16·3983	14·9920	13·7535	12·6593	11·6896
19	17·2260	15·6785	14·3238	13·1339	12·0853
20	18·0456	16·3514	14·8775	13·5903	12·4622
21	18·8570	17·0112	15·4150	14·0292	12·8212
22	19·6604	17·6580	15·9369	14·4511	13·1630
23	20·4558	18·2922	16·4436	14·8568	13·4886
24	21·2434	18·9139	16·9355	15·2470	13·7986
25	22·0232	19·5235	17·4131	15·6221	14·0939
26	22·7952	20·1210	17·8768	15·9838	14·3752
27	23·5596	20·7069	18·3270	16·3296	14·6430
28	24·3164	21·2813	18·7641	16·6631	14·8981
29	25·0658	21·8444	19·1885	16·9837	15·1411
30	25·8077	22·3965	19·6004	17·2920	15·3725
40	32·8347	27·3555	23·1148	19·7928	17·1591
50	39·1961	31·4236	25·7298	21·4822	18·2559

$$\frac{1 - (1 + r)^{-n}}{r}$$

Year	6%	7%	8%	9%	10%
1	0·9434	0·9346	0·9259	0·9174	0·9091
2	1·8334	1·8080	1·7833	1·7591	1·7355
3	2·6730	2·6243	2·5771	2·5313	2·4869
4	3·4651	3·3872	3·3121	3·2397	3·1699
5	4·2124	4·1002	3·9927	3·8897	3·7908
6	4·9173	4·7665	4·6229	4·4859	4·3553
7	5·5824	5·3893	5·2064	5·0330	4·8684
8	6·2098	5·9713	5·7466	5·5348	5·3349
9	6·8071	6·5152	6·2469	5·9952	5·7590
10	7·3601	7·0236	6·7101	6·4177	6·1466
11	7·8869	7·4987	7·1390	6·8052	6·4951
12	8·3838	7·9427	7·5361	7·1607	6·8137
13	8·8527	8·3577	7·9038	7·4869	7·1034
14	9·2950	8·7455	8·2442	7·7862	7·3667
15	9·7122	9·1079	8·5595	8·0607	7·6061
16	10·1059	9·4466	8·8514	8·3126	7·8237
17	10·4773	9·7632	9·1216	8·5436	8·0216
18	10·8276	10·0591	9·3719	8·7556	8·2014
19	11·1581	10·3356	9·6036	8·9501	8·3649
20	11·4699	10·5940	9·8181	9·1285	8·5136
21	11·7641	10·8355	10·0168	9·2922	8·6487
22	12·0416	11·0612	10·2007	9·4424	8·7715
23	12·3034	11·2722	10·3711	9·5802	8·8832
24	12·5504	11·4693	10·5288	9·7066	8·9847
25	12·7834	11·6536	10·6748	9·8226	9·0770
26	13·0032	11·8258	10·8100	9·9290	9·1609
27	13·2105	11·9867	10·9352	10·0266	9·2372
28	13·4062	12·1371	11·0511	10·1161	9·3066
29	13·5907	12·2777	11·1584	10·1983	9·3696
30	13·7648	12·4090	11·2578	10·2737	9·4269
40	15·0463	13·3317	11·9246	10·7574	9·7791
50	15·7619	13·8007	12·2335	10·9617	9·9148

$$\frac{1 - (1 + r)^{-n}}{r}$$

Year	12%	14%	15%	16%	18%
1	0·8929	0·8722	0·8696	0·8621	0·8475
2	1·6901	1·6497	1·6257	1·6052	1·5656
3	2·4018	2·3216	2·2832	2·2459	2·1743
4	3·0373	2·9137	2·8550	2·7982	2·6901
5	3·6048	3·4331	3·3522	3·2743	3·1272
6	4·1114	3·8887	3·7845	3·6847	3·4976
7	4·5638	4·2883	4·1604	4·0386	3·8115
8	4·9676	4·6389	4·4873	4·3436	4·0776
9	5·3282	4·9464	4·7716	4·6065	4·3030
10	5·6502	5·2161	5·0188	4·8332	4·4941
11	5·9377	5·4527	5·2337	5·0286	4·6560
12	6·1944	5·6603	5·4206	5·1971	4·7932
13	5·4235	5·8424	5·5832	5·3423	4·9095
14	6·6282	6·0021	5·7245	5·4675	5·0081
15	6·8109	6·1422	5·8474	5·5755	5·0916
16	6·9740	6·2651	5·9542	5·6685	5·1624
17	7·1196	6·3729	6·0472	5·7487	5·2223
18	7·2497	6·4674	6·1280	5·8178	5·2732
19	7·3658	6·5504	6·1982	5·8775	5·3162
20	7·4694	6·6231	6·2593	5·9288	5·3527
21	7·5620	6·6870	6·3125	5·9731	5·3837
22	7·6446	6·7429	6·3587	6·0113	5·4099
23	7·7184	6·7921	6·3988	6·0442	5·4321
24	7·7843	6·8351	6·4338	6·0726	5·4509
25	7·8431	6·8729	6·4642	6·0971	5·4669
26	7·8957	6·9061	6·4906	6·1182	5·4804
27	7·9426	6·9352	6·5135	6·1364	5·4919
28	7·9844	6·9607	6·5335	6·1520	5·5016
29	8·0218	6·9830	6·5509	6·1656	5·5098
30	8·0552	7·0027	6·5660	6·1772	5·5168
40	8·2438	7·1050	6·6418	6·2335	5·5482
50	8·3045	7·1327	6·6605	6·2463	5·5541

$$\frac{1 - (1 + r)^{-n}}{r}$$

Year	20%	22%	24%	25%	26%	28%
1	0·8333	0·8197	0·8065	0·8000	0·7937	0·7813
2	1·5278	1·4915	1·4568	1·4400	1·4235	1·3916
3	2·1065	2·0422	1·9813	1·9520	1·9234	1·8684
4	2·5887	2·4936	2·4043	2·6346	2·3202	2·2410
5	2·9906	2·8636	2·7454	2·6893	2·6351	2·5320
6	3·3255	3·1669	3·0205	2·9514	2·8850	2·7594
7	3·6046	3·4155	3·2423	3·1611	3·0833	2·9370
8	3·8372	3·6193	3·4212	3·3289	3·2407	3·0758
9	4·0310	3·7863	3·5655	3·4631	3·3657	3·1842
10	4·1925	3·9232	3·6819	3·5705	3·4648	3·2689
11	4·3271	4·0354	3·7757	3·6564	3·5435	3·3351
12	4·4392	4·1274	3·8514	3·7251	3·6059	3·3868
13	4·5327	4·2028	3·9124	3·7801	3·6555	3·4272
14	4·6106	4·2646	3·9616	3·8241	3·6949	3·4587
15	4·6755	4·3152	4·0013	3·8593	3·7261	3·4834
16	4·7296	4·3567	4·0333	3·8874	3·7509	3·5026
17	4·7746	4·3908	4·0591	3·9099	3·7705	3·5177
18	4·8122	4·4187	4·0799	3·9279	3·7861	3·5294
19	4·8435	4·4415	4·0967	3·9424	3·7985	3·5386
20	4·8696	4·4603	4·1103	3·9539	3·8083	3·5458
21	4·8913	4·4756	4·1212	3·9631	3·8161	3·5514
22	4·9094	4·4882	4·1300	3·9705	3·8223	3·5558
23	4·9245	4·4985	4·1371	3·9764	3·8273	3·5592
24	4·9371	4·5070	4·1428	3·9811	3·8312	3·5619
25	4·9476	4·5139	4·1474	3·9849	3·8342	3·5640
26	4·9563	4·5196	4·1512	3·9879	3·8367	3·5656
27	4·9636	4·5243	4·1542	3·9903	3·8387	3·5669
28	4·9697	4·5281	4·1566	3·9923	3·8402	3·5679
29	4·9747	4·5312	4·1585	3·9938	3·8414	3·5687
30	4·9789	4·5338	4·1601	3·9951	3·8424	3·5693
40	4·9966	4·5439	4·1659	3·9995	3·8458	3·5712
50	4·9995	4·5452	4·1666	3·9999	3·8461	3·5714

$$\frac{1 - (1 + r)^{-n}}{r}$$

Year	30%	35%	40%	45%	50%
1	0·7692	0·7407	0·7143	0·6897	0·6667
2	1·3609	1·2894	1·2245	1·1653	1·1111
3	1·8161	1·6959	1·5889	1·4933	1·4074
4	2·1662	1·9969	1·8492	1·7195	1·6049
5	2·4356	2·2200	2·0352	1·8755	1·7366
6	2·6427	2·3852	2·1680	1·9831	1·8244
7	2·8021	2·5075	2·2628	2·0573	1·8829
8	2·9247	2·5982	2·3306	2·1085	1·9220
9	3·0190	2·6653	2·3790	2·1438	1·9480
10	3·0915	2·7150	2·4136	2·1681	1·9653
11	3·1473	2·7519	2·4383	2·1849	1·9769
12	3·1903	2·7792	2·4559	2·1965	1·9846
13	3·2233	2·7994	2·4685	2·2045	1·9897
14	3·2487	2·8144	2·4775	2·2100	1·9931
15	3·2682	2·8255	2·4839	2·2138	1·9954
16	3·2832	2·8337	2·4885	2·2164	1·9970
17	3·2948	2·8398	2·4918	2·2182	1·9980
18	3·3037	2·8443	2·4941	2·2195	1·9986
19	3·3105	2·8476	2·4958	2·2203	1·9991
20	3·3158	2·8501	2·4970	2·2209	1·9994
21	3·3198	2·8519	2·4979	2·2213	1·9996
22	3·3230	2·8533	2·4985	2·2216	1·9997
23	3·3254	2·8543	2·4989	2·2218	1·9998
24	3·3272	2·8550	2·4992	2·2219	1·9999
25	3·3286	2·8556	2·4994	2·2220	1·9999
26	3·3297	2·8560	2·4996	2·2221	1·9999
27	3·3305	2·8563	2·4997	2·2221	2·0000
28	3·3312	2·8565	2·4998	2·2222	2·0000
29	3·3317	2·8567	2·4999	2·2222	2·0000
30	3·3321	2·8568	2·4999	2·2222	2·0000
40	3·3332	2·8571	2·5000	2·2222	2·0000
50	3·3333	2·8571	2·5000	2·2222	2·0000

Index

372